T0330165

Entrepreneurial Processes in a Changing Economy

Entrepreneurial Processes in a Changing Economy

Frontiers in European Entrepreneurship Research

Edited by

Friederike Welter

Jönköping International Business School, Sweden

David Smallbone

Small Business Research Centre, Kingston University, UK

Anita Van Gils

Maastricht University School of Business and Economics, The Netherlands

IN ASSOCIATION WITH THE ECSB

Edward Elgar
Cheltenham, UK • Northampton, MA, USA

Published by
Edward Elgar Publishing Limited
The Lypiatts
15 Lansdown Road
Cheltenham
Glos GL50 2JA
UK

Edward Elgar Publishing, Inc.
William Pratt House
9 Dewey Court
Northampton
Massachusetts 01060
USA

A catalogue record for this book
is available from the British Library

Library of Congress Control Number: 2012930625

MIX
Paper from
responsible sources
FSC® C018575

ISBN 978 1 78100 472 2

Typeset by Servis Filmsetting Ltd, Stockport, Cheshire
Printed and bound by MPG Books Group, UK

Contents

Contributors

Olga Belousova, Université catholique de Louvain, Belgium

Maryse Brand, University of Groningen, The Netherlands

Alejandro Campos, University of Barcelona, Spain

Tommy Høyvarde Clausen, Nordland Research Institute, Norway

Evelien Croonen, University of Groningen, The Netherlands

Benoit Gailly, Université catholique de Louvain, Belgium

Pedro M. García-Villaverde, University of Castilla-La Mancha, Spain

David Helleboogh, University of Antwerp, Belgium

Esther Hormiga, University of Barcelona, Spain

Eddy Laveren, University of Antwerp and Antwerp Management School, Belgium

Roger Leenders, Tilburg University, The Netherlands

Nadine Lybaert, Hasselt University, Belgium

Colm O'Gorman, Dublin City University, Ireland

Gloria Parra-Requena, University of Castilla-La Mancha, Spain

Einar Rasmussen, University of Nordland, Norway

María J. Ruiz-Ortega, University of Castilla-La Mancha, Spain

Veronique Schutjens, Utrecht University, The Netherlands

Bart Sleutjes, Utrecht University, The Netherlands

David Smallbone, Kingston University, UK

Anita Van Gils, Maastricht University School of Business and Economics, The Netherlands

Frank Van Oort, Utrecht University, The Netherlands

Friederike Welter, Jönköping International Business School, Sweden

Mike Wright, Imperial College, UK

Foreword

Dear reader,

As President of the European Council for Small Business, I am delighted to welcome you to the latest volume in the 'Frontiers in European Entrepreneurship Research' series. This publication is based upon papers presented at the annual RENT Conference and once again it highlights the exciting breadth, depth and sophistication of the research that is currently being undertaken by entrepreneurship researchers across Europe. The book also offers a stimulating array of topics and interests that propose important insights for entrepreneurs, policy makers, enterprise support agents and fellow academics into the current and future worlds of entrepreneurship.

Every November, academics from around the globe gather in Europe for the annual RENT Conference. Since its early days in 1987, the conference has been an energizing collaboration between ECSB and EIASM, and it is now recognized as being one of the premier conferences internationally on the topic of entrepreneurship. Over the years a substantial investment has been made towards ensuring that the quality of the papers presented is of a very high standard, and this commitment has led directly to the current position whereby only a minority of submitted papers now get accepted for the conference. Interestingly, while the percentage of papers accepted is being continuously lowered, the number of people wishing to attend the conference without presenting a paper is increasing annually as a growing number of academics are recognizing the many benefits of participating in such a high-quality conference. The philosophy of the conference is focused upon maintaining its intimate nature which allows for thought-provoking discussions to evolve, and this opportunity to engage positively with the authors is very much seen as part of its appeal.

There have been a number of exciting developments to the conference over the years as it now incorporates a Policy Forum, a Doctoral Consortium, a Post-Doc Roundtable and a Case Writing Workshop. Additionally, some of the keynote speeches are now streamed live via the Internet, and initiatives such as Inter-RENT help less experienced researchers to develop their papers to the standard required for publication by top-quality academic journals. The conference has steadily and progressively enhanced the benefits that it offers to its audience, which explains in some way the reasoning for its continued success.

The series 'Frontiers of European Entrepreneurship Research' was born from a desire to promote to a much broader audience the high-quality papers being presented at the RENT Conference, and to communicate its cutting-edge research to stakeholders across the full spectrum of the entrepreneurship community. This series of publications has quickly established itself as a key resource for all who are seeking to identify where the boundaries of research and thinking are now being expanded, and what opportunities might be arising from this new knowledge. This work is an exciting and valuable addition to the canon of knowledge already at our disposal, and I thank most sincerely all of those people who have given their time freely to ensure its success.

Yours sincerely,
Thomas M. Cooney
President, ECSB

1. Introduction

Friederike Welter, David Smallbone and Anita Van Gils

INTRODUCING RENT XXIV IN MAASTRICHT

This volume represents a selection of the best papers from the 127 presented at the RENT XXIV Conference, held at the Maastricht University in the Netherlands in November 2010. As such, it provides a window on contemporary European research in the field of entrepreneurship and small business. The selected papers contribute to the overall conference theme of 'Entrepreneurial processes in a changing economy', by taking a closer look at what constitutes entrepreneurial processes, how entrepreneurs develop their businesses and access critical resources in times of crisis and which roles knowledge and innovation play in continuous venture development.

INTRODUCING THE CHAPTERS

Chapter 2 represents a revised version of the keynote address presented by Mike Wright at the RENT conference. The author discusses the links between entrepreneurial mobility, resource orchestration and different facets of context. In a world that appears to be struggling to maintain economic growth, where corporate insolvencies increase and access to financial resources are severely constrained, entrepreneurial adaptability and mobility are challenged. While today's economic conditions might offer opportunities for new types of entrepreneurial mobility, they also pose challenges for assembling the resources required for opportunity exploitation and venture development. It is here that the author draws attention to the context in which entrepreneurship takes place as the changing economy emphasizes the need to understand contexts and their impact on venture survival, success and entrepreneurial processes. Entrepreneurial mobility includes organizational mobility, and the chapter focuses on two types, namely habitual entrepreneurs (that is, entrepreneurs who shift from one organization to another) and entrepreneurs involved in management buyouts (MBOs). Furthermore, the author distinguishes four contexts (temporal, social, institutional and spatial). He identifies research themes and challenges for future research, contributing towards an integration of the process and contextual perspectives on entrepreneurship.

Chapters 3 to 6 discuss various facets of venture growth. In Chapter 3, Bart Sleutjes, Frank Van Oort and Veronique Schutjens study the effects of neighbourhoods on firm success. While neighbourhoods are expected to benefit in several ways from the presence of local firms, it is not known whether local firms also benefit from their neighbourhood. The authors draw on unique datasets, including the Dutch Survey of Social Networks of Entrepreneurs and a longitudinal database of firms registered in selected neighbourhoods. They study how neighbourhood cohesiveness and liveability relate to local firms' chances for survival and growth. Their results show a differentiated picture. Social and physical neighbourhood aspects seem to be especially relevant for employment growth, but not for firm survival, while the market function of the neighbourhood seems to influence firm survival through building density. The authors conclude that more research is needed to study the underlying mechanisms and causality of aspects of neighbourhood and firm survival and growth.

In Chapter 4, Colm O'Gorman looks at the role of the entrepreneur in determining growth, drawing on a longitudinal case study of Cooley Distillery plc, the only Irish-owned distiller of Irish whiskey, which started up in 1986. The case analysis suggests that growth was an objective of the founder right from the beginning, and was one of the reasons why he started the firm, while choice of sector was an outcome of the resources available. Thus, an objective of growing the firm appears to be an intrinsic element of the decision to found the firm, rather than, as much of the current literature assumes, a consequence of the decision to found the firm. Furthermore, the author concludes that studies of venture growth need a longitudinal aspect. His results show that over extended periods of time, chance is not the 'key' explanation for growth. Consequently, studying growth over short timeframes may produce conflicting results as in any given time period either markets or resources might account for growth, but it is the interaction of both which explains growth paths over extended periods of time.

Chapter 5, co-authored by Pedro M. García-Villaverde, María J. Ruiz-Ortega and Gloria Parra-Requena, aims to analyse the moderating effect of market intelligence, cross-functional integration and internal commitment on the relationship between pioneering and new product performance. Their empirical study focuses on the Information and Communication Technology (ICT) Industry in Spain. This is a sector with a strong degree of dynamism and rivalry in which the advantages of a pioneering strategy can be easily eliminated or imitated by competitors; therefore a pioneering strategy might be a high risk strategy for ICT companies. The authors conclude that their study demonstrates a more complex and holistic approach to those internal factors that moderate the relationship between pioneering firms and new product performance.

Chapter 6, authored by Eddy Laveren, David Helleboogh and Nadine Lybaert, takes a look at the use of financial bootstrapping in small and medium-sized ventures and the impact on venture growth. The authors draw on a sample of 368 Belgian small and medium-sized enterprises, created between 2002 and 2003. The chapter contributes to the general knowledge of bootstrap financing among small ventures in two ways. First, the study reveals which human capital characteristics of the owner-manager have an impact on financial bootstrapping use. The empirical results indicate that bootstrapping is a skill which is absorbed from self-employed parents or during the founder's prior work and management experiences. Second, in line with resource-dependency theory, the authors demonstrate a relationship between financial bootstrapping and venture growth. Specifically, their study shows that joint-utilization bootstrapping is negatively related and owner-related bootstrapping is positively related to employment growth. Thus, small business owners need to be aware that different bootstrapping types do not appear to relate consistently to venture growth in the same way, since some bootstrapping types ameliorate, while others deteriorate their venture's growth. The authors conclude that such knowledge about non-traditional sources of financing may be especially valuable in times of economic crisis where access to financial resources can be a serious constraint.

Chapters 7 to 10 focus on innovation and knowledge in relation to venture development. In Chapter 7, Maryse Brand, Evelien Croonen and Roger Leenders develop a conceptual model of knowledge acquisition through strategic networks for franchising companies. Extant research has typically looked at franchisors distributing their codified knowledge in the form of a business format to their franchisees. The authors argue that franchisees also need local knowledge to adapt the management of their units to local circumstances. Taking an entrepreneurship perspective, they link the use of local knowledge to entrepreneurial behaviour and firm performance. As local knowledge often is not codified and not possessed by the franchisor, it is of interest to study where and how franchisees acquire the local knowledge needed to achieve a local fit in their specific locations, and how this influences their units' performance. The chapter adopts a network perspective to develop propositions on how network characteristics such as strength, size and diversity of individual franchisees influence the performance of their units. The authors conclude with the presentation of specific methodological guidelines for future empirical work.

Chapter 8, co-authored by Einar Rasmussen and Tommy Høyvarde Clausen, deals with the openness and innovativeness within science-based entrepreneurial firms (SBEF), which play a key role in converting scientific knowledge into new breakthrough products and services. Similar to other start-ups, these firms must also assemble resources in order to survive and succeed. In this regard, the authors examine the role of openness, understood as external sourcing of technology, organization building and legitimacy, for the ability of SBEFs to innovate, as reflected in their ability to commercialize basic research. Based on a sample of 84 SBEFs established from public research institutions between 2003 and 2008 in Norway, the authors find empirical support for their conceptualization of openness and also confirm that openness is a positive and significant predictor of the innovativeness of SBEFs. They conclude that it is not only external technology sourcing which is of importance to the innovation process, but, at least in the new venture context, also the sourcing of resources for organizational building and legitimacy are key aspects of open innovation.

In Chapter 9, Olga Belousova and Benoit Gailly explore corporate entrepreneurship (CE) within a large company. Drawing on an in-depth case study, the authors analyse the behavioural component of CE along a process dimension, covering the key elements of CE action (discovery, evaluation, legitimation and exploitation) and a hierarchical dimension including operating, middle and top levels of management. Their case is a business unit with more than 1000 employees of a large, European based industrial company. The case covers the development of various entrepreneurial initiatives within the business unit from 2003 to 2011. Based on their case analysis, which shows interesting facets such as co-creation and co-discovery of opportunities through teams, the authors develop propositions which aim at providing a more in-depth view on the influence that CE activities may have on the organizational environment. Their analysis contributes to a deeper understanding of the very essence of entrepreneurial process – the nature of entrepreneurial behaviour, in particular within established and large organizations.

In Chapter 10, Alejandro Campos and Esther Hormiga look at the state of the art of knowledge research in entrepreneurship. The authors review articles published between 2000 and 2010 in the six major academic journals in the entrepreneurship field in terms of impact. A total of 143 articles were identified and analysed, searching for specific characteristics, amongst them the academic theories used to support the study, indicators, sample used for analysis, size of company, ontological level of learning and main conclusions. Knowledge in entrepreneurship is mainly understood as the stock of knowledge possessed by the entrepreneur as an individual, and related articles draw on management or entrepreneurship theories. On the other hand, when researchers discuss knowledge creation of entrepreneurs and organizations, they draw on theories from psychology. The authors conclude that there is no agreement as to the way knowledge is conceived and measured, arguing for that the entrepreneurship field needs a specialized theory which explains the knowledge construction process of entrepreneurs.

CONCLUDING REMARKS

The selection of chapters included in this volume gives a flavour of the themes and approaches featuring in contemporary entrepreneurship and small business research in Europe. The collection reflects the methodological diversity that is typical of European research, as well as heterogeneity in terms of topics studied. Despite the fact that RENT is a scientific rather than a policy oriented conference, all chapters included in this volume have potential implications for policy makers and also practitioners as well as entrepreneurs.

Policy and practitioner relevant topics covered in this volume refer to different types of entrepreneurial mobility with implications for resource orchestration, the importance of including business aspects in local neighbourhood policies, growth as intentional entrepreneurial imperative which already drives the start-up, the role of new product development for pioneering strategies, the importance of tailor-made bootstrapping strategies, network-related factors influencing franchisees' performance, the role of intermediary actors for science-based entrepreneurial firms, the behavioural aspects of corporate entrepreneurship and the effect of knowledge-related practices in companies.

As an applied field of study, it is important that academic researchers maintain a dialogue with policy makers and practitioners. Organizations such as the European Council for Small Business and Entrepreneurship (ECSB), and the International Council for Small Business (ICSB), its global equivalent, provide a forum in which such a dialogue can take place.

2. Entrepreneurial mobility, resource orchestration and context

Mike Wright

1. INTRODUCTION

The global economy has been marked, and continues to be affected, by traumatic turbulence. Economies are always changing but we appear to be witnessing a paradigm shift rather than any short-term blip in fortunes. Many developed economies especially are struggling to maintain GDP growth and avoid a double-dip recession. There has been a significant increase in corporate insolvencies, and access to bank finance is severely constrained.

Such conditions emphasize the need for adaptability by entrepreneurs if they are to survive and prosper. These conditions introduce opportunities for new types of entrepreneurial firms that involve the adaptability and mobility of entrepreneurs. Further, these conditions pose challenges to entrepreneurs in assembling and coordinating the resources and capabilities they need to exploit these opportunities. While the strategic entrepreneurship literature is beginning to make great strides in linking opportunities to resources, it has so far had little to say about the role of context in introducing contingencies to this process. A changing economy stresses the need to understand the context in which entrepreneurship occurs, since this may contribute to the success of ventures and help in identifying the heterogeneity of entrepreneurial activities. Although context has received some recognition in the entrepreneurship literature (Welter 2011), generally this has been quite fragmented and has not fully recognized the heterogeneity of context (Zahra and Wright 2011). My purpose in this chapter is to contribute to an integration of the process and contextual perspectives on entrepreneurship. Specifically, I examine how the resource coordination or orchestration process in two particular cases that involve entrepreneurial mobility is influenced by different dimensions of context.

In what follows, I first outline the dimensions of resource orchestration. Second, I discuss four aspects of context. The relationship between these

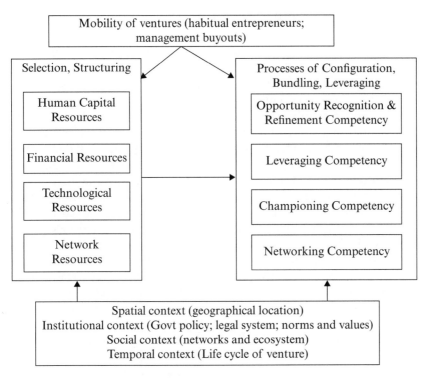

Source: Adapted from Wright et al. (2011).

Figure 2.1   Entrepreneur mobility, resource orchestration and context

dimensions is presented schematically in Figure 2.1. Third, I define entrepreneurial mobility and outline the focus on two particular aspects, that is, habitual entrepreneurs and management buyouts. In the next section, I synthesize these three elements to identify emerging research themes. A final section discusses further aspects of a future research agenda that focuses upon empirical and other issues.

This chapter makes several contributions to the entrepreneurship literature. First, I develop the literature on entrepreneurial mobility to elaborate the processes involved in two particular aspects, habitual entrepreneurs and management buyouts, that focus upon organizational mobility. Second, I extend the emerging strategic entrepreneurship literature by focusing upon the challenges involved in resource orchestration processes in different contexts and types of organization. Third I extend the literature on organizational context by considering how entrepreneurial processes are influenced by different types of context.

2.   RESOURCE ORCHESTRATION

Building upon the resource-based view of the firm (Barney et al. 2011), the strategic entrepreneurship perspective emphasizes the need to select and structure human, social/network, financial and technological resources in order to exploit opportunities and gain competitive advantage, achieve growth and create value (Ireland et al. 2003). Human capital refers to the general (for example, general management skills) and specific (for example, sector, venture creation experience) skills of entrepreneurs and entrepreneurial teams. Social/network resources refer to resources emanating from the embeddedness and ties that entrepreneurs have with trading partners and other stakeholders. Financial resources refer to the specific finance that fits the needs of the entrepreneur, such as venture capital, which typically involves both the provision of finance as well as monitoring and added value expertise. Technological resources include both formal technology (such as patents) and informal technology (skills of the entrepreneur). Technological resources may be quite specific or broad based (platform) resources. Recent developments in the resource based theory of the firm have demonstrated the need for firms to be able to orchestrate or better coordinate their resources and capabilities (Maritan and Peteraf 2011; Sirmon et al. 2007; 2011). Success along these dimensions involves both selecting and structuring the requisite types of resources and capabilities just noted (left-hand box in Figure 2.1) and knowing how to accumulate, bundle and leverage them to generate sustainable returns (right-hand box in Figure 2.1). This process of configuring and bundling resources requires the identification of opportunity recognition, leveraging, championing and networking competencies (Rasmussen et al. 2011). Opportunity refinement refers to the ability iteratively to refine initial ideas into a viable business concept. The leveraging competency concerns the ability of entrepreneurs to build on their own resources and expertise to access resources from trading partners and external investors. The championing competency refers to the ability of someone in the team to take the lead in developing a venture. The networking competency is important since it is the ability to build links or ties with other parties that can help acquire the three other competencies. I examine resource selection and structuring, and the configuration, bundling and leveraging of resources in habitual entrepreneurs and MBOs in different contexts.

3.   CONTEXT

The bottom box in Figure 2.1 refers to different types of context. Although context has received relatively little attention in the entrepreneurial literature (Welter 2011), studying entrepreneurs in the context in which they find themselves is central to understanding the entrepreneurial process (Shane and Venkataraman 2000). Context is, however, not a homogeneous construct, and four dimensions have been identified by Zahra and Wright (2011): temporal, institutional, social and spatial.

The temporal dimension concerns the emergence of ventures over time (life cycle). This emergence has implications for the development of leadership of these companies, and how and whether entrepreneurs and companies learn through this process of emergence and become sustainable ventures (Zahra et al. 2009). Second, the institutional dimension concerns the effect of different institutional contexts. This context includes the characteristics of the external environment and institutional contexts in which ventures emerge. Institutional contexts are taken to include both formal (that is, legal systems and regulations) and informal (that is, norms and values) institutions. Third, the social dimension concerns the business relationships between the various parties that influence the emergence and development of ventures, such as alliance and trading partners, investors, parent corporations and other stakeholders. Finally, the spatial dimension (Welter 2011) denotes the geographical locus and concentration of entrepreneurial ventures and the dispersion of institutions that support these ventures.

4.   ENTREPRENEURIAL MOBILITY

The literature has principally focused on geographical mobility, so far as entrepreneurial mobility is concerned. This has typically involved immigrant entrepreneurship (Levie 2007) although there are emerging studies on returnee and transnational entrepreneurship (Drori et al. 2009; Filatotchev et al. 2011; Liu et al. 2010; Wright et al. 2008).

However, entrepreneurial mobility also involves organizational mobility, which is the focus of this chapter (Wright 2011). Entrepreneurs may shift from one organization or venture to another, becoming habitual entrepreneurs. Alternatively, they may shift part of the organization in which they are employed to become owner-managers of an independent entity through a management buyout (MBO).

4.1   Habitual Entrepreneurs

Many ventures are owned by habitual entrepreneurs and their subcategories of serial entrepreneurs (who own multiple ventures sequentially) and portfolio entrepreneurs (who own multiple ventures concurrently)

(Ucbasaran et al. 2008b). Few habitual entrepreneurs change the geographical location of their subsequent ventures or their industrial sectors.

Increasing interest has been focused upon the cognitive factors influencing how habitual entrepreneurs create new ventures. In particular, attention has been devoted to examining the heuristics and biases used by habitual entrepreneurs in processing information related to opportunities. Entrepreneurial experience enables habitual entrepreneurs to direct their attention in a more focused manner and to be able to interpret information more efficiently so as to better facilitate the generation of ideas. As experts have more developed knowledge structures and schemas, this allows them to unify superficially disparate information and to process more fragmentary information. Habitual entrepreneurs identify more opportunities in a given period than novices, and more innovative opportunities (Ucbasaran et al. 2008a).

Prior entrepreneurial experience may increase the likelihood of pursuing opportunities (Ucbasaran et al. 2008b) as it provides for learning that reduces the costs and risks associated with exploitation. The skills and networks developed as part of prior experience may lead to the identification of better quality opportunities. Concomitantly, such human and social capital may enable experienced entrepreneurs to access and combine the resources they need more cheaply and effectively.

Entrepreneurial experience helps entrepreneurs develop richer knowledge structures that enable faster and more effective information processing. Not only is this likely to make entrepreneurs more likely to be able to identify and process information relating to opportunities, but it is also likely that they will be better able to process information concerning the location of the most advantageous resources and also be able to combine them effectively. However, prior experience may convince habitual entrepreneurs that they should become more risk averse and avoid highly innovative ventures.

The nature of habitual entrepreneurs' prior experience may influence learning. Prior success may have a different impact on learning compared to prior failure. Prior failure may either dissuade entrepreneurs from re-entering entrepreneurship or may make them less optimistic and more cautious in subsequent ventures. However, if entrepreneurs experience success as well as failure, the impact of a single failure event may be less marked. Further, failure of part of a portfolio of ventures may have a less negative impact, and portfolio entrepreneurs may learn more effectively than serial entrepreneurs. Serial entrepreneurs who experience failure of what is their sole current venture may be more likely to blame external factors rather than themselves (Ucbasaran et al. 2009; Ucbasaran et al. 2010).

4.2   Management Buyouts

Distinct from corporate spin-offs (Phan et al. 2009) that involve employees quitting their current employers to create a new venture (Agarwal et al. 2004), MBOs of a divested division or subsidiary of a corporation involve the acquisition by a small group of incumbent management of a set of trading activities that already exist. Management obtain a significant, if not majority equity stake in the new independent entity, with the purchase also being funded by a private equity firm as well as debt providers (Gilligan and Wright 2010). Relatedly, management buy-ins (MBIs) concern acquisition of a division by a new external management team with experience in other organizations. Often the MBO or MBI involves activities that are peripheral to the main business of the parent. However, there may be a continuing trading relationship, and the former parent may retain an equity stake to support this relationship (Wright 1986).

MBOs have traditionally been seen in the finance literature to be concerned with addressing agency issues. However, a long-standing parallel literature has focused upon their entrepreneurial dimensions, especially with respect to the buyout enabling managers to pursue opportunities that they were prevented from doing under the previous ownership regime (Wright and Coyne 1985).

Wright et al. (2000) integrate insights from agency theory and cognition perspectives to present a *conceptual typology* of buyout types. In efficiency buyouts, executives with a managerial mindset are expected to respond positively to enhanced monetary incentives and control mechanisms designed to reduce agency costs by improving efficiencies in mature firms with stable cash flows. In revitalization buyouts, the change of ownership creates the discretionary power for the newly independent management team to decide what is best for the business and to engage in catch-up innovations which have been frustrated by the former corporate owner.

An entrepreneurial perspective recognizes that incumbent management have capabilities with respect to identifying and exploiting growth opportunities. Prior to an MBO, managers might be unable or unwilling to utilize their knowledge to achieve value-creating growth. Management in buyouts may not merely respond to greater incentives. Rather, managers may have an entrepreneurial mindset that enables them to perceive entrepreneurial opportunities; however, such opportunities cannot be realized within the existing ownership and control structure (Wright et al. 2000). In entrepreneurial buyouts, management with an entrepreneurial cognition or mindset, who adopt heuristic-based decision-making, may be able to pursue entrepreneurial opportunities that they have identified, but which could not previously be pursued within a larger group. This change in direction of the firm resulting from a buyout helps highlight a further aspect of how entrepreneurs and managers may be able to change the path dependencies of firms (Ahuja and Katila 2004).

Evidence from divisional buyouts shows significant increases in corporate entrepreneurship, including new product development, better use of research and development, and increased patent citations (Lerner et al. 2008; Wright et al. 1992; Zahra 1995). Post-MBO these firms do achieve growth and the experience of private equity firms aids this achievement (Meuleman et al. 2009). The heterogeneity of private equity firms involved in MBOs is beginning to be examined, in terms of prior sector experience and intensity of monitoring models. However, the processes by which management and their private equity firm backers identify and exploit the new opportunities facilitated by the buyout are little understood. Similarly, while the Wright et al. (2000) typology has provided a conceptual distinction between managers in buyouts who have a managerial or an entrepreneurial mindset, empirical evidence exploring this distinction is lacking.

Private equity (PE) investors in MBOs may play a central role in ensuring that resources are accessed and configured in a more effective way to exploit opportunities than prior to the ownership change (Bruining and Wright 2002). Bruining et al. (2012) show not only that buyouts are efficiency driven but that PE backed buyouts significantly increase entrepreneurial management practices.

5. ENTREPRENEURIAL MOBILITY, RESOURCE ORCHESTRATION AND CONTEXT

In this section, I consider themes relating to resource orchestration for habitual entrepreneurs and entrepreneurs involved in MBOs in each of the four contexts. These themes are summarized in Table 2.1.

5.1 Temporal

As noted above, evidence shows that habitual entrepreneurs identify more opportunities than novice entrepreneurs, but also may change the nature of the opportunities they pursue according to whether prior experience was successful or not. However, how habitual entrepreneurs acquire or develop resources and whether these processes change between earlier and later ventures is little understood.

We know little about whether and how habitual entrepreneurs develop the processes by which they access and configure resources over time from

Table 2.1 Summary of potential themes for a research agenda: context, orchestration and mobility

Mobility Type	Context			
	Temporal	Institutional	Social	Spatial
Habitual entrepreneur	How do habitual entrepreneurs develop access to sufficient human capital, sources of finance, technology, and networks over the time from initial to later ventures? Is this development process linear or non-linear?	What are the implications for different approaches to resource orchestration for habitual entrepreneurs in different institutional contexts?	How do habitual entrepreneurs access and evolve with business ecosystems?	To what extent and how are habitual entrepreneurs better placed than novice entrepreneurs to overcome the problems of geographical concentrations of finance providers?
	How does the way in which habitual entrepreneurs configure their resource develop across their different ventures over time? Does this depend on whether ventures are created or acquired?	How do differences in institutional regulations regarding bankruptcy affect the ability of individuals to be able to assemble the resources they need for new ventures following failure?	How do habitual entrepreneurs facilitate local networks to enable local resources to be assembled that signal credible quality to venture capital firms?	To what extent do particular local business ecosystems involve different forms of entrepreneurship? For example, what role do habitual entrepreneurs play in different ecosystems?

Table 2.1 (continued)

Mobility Type	Context			
	Temporal	Institutional	Social	Spatial
Habitual entrepreneur	How do the processes of resource access and configuration vary according to whether prior experience was successful or not?	How do equity gaps vary between institutional contexts and how can these be addressed?	How do habitual entrepreneurs draw upon their social context to develop their teams and boards in subsequent ventures to introduce new competencies?	To what extent do habitual entrepreneurs move between spatial contexts and how is this achieved in terms of resource orchestration?
Management buyouts	How do MBO entrepreneurs change their access to resources and skills to identify opportunities following buyout from the parent?	How do different labour laws influence changes in the configuration of human capital following buyout?	To what extent do private equity firms provide a new set of social relationships that replace those previously provided by the parent corporation?	How do MBOs of divisions address challenges posed by concentrations of private equity providers in major cities?

How do private equity firms contribute to resource access and configuration in the period from buyout to exit?

How do resource orchestration processes differ between first time, secondary and tertiary buyouts?

How do different labour regulations affect how employees influence the direction of the firm through board and works councils representation?

To what extent is the human and social capital of PE firms mobile across institutional contexts to be able to add value to buyout deals with internationalization prospects?

To what extent do trading relationships with former parents create challenges in addressing asymmetries of interdependencies with the dominant firm in the business ecosystem?

How do MBO managers build new social networks to reduce their dependence on former parent corporations?

In mature sectors, to what extent does geographical concentration of firms in the same sector provide opportunities for alliances and/or consolidation to gain better access to resources?

To what extent does the MBO provide the opportunity to relocate the business to a spatial context more conducive to resource orchestration?

Source: Author.

initial to subsequent ventures. If habitual entrepreneurs learn from prior experience it may be expected that they will be better able to identify the most efficient and appropriate resources and combine them more effectively. But we know from prior research that habitual entrepreneurs may be fixated on identifying the same kinds of opportunities and that learning may be imperfect. Following this line of reasoning, it may also be the case that they do not necessarily learn to seek out resources and combine them more effectively.

The modes used by habitual entrepreneurs may involve start-ups and/ or purchases of existing ventures (Ucbasaran et al. 2008). Habitual entrepreneurs may change their mode of exploitation between initial and subsequent ventures. The reasons for these differences relate both to the nature of the opportunity identified and to the resource orchestration processes involved. At present, we know little about these resource orchestration processes and how they may change across venture modes.

Many entrepreneurial ventures are created by teams (Wright and Vanaelst 2009). Habitual entrepreneurs may change their teams between ventures in order both to access different mixes of human and social capital resources but also to bring in different championing and networking competencies that may be required in new situations. There is little evidence on whether and how habitual entrepreneurs change their teams. Similarly, habitual entrepreneurs may develop improved governance arrangements such as boards as they become more experienced at entrepreneurial activities. Habitual entrepreneurs developing multiple ventures concurrently may also need to develop the governance arrangements needed to monitor their portfolio of activities. The effectiveness with which the board operates can be an important resource for habitual entrepreneurs, particularly if they themselves have a comparative advantage in identifying and exploiting opportunities. Further analysis is needed of this topic.

With respect to MBOs, managers who become entrepreneurs need initially to orchestrate resources to establish the business as an independent entity. MBO entrepreneurs may need to ensure that suppliers and customers will remain with the business when ownership changes hands, since trading partners may be concerned about the viability of the business once it is no longer part of a larger corporate entity.

Many MBOs have private equity firms as investors, and much debate has concerned their contribution to improved performance. While private equity firms typically will take board seats and engage in extensive involvement in setting the strategy for the buyout during the first 100 days, the process by which this is achieved has been little studied. Further the process of reconfiguration where MBOs underperform, which involves replacement of senior management and financial restructuring, requires further analysis. Similarly, the process of preparing MBOs for exit and effecting an exit is also an interesting area for further study.

A subsequent temporal aspect concerns MBOs that become secondary buyouts following the exit of the initial investors. Incoming investors will also need to have been convinced that there are further opportunities for value creation. This appears to pose a major challenge since studies of secondary buyouts indicate that performance outcomes are not as great as in first-time buyouts (Jelic and Wright 2011).

5.2 Institutional

Variations between institutional contexts may influence the extent to which habitual entrepreneurs can assemble and configure the resources they need for their various ventures. To some extent, this may relate to the tax regime which may or may not provide incentives to create further businesses.

Not all habitual entrepreneurs, of course, have been successful in their earlier ventures. Differences in institutional regulations regarding bankruptcy may affect the ability of individuals to be able to assemble the resources they need for new ventures following failure. For example, in some contexts it may simply be illegal to start another business, or failure may carry with it both a cultural and business related stigma that means that financiers, prospective customers and suppliers and potential employees will be unwilling to engage with prospective habitual entrepreneurs who have previously failed.

There has been extensive debate about the nature of equity gaps for entrepreneurial firms. This debate has primarily focused on access to funding for nascent and novice entrepreneurs. The existence and nature of an equity gap may vary between institutional contexts. There may be a need for more fine-grained analysis of the nature of equity gaps and the targeting of policy to fill these specific gaps that enables support for habitual entrepreneurs as well as novice entrepreneurs (Ucbasaran et al. 2008b).

MBO activity has been growing in different countries (Wright and Bruining 2008). An important aspect of buyout value creation involves the reconfiguration of the businesses acquired, especially in relation to human resources (Amess and Wright 2007; 2011; Bacon et al. 2010). For MBOs completed in institutional contexts with different labour regulations, there may be significant challenges in effecting such reconfigurations.

MBOs in different countries are increasingly invested in by foreign private equity firms. A major challenge concerns the extent to which the human and social capital of private equity firms can be transferred to other institutional contexts (Meuleman and Wright 2011). Certain resources and capabilities may be fungible across borders while others are not (Meyer et al. 2009). To the extent that such resources are fungible, MBOs may be able to benefit from having overseas investors.

5.3 Social

The business-related social contexts within which habitual entrepreneurs operate may provide access to different kinds of networks that enable them to identify and exploit opportunities. Habitual entrepreneurs may need to draw upon these social contexts to access the expertise they need to configure boards with the expertise to develop subsequent ventures.

However, all entrepreneurs face the challenges of entering into existing business ecosystems, often dominated by incumbents. A business ecosystem is an economic community supported by a foundation of interacting organizations and individuals that include customers, suppliers, lead producers, competitors, and other stakeholders (Moore 1996). Business ecosystems develop over time and, by virtue of their experience, habitual entrepreneurs may be better able to access these business ecosystems than are novice entrepreneurs. Further, the development of the various ventures by the habitual entrepreneur may co-evolve with the business ecosystem. For example, being part of an evolving business ecosystem may enable the habitual entrepreneur to identify new opportunities but also to access the resources and capabilities needed to exploit them.

MBOs do not face the same challenges in entering business ecosystems, but as noted above, their position within the ecosystem may be under some strain once they become independent from the parent corporation. Further, where trading relationships continue with the former parent, particular challenges regarding resource access and configuration may arise if the buyout is heavily dependent on the former parent (Wright 1986). To some extent there may be some form of mutual interdependence that may be appropriate if both parties are involved in collaborating in the development and production of complex products. But the interdependence may be asymmetrical and the MBO entrepreneurs may need to engage in activities to diversify the resource and customer base with other participants in the ecosystem or may need to forge links to other business ecosystems.

5.4 Spatial

Financial availability may be concentrated in certain geographical regions and it is sometimes argued that firms may benefit from spatial proximity. However, this argument is being challenged (Huggins 2008). Habitual entrepreneurs may be able to overcome these geographical constraints.

Mueller et al. (2011) find in the case of university spin-offs that those ventures geographically located outside main financial centres are more likely to obtain venture capital funding if their founders have previous venture creation experience. Similarly, habitual entrepreneurs not involved with university spin-offs may also be able to signal their quality. At present, though, there is a lack of evidence on when habitual entrepreneurs undertake such signalling and on the processes through which they do so.

We noted earlier the involvement of habitual entrepreneurs in business ecosystems. There may also be a spatial dimension to these challenges. For example, particular local business ecosystems involve different forms of entrepreneurship, and habitual entrepreneurs with experience of the local context may play a more important role. Habitual entrepreneurs may also play a role in helping develop spatial ecosystems towards regional innovation systems or milieux.

For smaller MBOs especially, concentrations of investors may raise issues concerning access to funding to purchase the business in the first place but also for follow-on funding to enable the business to grow. In mature and fragmented sectors, geographical concentration of firms may provide opportunities for alliances and/or consolidation to gain better access to resources and compete in the face of dominant customers. Alternatively, the MBO may provide the opportunity for management to implement options to relocate the business to a spatial context more conducive to resource orchestration that was not possible under the previous ownership.

6. CONCLUSIONS

The analysis in this chapter raises several opportunities and challenges for further research. First, the research themes identified suggest a need for further theory-building research, qualitative studies and quantitative analysis. Focusing upon how resources are orchestrated opens up opportunities for in-depth process studies in the different contexts. The temporal context especially suggests a need for longitudinal studies.

Quantitative analysis can help shed light upon the profiles of the entrepreneurs engaging in the two forms of entrepreneurial mobility presented here, focusing upon their human and social capital as well as their cognitive attributes. Quantitative analysis could also make the link to firm performance. Quantitative analysis also needs to consider the development of more fine-grained measures of context. Further, although I have discussed the four contexts separately, there are overlaps between them and empirical analysis may need to consider interaction effects.

Of course, developing datasets for quantitative analysis poses major challenges. Archival datasets of private firms are available in some jurisdictions (for example, the UK and Sweden) and may provide performance measures. However, such datasets may not distinguish novice from habitual entrepreneurs, or between serial and portfolio entrepreneurs. Similarly, these datasets may not distinguish MBOs from other private firms. Datasets of private equity backed buyouts are available (for example CapitalIQ) and there is a need in these datasets to distinguish divisional buyouts from buyouts from other vendor sources. There may also be a need either to integrate these datasets with other datasets that contain relevant variables relating to context and/or to integrate them with questionnaire survey data. Private company registration documents that contain information on founding directors, changes in directors, and director characteristics and their experience may be accessible in some jurisdictions.

The discussion I have presented has treated habitual and MBO entrepreneurs separately. Further research could also consider differences in resource orchestration processes between these two types. For example, there may be significant differences in approach between entrepreneurs who have built up the experience from starting multiple ventures compared to individuals who have become entrepreneurs through purchasing the business in which they worked and taking it out from the corporate umbrella.

Finally, my focus in this chapter has been on entrepreneurial mobility between organizations. As noted at the outset, entrepreneurial mobility is often discussed in terms of geographical mobility. Such mobility also presents opportunities to analyse the challenges of resource orchestration in the different contexts examined here.

REFERENCES

Agarwal, R., R. Echambadi, A. Franco and M. Sarkar (2004), 'Knowledge transfer through inheritance: spin-out generation, development and survival', *Academy of Management Journal*, **47**, 501–22.

Ahuja, G. and R. Katila (2004), 'Where do resources come from? The role of idiosyncratic situations', *Strategic Management Journal*, **25**, 887–907.

Amess, K. and M. Wright (2007), 'The wage and employment effects of leveraged buyouts in the UK', *International Journal of Economics and Business*, **14** (2), 179–95.

Amess, K. and M. Wright (2011), 'Leveraged buyouts, private equity and jobs', *Small Business Economics*, forthcoming.

Bacon, N., M. Wright, L. Scholes and M. Meuleman (2010), 'Assessing the impact of private equity on industrial relations in Europe', *Human Relations*, **63** (9), 1343–70.

Barney, J.B., D. Ketchen and M. Wright (2011), 'The future of resource-based theory: revitalization or decline?', *Journal of Management*, **37**, 1299–315.

Bruining, H. and M. Wright (2002), 'Entrepreneurial orientation in management buyouts and the contribution of venture capital', *Venture Capital*, **4** (2), 147–68.

Bruining, H., E. Verwaal and M. Wright (2012), 'Private equity and entrepreneurial management in management buyouts', *Small Business Economics*, forthcoming.

Drori, I., B. Honig and M. Wright (2009), 'Transnational entrepreneurs', *Entrepreneurship Theory and Practice*, **33**, 1001–22.

Filatotchev, I., X. Liu, J. Lu and M. Wright (2011), 'Knowledge spillovers through human mobility across national borders: evidence from Zhongguancun Science Park in China', *Research Policy*, **40** (3), 453–62.

Gilligan, J. and M. Wright (2010), *Private Equity Demystified*, 2nd ed, London: ICAEW.

Huggins, R. (2008), 'Universities and knowledge-based venturing: finance, management and networks in London', *Entrepreneurship and Regional Development*, **20**, 185–206.

Ireland, R.D., M.A. Hitt and D.G. Sirman (2003), 'A model of strategic entrepreneurship: the construct and its dimensions', *Journal of Management*, **29** (6), 963–89.

Jelic, R. and M. Wright (2011), 'Exits, performance, and late stage capital: the case of UK management buy-outs', *European Financial Management*, **17** (3), 560–93.

Lerner, J., P. Strömberg and M. Sørensen (2008), 'Private equity and long-run investment: the case of innovation', in J. Lerner and A. Gurung (eds), *The Global Impact of Private Equity Report 2008, Globalization of Alternative Investments*, Working Papers Volume 1, World Economic Forum, pp. 27–42.

Levie, J. (2007), 'Immigration, in-migration, ethnicity and entrepreneurship: insights from the GEM UK database', *Small Business Economics*, **28** (2), 143–69.

Liu, X., J. Lu, I. Filatotchev, T. Buck and M. Wright (2010), 'Returnee entrepreneurs, knowledge spillovers and innovation in high-tech firms in emerging economies', *Journal of International Business Studies*, **41**, 1183–97.

Maritan, C. and M.A. Peteraf (2011), 'Building a bridge between resource acquisition and resource accumulation', *Journal of Management*, **37**, 1374–89.

Meuleman, M. and M. Wright (2011), 'Cross-border private equity syndication: institutional context and learning', *Journal of Business Venturing*, **26** (1), 35–48.

Meuleman, M., K. Amess, M. Wright and L. Scholes (2009), 'Agency, strategic entrepreneurship, and the performance of private equity-backed buyouts', *Entrepreneurship Theory and Practice*, **33** (1), 213–39.

Meyer, K., M. Wright and S. Pruthi (2009), 'Managing knowledge in foreign entry strategies: a resource-based analysis', *Strategic Management Journal*, **30** (5), 557–74.

Moore, J.F. (1996), *The Death of Competition: Leadership & Strategy in the Age of Business Ecosystems*, New York: HarperBusiness.

Mueller, C., P. Westhead and M. Wright (2011), 'Formal venture capital acquisition: can entrepreneurs compensate for the spatial proximity benefits of south east of England and "star" golden triangle universities?', *Environment and Planning A*, forthcoming.

Phan, P., M. Wright, D. Ucbasaran and W.-L. Tan (2009), 'Corporate entrepreneurship: current research and future directions', *Journal of Business Venturing*, **24**, 197–205.

Rasmussen, E., S. Mosey and M. Wright (2011), 'The evolution of entrepreneurial competencies: a longitudinal study of university spin-off venture emergence', *Journal of Management Studies*, **48**, 1314–46.

Shane, S.A. and S. Venkataraman (2000), 'The promise of entrepreneurship as a field of research', *Academy of Management Review*, **26**, 217–26.

Sirmon, D.G., M.A. Hitt and R.D. Ireland (2007), 'Managing firm resources in dynamic environments to create value: looking inside the black box', *Academy of Management Review*, **32** (1), 273–92.

Sirmon, D.G., M.A. Hitt, R.D. Ireland and B.A. Gilbert (2011), 'Resource orchestration to create competitive advantage: breadth, depth and life cycle effects', *Journal of Management*, **37**, 1390–412.

Ucbasaran, D., P. Westhead and M. Wright (2008a), 'Opportunity identification and pursuit: does an entrepreneur's human capital matter?', *Small Business Economics*, **30** (2), 153–73.

Ucbasaran, D., P. Westhead and M. Wright (2009), 'The extent and nature of opportunity identification by repeat entrepreneurs', *Journal of Business Venturing*, **24**, 99–115.

Ucbasaran, D., P. Westhead, M. Wright and M. Flores (2010), 'The nature of entrepreneurial experience, business failure and comparative optimism', *Journal of Business Venturing*, **25**, 541–55.

Ucbasaran, D., G. Alsos, P. Westhead and M. Wright (2008b), 'Habitual entrepreneurs', *Foundations and Trends in Entrepreneurship*, **4** (4), 1–93.

Welter, F. (2011), 'Contextualizing entrepreneurship – conceptual challenges and ways forward', *Entrepreneurship Theory and Practice*, **35** (1), 165–78.

Wright, M. (1986), 'The make–buy decision and managing markets: the case of management buy-outs', *Journal of Management Studies*, **23** (4), 443–64.

Wright, M. (2011), 'Entrepreneurial mobility', in D. Bergh and D. Ketchen (eds), *Research Methodology in Strategy and Management*, Vol. 6., forthcoming.

Wright, M. and H. Bruining (2008), *Private Equity and Management Buyouts*, Cheltenham, UK and Northampton, MA, USA: Edward Elgar Publishing.

Wright, M. and J. Coyne (1985), *Management Buyouts*, Beckenham: Croom Helm.

Wright, M. and I. Vanaelst (2009), *Entrepreneurial Teams*, Cheltenham, UK and Northampton, MA, USA: Edward Elgar Publishing.

Wright, M., S. Mosey and B. Clarysse (2011), 'Challenges in growing spin-offs from universities', *Imperial College Business School Working Paper*, London.

Wright, M., S. Thompson and K. Robbie (1992), Venture capital and management-led leveraged buy-outs: a European perspective', *Journal of Business Venturing*, **7** (1), 47–71.

Wright, M., R. Hoskisson, L. Busenitz and J. Dial (2000), 'Entrepreneurial growth through privatization: the upside of management buy-outs', *Academy of Management Review*, **25** (3), 591–601.

Wright, M., X. Liu, T. Buck and I. Filatotchev (2008), 'Returnee entrepreneur characteristics, science park location choice and performance: an analysis of high technology SMEs in China', *Entrepreneurship Theory and Practice*, **32** (1), 131–56.

Zahra, S.A. (1995), 'Corporate entrepreneurship and financial performance: the case of management leveraged buyouts', *Journal of Business Venturing*, **10**, 225–47.

Zahra, S.A. and M. Wright (2011), 'Entrepreneurship's next act', *Academy of Management Perspectives*, **25**, 67–83.
Zahra, S., I. Filatotchev and M. Wright (2009), 'How do threshold firms sustain corporate entrepreneurship? The role of boards of directors and knowledge', *Journal of Business Venturing*, **24**, 248–60.

3. Cohesion, liveability and firm success in Dutch neighbourhoods

Bart Sleutjes, Frank Van Oort and Veronique Schutjens

1. INTRODUCTION

Residential neighbourhoods function as 'breeding places' for firm activity. Many small-scale firms are started within inner-city milieux or within residential neighbourhoods because of their limited demand for space and the proximity of network contacts, which are important for the provision of resources and reputational development in the early stages of a firm's life cycle. As a result, an increasing number of small and medium-sized firms are located within residential districts, including those with visible functions, such as shops, and invisible business services firms that are operated from the entrepreneurs' homes (Aalders et al. 2008). For many of these neighbourhood-based entrepreneurs, their own neighbourhood is where most of their daily life takes place. This 'everydayness' of entrepreneurship makes the neighbourhood a potentially important arena for entrepreneurial processes, because it is a 'relational space' that brings together different transaction benefits (Johannisson 2011).

In recent years, the neighbourhood economy has regained the attention of policy makers in several European countries, including the Netherlands and Germany. Dutch urban policy has adopted a neighbourhood-targeted approach to urban social and economic problems (Van Gent et al. 2009). Stimulating local entrepreneurship is regarded as a way to improve the economic profile of neighbourhoods and to help unemployed neighbourhood residents obtain jobs. It is assumed that local businesses also have positive, non-economic side effects; for example, entrepreneurs' input plays a significant role in improving local social and physical order (Schutjens and Steenbeek 2010). In other words, neighbourhoods are expected to benefit in several ways from the presence of local firms. However, it is not known whether local firms also benefit from their neighbourhood.

The urban geographical literature dealing with 'neighbourhood effects' states that living in a disadvantaged neighbourhood negatively influences individuals' development opportunities (Andersson et al. 2007, Musterd and Andersson 2006). We expect that such neighbourhood effects also exist for the performance of local firms. The social, physical and economic characteristics of neighbourhoods influence both local market prospects (via average income levels, the attractiveness of the business environment and competition forces) and opportunities for networking (via cohesiveness). Thus far, policy makers have assumed that these neighbourhood effects on local firms exist, but empirical evidence on the existence and magnitude of these effects is lacking. However, a recent study by PBL (2010) showed that local firm dynamics in Dutch urban neighbourhoods are influenced by the physical characteristics and disorder of the neighbourhood, in addition to economic and market factors. In this study, we further investigate the relationship between firms and their environment at the neighbourhood level, with a specific focus on local social and physical order – specifically, cohesiveness and liveability. The main research question of this chapter is as follows: how do neighbourhood cohesiveness and liveability relate to local firms' chances for survival and growth?

This study makes a threefold contribution to the existing literature. First, by linking firm performance to social neighbourhood aspects, we address a relatively unexamined but important research field (Welter et al. 2008). Second, we focus on the smallest spatial scale, the local neighbourhood, while most previous studies have been conducted at the district level or even the metropolitan level (e.g., Audretsch and Dohse 2007, Love and Crompton 1999). We argue, however, that aspects such as local liveability and social cohesion are relevant at a much smaller spatial range: the immediate neighbourhood environment or even the block level. Third, instead of focusing on districts only within urban regions, we study the firms within and characteristics of both urban and rural areas, thereby providing a representative picture of Dutch neighbourhoods.

Furthermore, we contribute to recent policy debates. The recent turn by several European governments (e.g., the Netherlands and Germany) and the European Union (URBAN II programme) to the neighbourhood economy as a solution for urban social and economic problems demands insight into the intra-urban patterns of the new economic potential. Some of the factors that relate to the success of local firms may be in the realm of local policy makers.

This chapter is structured as follows. In the second section, we examine the existing literature on firm success and the potential influence of the neighbourhood context. After describing the data and methodology in the third section, the fourth section presents the analyses of firm survival and firm growth with a focus on the role of neighbourhood influences. Finally, the fifth section provides an answer to our research question and concludes with a discussion of the findings, followed by policy implications.

2.   LITERATURE REVIEW AND HYPOTHESES

2.1   The Role of 'the Local' in Firm Success

Firm success is generally understood as firm survival and firm growth. Firm survival implies that a firm does not leave the market within a given period. Firm growth is a broad term, and stakeholders attach different values to its various forms. Whereas for entrepreneurs growth in terms of profits and sales is likely to be the most important aspect, local governments are more concerned with employment growth because of its beneficial effects for society (Bridge et al. 2003).

Studies have examined the differences between urban and rural districts in terms of the influence of the spatial context on local firm success. In general, urban areas are regarded as better production milieux than rural areas because of the larger local demand (Davidsson et al. 2010). The concentration of firms in a certain location leads to 'agglomeration advantages' or 'externalities', such as the availability of skilled and specialized labour, intermediary goods and the potential to quickly exchange ideas and innovations – the old 'Marshallian' economies. Through face-to-face contacts in clusters, both codified and tacit knowledge is easily transmitted from one firm to another (Storper and Venables 2004). Geographical proximity also strengthens competition through a common market, and enables the sharing of suppliers (RPB 2006).

However, the positive effect of clustering on the survival and growth chances of firms is disputed. Firms do not necessarily have to be located in close spatial proximity to benefit from knowledge and resource spillovers. Most firms are 'embedded' within a network of suppliers, customers and institutions (Bathelt and Glückler 2003), which, by definition, is not local. In addition, a negative aspect of clustering is the related strong level of competition that decreases firms' survival prospects, especially when there is a large concentration of similar firms (Sorenson 2003).

The literature on clusters and (knowledge) externalities focuses on the regional level. However, there are reasons to believe that determinants at a smaller spatial level (that is, specific neighbourhood characteristics) also influence local firms' survival and growth prospects. We distinguish three functions of neighbourhoods that relate to economic potential.

The first function is the neighbourhood as a *living environment*, which is relevant because many entrepreneurs within residential neighbourhoods work from or close to home (Ouwehand and Van Meijeren 2006). Therefore, personal preferences for housing or the residential environment, rather than purely economic reasons, determine entrepreneurs' location choices and relocation likelihood. Research over the past two decades has focused on the importance of so-called 'quality-of-life' factors on firms' location decisions (e.g., Glaeser et al. 2001, Love and Crompton 1999). Local liveability aspects, in particular (perceived) crime rates, are often mentioned as potential bottlenecks for entrepreneurs, especially by entrepreneurs that are located in disadvantaged neighbourhoods (Bates and Robb 2008). Nuisances and crime are more likely to occur in low-income neighbourhoods with an unattractive housing stock (Marlet et al. 2008). In particular, locally oriented firms are affected by the local liveability situation through its effect on local customer potential. Both actual and potential customers are more likely to search for shopping alternatives if they do not feel safe in the neighbourhood or if they consider the local environment unattractive.

However, little research has examined the relationship between local liveability and firm performance. A recent study by PBL (2010) showed that local crime, nuisance and deterioration influence firm survival and firm growth negatively. However, the relationship between liveability and local firms is two-sided because certain types of economic activity, such as shopping malls and bars, tend to attract various forms of nuisance and petty crime (Marlet 2010). In addition to a direct relationship between local liveability and firm success, local liveability may indirectly influence firm success by prompting middle-class residents to move, beginning a vicious circle of neighbourhood decline (Wilson 1987). Amenities tend to follow the middle class to other neighbourhoods, leading to a further downgrading of the local amenity structure and, eventually, the out-migration of larger numbers of higher-income households and a further decrease in spending power.

Second, the neighbourhood functions as a *community* (Ouwehand and Van Meijeren 2006) where residents and entrepreneurs interact. Neighbourhoods that are characterized by intensive and high-quality interactions between residents, as well as high levels of interpersonal trust, are generally perceived to be *cohesive* (Forrest and Kearns 2001). Neighbourhood cohesiveness can be conceptualized in several ways. The first conceptualization is 'community', which combines the factors of affection, comfort, stimulation and status (Völker et al. 2007). In the context of residential neighbourhoods, this concept refers to the intensity and quality of contacts between neighbourhood residents, the number of common activities, and the extent to which residents feel safe and respected in their neighbourhood. The second concept, which involves the factors of social cohesion, trust and social control, is 'collective efficacy' (Sampson et al. 1997). Collective efficacy is the perception of individuals within a group (in this case, a neighbourhood) about the capability of the group as a whole to achieve common goals. This belief in the capabilities of the group positively affects individual decisions to engage in certain behaviours. An example relevant to the context of urban neighbourhoods is the expectation that others will intervene in cases of nuisance and petty crime.

Hackler and Mayer's (2008) empirical study on entrepreneurs and their environment stressed the importance of entrepreneurs' social environments in obtaining skills, human capital, financial resources and market areas. According to a conceptual study by Lambooy (2010), social capital is often restricted to the region in which the firm is located, where inter-personal interactions enable the transfer of knowledge. Neighbourhood cohesiveness and local firm success are linked through trust and local social contacts. Dubini's (1989) empirical study on the interaction between peripheral Italian firms and their local context showed that 'munificent environments', characterized by strong social contacts, benefit the net-working potential of entrepreneurs. Some empirical evidence suggests that firms benefit from their entrepreneurs' local inter-firm networks and localized personal contacts, particularly for small firms (Schutjens and Völker 2010).

The third neighbourhood function is the *market* function (Ouwehand and Van Meijeren 2006), including competition, sales relationships and employees. Some firms rely heavily on neighbourhood residents, but there is significant variation between sectors in this respect. The retail, catering and consumer services sectors ('locally oriented sectors'), for example, have many more local customers than firms in business services or manu-facturing (Bulterman et al. 2007). The performance levels of locally ori-ented firms in different neighbourhoods are therefore likely to vary with differences in levels of local spending power. It is assumed that affluent neighbourhoods, through high spending power, offer more favourable market conditions for firms that depend on local customers than low-income districts do. Dutch empirical studies confirm that locally oriented firms in disadvantaged districts not only have lower sales growth levels than firms in affluent areas, they are even outperformed by non-locally oriented firms in disadvantaged neighbourhoods (Aalders et al. 2008, Bulterman et al. 2007).

The neighbourhood can also function as a market for employees. Retail firms (that is, shops), in particular, often make use of local employees

(Bulterman et al. 2007), presumably because this kind of labour does not require specific skills and is widely available. The market for skilled labour is a regional, rather than a local, phenomenon (Audretsch and Dohse 2007).

The 'living environment' and 'community' functions are the focus of this study. The 'market' function will be considered to be a control because of its obvious relevance for local firm success.

2.2   The Traditional Determinants of Firm Success

In addition to neighbourhood-level determinants, the literature on industrial organization and firm performance shows that the most robust determinants of firm success are at the firm and entrepreneur levels. Firm survival is mainly influenced by factors internal to the firm, such as firm size and firm age. Small firms (with few or no employees) are less likely to survive than relatively large firms, in a 'liability of smallness' (Brüderl and Schüssler 1990). Small firms are often not well endowed with knowledge, resources and financial reserves, which makes them more vulnerable in times of economic decline or increasing competition. In contrast, larger firms have access to more resources and knowledge and are therefore more capable of withstanding economic downturns or increasing competition, and more likely to survive (Tamásy 2006).

Regarding firm age, most evidence is in favour of the 'liability of newness': the probability of failing is the greatest within the crucial early stages in a firm's life cycle (Brüderl and Schüssler 1990), and hazard rates decrease with age (Santarelli and Vivarelli 2007). Empirical evidence shows that approximately 20 to 40 per cent of all new firms fail within the first two years (Garnsey 1998).

There are also differences in firm survival rates between sectors. A high degree of competition and a high share of mature firms within the sector negatively influence the survival prospects of new firm entrants, especially for business service firms (Kaniovski and Peneder 2008). The organization structure of the firm influences survival as well. Having a business partner improves survival prospects through the sharing of knowledge and resources but may also increase the risk of failure if conflicts between partners occur (Tamásy 2006).

Firm characteristics also influence the hiring of employees. In general, young firms show the highest growth rates, and a quarter of all firms, at most, will continue to grow after the first few years (Garnsey 1998). Firms that start with one or more employees tend to show higher rates of employment growth than firms that started without employees (Tamásy 2006), and past growth often leads to future growth (Davidsson et al.

2010). Finally, having a business partner increases the financial capital and consequently the growth chances of entrepreneurs (Bosma et al. 2004).

Firm growth is further related to the personality and individual characteristics of the entrepreneur. First, the entrepreneur's ambition strongly influences whether a firm considers growth in the first place and, in turn, whether this growth is realized or not. However, many business founders have only modest growth ambitions (Davidsson et al. 2010).

Second, in general, entrepreneurs with high human capital (that is, highly-educated and experienced individuals) are expected to be better at perceiving profitable opportunities for new economic activity (Davidsson and Honig 2003). This assumption is supported by empirical evidence (Tamásy 2006, Santarelli and Vivarelli 2007).

Third, in addition to the knowledge and experience necessary to run a business successfully, most entrepreneurs need financial input, and not all entrepreneurs have equal access to financial resources (Garnsey 1998). Credit constraints and a lack of financial capital limit firms' growth prospects (Santarelli and Vivarelli 2007).

2.3   Hypotheses

We formulate three hypotheses based on the above-mentioned literature. First, we expect that the local liveability situation influences local firms' survival and growth prospects, especially through the image of the neighbourhood that trickles down to the firm's reputation. A location in a neighbourhood with high levels of crime and deterioration may negatively affect a firm's reputation and its attractiveness to customers, while a clean and safe environment may attract customers and ultimately boost the image of both the firm and the neighbourhood.

H1:   Neighbourhood liveability is positively related to firm success.

Second, regarding neighbourhood cohesiveness, we expect that the degrees of community and collective efficacy contribute positively to a firm's success by providing access to relevant network contacts and potential customers or employees.

H2:   Neighbourhood cohesiveness is positively related to firm success.

Third, we expect differences between sectors. An attractive local liveability situation and a high degree of cohesiveness within the neighbourhood will especially benefit those firms that depend on local customers, such as the retail sector. We expect that retail firms are affected most by local liveability because the local market orientation of this sector requires an attractive public space for (potential) customers.

H3: Retail firms are more influenced by the neighbourhood context than business services firms.

3. DATA AND METHODOLOGY

3.1 Selection of Neighbourhoods

This study makes use of the neighbourhood selection used in the Survey of Social Networks of Entrepreneurs (SSNE 2008), which focuses on the relationship between local entrepreneurs and neighbourhoods. First, we took a stratified random sample of 40 representative urban and rural areas of the approximately 500 Dutch municipalities and took into account the building density and the number of residents. Second, within those 40 municipalities, we randomly selected four (in one municipality, five) neighbourhoods using the postal code system. This selection yielded 161 neighbourhoods, 16 of which were excluded from the analysis due to a lack of data. It should be noted that our study defines neighbourhoods as five-digit postal code districts. This spatial level is regarded as a good approximation of what people understand as their 'local context' (Völker et al. 2007). Such an area includes 230 addresses, on average, and does not include significant physical barriers, such as rivers or highways.

We used a longitudinal dataset (LISA) that provides data on the sector and the number of employees for all registered firms located within the selected districts. We selected all firms that did not move during the 1999–2006 period, excluding non-profit sectors such as healthcare, education and government. Although we are aware of a potential bias in our data, we decided to omit the movers for four reasons. First, the survival and growth levels of firms that moved away may have been influenced by characteristics of the new neighbourhood instead of the old neighbourhood. Second, we wanted to measure firm success on site, within the selected neighbourhood. Third, we did not know the motivations for relocation, such as the contribution of aspects of the research neighbourhood. Fourth, the share of firm movements is quite low, as only 16 per cent of the total firm population from 1999 moved between 1999 and 2006.[1] Because previous research has shown that aspects of neighbourhoods only marginally influence firm relocations – less than 5 per cent of variance is explained at the neighbourhood level (PBL 2010) – we did not expect this bias to

Table 3.1   Composition of industries within the 145 neighbourhoods

Sector	Share in total firm population (per cent)
Agriculture	2.1
Manufacturing	8.3
Construction	9.3
Trade	3.6
Wholesale	9.3
Retail	21.2
Catering	7.2
Transport and communication	3.4
Financial services	2.2
Business services	21.2
Driving schools and private education	1.9
Culture and recreation	4.1
Personal services	5.6
Total number of firms (2938)	100.0

Source: LISA (2007).

dramatically affect our results. This selection of non-movers resulted in a sample of 2938 firms, with an average size of 5.7 employees (see Table 3.1). The firms were distributed as follows across different industries: 21 per cent were active within retail, 21 per cent were in business services and 8 per cent were in manufacturing. In total, 36 per cent of the firms were active within a locally oriented sector, including retail, consumer services and the catering sector.

3.2   Variables

3.2.1   Dependent variables
We used two indicators of past firm performance as our dependent variables: firm survival and employment growth between 1999 and 2006, derived from the LISA 2007 database. Firms that still existed in 2006 without having moved were coded as 'survivors' (1), whereas firms that ceased activities between 1999 and 2006 were labelled 'non-survivors' (0). Employment growth was a measure of the relative increase or decrease of the number of employees for each firm that survived. This concept was measured as the exact difference between the number of jobs in 2006 and in 1999, which is recoded under three categories. The category 'decline' (1) included all firms that had fewer employees in 2006 than in 1999

Table 3.2   The statements regarding 'community'

---

1   'I feel safe in this neighbourhood'
2   'Contact among the people here is generally good'
3   'There are not many conflicts between people in this neighbourhood'
4   'If something has to be done together, everybody participates'
5   'If somebody needs help s/he can always rely on the neighbours'
6   'In this neighbourhood, people keep to an agreement, even if it is not in their interest'
7   'If somebody is responsible for an inconvenience, s/he apologizes and tries to set things right'
8   'I really belong to this neighbourhood'
9   'If I meet a person on the street, I know where s/he lives'
10   'I trust most of the people who live here'

Source: SSND (2000).

(score < 0). The category 'stabilization' (2) includes all firms that did not see a change in the number of employees (score = 0). The category 'growth' (3) encompasses all firms with a larger number of employees in 2006 than in 1999 (score > 0).

3.2.2   Key independent variables

The key independent variables, liveability and cohesiveness, are related to local physical and social order. Regarding liveability, the Police Population Monitor (PPM) from 2005 provided us with indicators of how neighbourhood residents perceive the occurrence of the following four aspects of neighbourhood disorder: crime against property, physical deterioration, violence and harassment, and insecurity.[2] The PPM is a nationwide biannual Computer Assisted Telephone Interviewing (CATI) survey among residents with questions about residents' perceptions of neighbourhood disorder.

For each of the neighbourhoods under investigation, we included two indicators of neighbourhood cohesiveness. First, the indicator 'community' is based on the score of neighbourhood residents within the same five-digit postal code districts on ten propositions (Table 3.2) in the 2000 Survey of the Social Networks of the Dutch (SSND). Taken together, these statements result in a Cronbach's alpha of 0.801 and provide an indication of the quality of contacts among neighbourhood residents (Forrest and Kearns 2001). Respondents could answer with 'I do not agree at all' (1), 'I do not fully agree' (2) or 'I agree' (3). The aggregate of these scores on ten propositions divided by the number of neighbourhood respondents

Table 3.3   The statements regarding collective efficacy

---

1 'Children who are truant: would someone from the neighbourhood do something?'
2 'Adolescents who spray graffiti: would someone from the neighbourhood do something?'
3 'Violent arguing: would someone from the neighbourhood do something?'
4 'Burglary observed: would someone from the neighbourhood do something?'
5 'Vandalizing parked cars: would someone from the neighbourhood do something?'

Source: SSND (2000).

produce the level of neighbourhood cohesiveness. The average score for all districts is 24.42. The higher the score, the more cohesive the neighbourhood is.

Second, we included a measure of 'collective efficacy', the degree to which neighbourhood residents expect that others in the neighbourhood would intervene in situations in which local social or physical order was violated (Sampson et al. 1997). This variable was constructed by taking the average score of five statements regarding the expected response of other neighbourhood residents to inappropriate behaviour (Table 3.3). Respondents could answer with 'Not true' (1), 'Not really true' (2) or 'True' (3). A high average score corresponds with a high degree of collective efficacy.

3.2.3 Control variables

We included in our model control variables at the firm level and at the neighbourhood level only, as the LISA database does not contain information on firm owners. At the firm level, we included firm size, in terms of the number of employees in 1999, and firm sector ('locally oriented' versus 'non-locally oriented'). 'Locally-oriented sectors' are defined as those sectors that traditionally depend on (customers in) the neighbourhood and the area immediately surrounding it. Examples of locally oriented sectors are retail, the catering sector and consumer-based services. Those sectors offer products or services for which people are not prepared to travel long distances. The group of 'non-locally oriented sectors' consists of business services, manufacturing, building, and cultural activities that mainly serve non-local markets (Bulterman et al. 2007).

At the neighbourhood level,[3] we controlled for factors related to the local market. From Statistics Netherlands (2006), we derived the building density and the average monthly income. The building density variable indicates the number of addresses per square kilometre and is subdivided into five categories, ranked from very high urban (1) to very low urban (5). Average income measures the average monthly household income for the neighbourhood in euros. These factors determine the size of the local market and the level of local spending power, respectively.[4]

Table 3.4 summarizes the definitions of the variables included in the model and provides an overview of the mean values and standard deviations of all of the variables under study. Table 3.5 presents the correlation matrix, including all neighbourhood-level variables. The table shows that there are no strong correlations between the neighbourhood characteristics.

3.3 Methodology

The research question calls for an analysis that includes factors of different hierarchical levels. We explain phenomena at the firm level using the characteristics of both the firm and the neighbourhood. This is regarded as a 'multilevel problem' because explanatory variables at the neighbourhood level may serve as moderators of individual-level relationships (Hox 2002). Multilevel analysis is an appropriate method to examine the different levels because firms are nested within neighbourhoods. Accounting for this nested structure acknowledges that the assumption of independent observations is violated in grouped data.

The co-variation between individuals' behaviour when sharing the same neighbourhood externalities is expressed by the *intraclass correlation*. This correlation indicates how much of the variance is being explained at the neighbourhood level. For the group of surviving firms, we analysed employment growth between 1999 and 2006. The analysis was repeated for the retail and business services sectors separately, to test Hypothesis 3.

4. RESULTS

Of our sample of almost 3000 firms, 58 per cent survived during the period of 1999–2006. This indicates that the firms did not leave the market and did not move out of the neighbourhoods where they were located in 1999. Of all surviving firms, 27 per cent achieved employment growth during this time span, whereas an almost equal number of firms witnessed a decrease in the number of employees. Nearly half of all surviving firms remained stable in terms of the number of employees.

An interesting finding is that none of the key independent variables at the neighbourhood level are related to survival (Table 3.6). This is true not

Table 3.4 Description and source of variables

Type of variable		Source	Value	Percentage	Mean	Standard deviation
Firm survival	Firm survived during the 1999–2006 period	LISA 2007	0 = no 1 = yes	42 58		
Employment growth	The relative employment growth that was achieved between 1999 and 2006, proxied by the difference in the number of jobs in 2006 and 1999	LISA 2007	1 = decline (< 0) 2 = stable (0) 3 = growth (> 0)	26 47 27		
Employees in 1999	The number of employees at start of measurement (1999)	LISA 2007			5.71	19.36
Locally oriented sector	Firm is active within a locally oriented sector (retail, catering, personal services)	LISA 2007	0 = no 1 = yes	64 36		
Building density	The average building density within the neighbourhood, based on the number of addresses per square kilometre (data: 2004)	CBS 2006	1 = very high urban (2500 addresses/km²) 2 = high urban (1500 to < 2500 addresses/km²) 3 = moderately urban (1000 to < 1500 addresses/km²) 4 = low urban (500 to < 1000 addresses/km²)	15.5 21.5 7.3 21.5		

			5 = very low urban (< 500 addresses/km²) 34.2		
Average income	The average monthly household income, in euros (data: 2004)	CBS 2004	2107.97	543.88	
Cohesiveness	The degree of social cohesion within the neighbourhood	SSND 2000	24.42	2.87	
Collective efficacy	The extent to which residents expect that others will intervene in certain situations that affect the community as a whole	SSND 2000	14.43	2.38	
Property crime	The extent to which residents perceive property crime to occur within the neighbourhoods	PPM 2005	3.07	1.84	
Deterioration	The extent to which residents perceive deterioration to occur within the neighbourhoods	PPM 2005	3.13	1.72	
Violence and harassment	The extent to which residents perceive violence and harassment to occur within the neighbourhoods	PPM 2005	1.09	1.29	
Insecurity	The extent to which residents perceive insecurity within the neighbourhood	PPM 2005	2.07	1.46	

Source: Authors.

Table 3.5 Correlations between neighbourhood-level independent key and control variables

	Building density	Average income	Property crime	Deterio-ration	Violence and harassment	Insecurity	Neighbourhood cohesiveness	Collective efficacy
Building density	1							
Average income	−0.055**	1						
Property crime	−0.346**	0.130**	1					
Deterioration	−0.445*	0.043*	0.493**	1				
Violence and harassment	−0.510**	0.026	0.597**	0.480**	1			
Insecurity	−0.199**	0.128**	0.244**	0.316**	0.290**	1		
Neighbourhood cohesiveness	0.588**	−0.156**	−0.206**	−0.339**	−0.344**	−0.288**	1	
Collective efficacy	0.069**	−0.092**	0.034	−0.045*	−0.087**	−0.096**	0.401**	1

Notes:
** Correlation is significant at the 0.001 level (2-tailed).
* Correlation is significant at the 0.05 level (2-tailed).

Source: Authors.

only for firms in general and for business services, but also for the locally oriented retail firms. For growth, however, both the social and physical local orders have a small but significant influence.

Regarding neighbourhood cohesiveness, firms are more likely to have hired employees when the level of 'collective efficacy' is high. For retail firms, specifically, we found a contradictory result regarding neighbourhood cohesiveness. The degree of 'community' is positively associated with employment growth, which confirms our hypothesis that being located in a neighbourhood with numerous, high-quality contacts among neighbours and a high degree of interpersonal trust is beneficial for local firms' performance rates. Although the mechanism behind this association is unclear, it is possible that through interpersonal interactions with the local community, entrepreneurs become familiar with potential employees or receive advice on the recruitment of staff. However, in contrast to the results for firms in general, the degree of 'collective efficacy' is negatively related to employment growth. A possible explanation for this finding is that locally oriented firms are less successful in neighbourhoods where interventions in social and physical order are necessary. As expected, neighbourhood cohesiveness is not related to employment growth for business services, a typical non-locally oriented sector.

Contrary to our first hypothesis, the perception of physical deterioration is positively rather than negatively associated with firm growth. A possible explanation for this finding is that successful areas attract several forms of crime and nuisance. An earlier study by PBL (2010) has also shown that firm growth goes hand in hand with negative scores on several indicators of liveability. All other liveability aspects are unrelated to employment growth. We expected that locally oriented sectors would be especially affected by local liveability, but we found no empirical evidence for this assumption. The analyses for retail firms (locally oriented) and business services firms (non-locally oriented) show no relationship between neighbourhood liveability and employment growth.

Some of the control variables were related to firm survival and employment growth. At the neighbourhood level, we found that building density is positively related to firms' survival chances. This indicates that rural areas provide a better business climate than highly urban districts, in contrast to the findings of Davidsson et al. (2010). However, this result is only valid for firms in general and not for retail or business services firms specifically, and building density does not relate to employment growth. Surprisingly, local spending power, proxied by average income level, does not relate to firm survival and firm growth, not even for locally oriented retail firms.

The relationships between the firm-level control variables and firm success are in line with our expectations. Regarding firm survival, we found that the number of jobs at the beginning of the measurement period (1999) positively correlated with survival chances. Larger firms were more likely to have survived the period 1999–2006 than smaller firms, thereby confirming the 'liability of smallness' (Brüderl and Schüssler 1990). For firms without employees, not hiring staff is a deliberate strategy, whereas larger firms tend to increase the number of employees further. However, we found a negative relationship between initial firm size and employment growth. Firms with employees were less likely to have hired new employees between 1999 and 2006. There were also differences between different sectors. Firms active within locally oriented sectors (retail, catering and consumer services) were more likely to survive than non-locally oriented sectors, which is in line with previous studies (Kaniovski and Peneder 2008).[5]

Finally, the intraclass correlations show that both survival and growth are explained by factors at the firm level. A meagre 8 per cent of the variance in our models is explained by factors at the neighbourhood level (Table 3.6). For retail firms, the intraclass correlation is higher than for firms in general and business services, particularly concerning firm survival. This underlines the relatively high dependency of retail firms on the social and physical situation of their neighbourhood.

5. DISCUSSION AND CONCLUSIONS

This chapter used a multilevel analysis to investigate the relationship between firms and their local environment. The main research question of this study was: how do neighbourhood cohesiveness and liveability relate to local firms' chances for survival and growth?

When we controlled for firm characteristics and market aspects at the neighbourhood level, we identified some significant neighbourhood effects. Social and physical neighbourhood aspects seem to be especially relevant for employment growth, but these aspects are not significantly related to firm survival. Returning to the three main functions of the neighbourhood, we conclude that the *market* function relates to firm survival through building density, but is not at all related to employment growth. For retail firms in particular, we did not find a relationship between local market characteristics and firm success. Regarding the neighbourhood as a *living environment*, we discovered only one significant relationship, between physical deterioration and firm growth, which was not in the expected negative direction. Hypothesis 1, suggesting a positive relationship between liveability and firm success, therefore must be

Table 3.6 Determinants of firms' survival and firm growth

	All firms		Retail		Business services	
	Model 1 Survival	Model 2 Employment growth	Model 3 Survival	Model 4 Employment growth	Model 5 Survival	Model 6 Employment growth
FIRM LEVEL DETERMINANTS						
Jobs 1999	0.071*** (0.009)	−0.121*** (0.017)	0.109*** (0.024)	−0.155*** (0.048)	0.071** (0.028)	−0.052 (0.044)
Locally oriented sector	0.059*** (0.019)	0.032 (0.037)	X	X	X	X
NEIGHBOURHOOD-LEVEL DETERMINANTS (MARKET ASPECTS)						
Building density	0.026*** (0.008)	0.023 (0.016)	−0.012 (0.019)	−0.011 (0.036)	0.020 (0.019)	−0.019 (0.034)
Average income	0.000 (0.000)	0.000 (0.000)	0.000 (0.000)	0.000 (0.000)	0.000 (0.000)	−0.000 (0.000)
NEIGHBOURHOOD-LEVEL DETERMINANTS (LIVING ENVIRONMENT ASPECTS)						
Property crime	0.007 (0.007)	−0.010 (0.014)	0.025 (0.017)	0.024 (0.030)	0.014 (0.018)	0.010 (0.035)
Deterioration	−0.003 (0.007)	0.028** (0.014)	−0.028 (0.016)	0.024 (0.027)	−0.000 (0.019)	−0.007 (0.036)
Violence and harassment	−0.010 (0.010)	0.023 (0.020)	−0.037 (0.022)	−0.049 (0.046)	−0.013 (0.025)	−0.002 (0.045)
Insecurity	0.003 (0.007)	−0.010 (0.016)	−0.025 (0.022)	0.003 (0.039)	0.020 (0.019)	−0.009 (0.035)
NEIGHBOURHOOD-LEVEL DETERMINANTS (NEIGHBOURHOOD COHESIVENESS)						
Community	0.000 (0.001)	0.001 (0.001)	0.001 (0.002)	0.013*** (0.004)	−0.002 (0.002)	−0.002 (0.004)
Collective efficacy	−0.000 (0.001)	0.002** (0.001)	0.002 (0.002)	−0.006** (0.003)	0.000 (0.002)	0.004 (0.003)
Constant	*0.34*** (0.034)*	*2.060*** (0.072)*	*0.419*** (0.087)*	*2.097*** (0.164)*	*0.343*** (0.081)*	*2.095** (0.153)*
Observations	*2.936*	*1.702*	*601*	*353*	*456*	*231*
Intraclass correlation (intercept only)	*0.016*	*0.009*	*0.078*	*0.005*	*0.000*	*0.005*

Note: *** p < 0.001; ** p < 0.01; X = not applicable.

Source: Authors.

rejected. Further research will be needed on the interplay between safety and growth, taking into account that the relationship works both ways. Certain types of economic activity (that is, bars and malls) may also attract crime and nuisance (Marlet 2010).

Hypothesis 2 assumed that being located within a cohesive neighbourhood would improve firms' survival and growth chances. We can partially accept this hypothesis because collective efficacy positively relates to firm growth for firms in general, but we found no significant relationship between community and growth for the total sample of firms.

The third hypothesis stated that the retail sector, as a typical example of a locally oriented sector, would be affected more by neighbourhood aspects than non-locally oriented business services firms were. However, this is true only in relation to neighbourhood cohesiveness and can be directed both positively and negatively. Retail firms are more likely to grow when the local level of community is high, but they have lower growth chances when collective efficacy is high. For business services firms, there is no association between neighbourhood cohesiveness and firm success. Concerning liveability, we found no relationship between liveability and firm success in either the retail or the business services sector.

Despite the neighbourhood effects that were identified, it is clear from the intraclass correlation that firm-level determinants are the most significant and most robust determinants of firm success and that most variety is explained at the firm level. Because the results point in both positive and negative directions, more in-depth research, such as longitudinal studies, interviews or focus groups, is needed to further investigate how firm success relates to cohesiveness and liveability. Apart from entrepreneurs, this research should involve local policy makers and practitioners in the field for further insight into the applicability of research results to local policy.

Although the results provide some useful insights into the interplay between firms and their local contexts, we are aware of some limitations that must be addressed in future research. First, we need more detailed information about the characteristics of the firm and especially the entrepreneur. According to the literature this information is crucial for firm survival and firm growth. To draw conclusions about the contribution of neighbourhood characteristics to firm survival and firm growth, these data must be included in the model. Second, we cannot draw conclusions about causality. We can suggest associations between context variables and firm success, but we do not have information about the underlying mechanisms. Third, we are aware that by excluding moving firms for theoretical reasons, we might have created a bias in our research population.

Because the most convincing results were related to neighbourhood cohesiveness, policy makers may be advised to stimulate contacts between neighbourhood residents. Although interpersonal contacts cannot be guided easily, authorities have a number of tools to stimulate interactions, such as the creation of physical meeting places (that is, community centres, benches and playgrounds) where encounters between local residents may occur naturally. However, the effectiveness of such measures is disputed. For example, Marlet (2010) states that meeting places also attract nuisance and petty crime.

It is significant that area-based policies related to improving local liveability and social cohesion, such as the Dutch neighbourhood improvement programme, are likely to affect local entrepreneurs as well as local residents. Neighbourhood improvement programmes have rarely considered economic actors, and if these elements are included, the emphasis is only on how local economic developments, such as stimulating local entrepreneurs, may influence local liveability and cohesiveness. Entrepreneurs have different stakes in a neighbourhood than regular residents do, and they are therefore more likely to intervene in situations of neighbourhood social and physical disorder (Steenbeek 2011). Similarly, locally oriented firms, such as retailers, catering and personal services, may function as meeting places for local residents, thereby stimulating neighbourhood cohesiveness (Völker et al. 2007). However, the opposite relationship, the effect of local liveability and cohesiveness on local business performance, has been neglected despite increasing demand for knowledge in this field (e.g., Welter et al. 2008). The results of our study suggest that both social and physical local aspects are related to firm success. For local policy, this means that investing in the social and physical pillars of neighbourhood policy will indirectly influence local economic developments.

ACKNOWLEDGEMENTS

Establishment level data on economic activity are courteously provided by Stichting LISA. Data on (perceptions of) neighbourhood disorder are taken from the Politiemonitor (PPM 2005), which was courteously provided by the 'DirectiePolitie en Veiligheidsregio's' of the Ministry of Internal Affairs, The Hague.

NOTES

1. Compared to firms that stayed, firms that moved between 2000 and 2006 were active relatively more often within non-locally oriented sectors: 90 per cent compared to 82 per cent of firms that stayed. Firms that moved appear to be relatively more successful than

firms that stayed: 76.5 per cent of all firms that moved survived between 1999 and 2006 compared to 58 per cent of firms that stayed. Similarly, firms that moved grew relatively more often between 1999 and 2006: 28 per cent compared to 16 per cent for firms that stayed.

2. The liveability indicators were measured at one point in time only, but this is not likely to bias our results. According to a recent empirical study, the scores on liveability indicators within Dutch neighbourhoods have hardly changed between 1999 and 2008, and disadvantaged neighbourhoods in general remain problematic over time (Wittebrood and Permentier 2011).

3. Neighbourhood-level factors are measured at the five-digit postal code level.

4. Additionally, we controlled for the degree of turbulence (average sum of firm entry and firm exit rates 1999–2006) within the neighbourhood but found no significant relationships between turbulence and firm survival or firm growth.

5. In order to control for different industries, we tested a model where the 'locally oriented sector' dummy has been replaced by sector dummies for retail, business services and manufacturing. These analyses have shown that business services firms are less likely to survive, whereas retail and manufacturing firms have a lower likelihood to achieve employment growth. Including these sector dummies instead of the 'locally oriented sector' dummy hardly alters the rest of the results.

REFERENCES

Aalders, R., A. Bakkeren, J. Kok and T. Twigt (2008), 'De kracht van de wijk. Belang van wijkeconomie voor de leefbaarheid in Amsterdamse krachtwijken', Amsterdam: Rabobank Amsterdam en Omstreken/EZ Amsterdam/MKB Amsterdam.

Andersson, R., S. Musterd, G. Galster and T.M. Kauppinen (2007), 'What mix matters? Exploring the relationships between individuals' incomes and different measures of their neighbourhood context', *Housing Studies*, **22** (5), 637–60.

Audretsch, D.B. and D. Dohse (2007), 'Location: a neglected determinant of firm growth', *Review of World Economics*, **143** (1), 79–107.

Bates, T. and A. Robb (2008), 'Crime's impact on the survival prospects of young urban small businesses', *Economic Development Quarterly*, **22** (3), 228–38.

Bathelt, H. and J. Glückler (2003), 'Toward a relational economic geography', *Journal of Economic Geography*, **3**, 117–44.

Bosma, N., M. Van Praag, R. Thurik and G. De Wit (2004), 'The value of human and social capital investments for the business performance of startups', *Small Business Economics*, **23**, 227–36.

Bridge, S., K. O'Neill and S. Cromie (2003), *Understanding Enterprise, Entrepreneurship and Small Business*, Basingstoke and New York: Palgrave Macmillan.

Brüderl, J. and R. Schüssler (1990), 'Organizational mortality: the liabilities of newness and adolescence', *Administrative Science Quarterly*, **35**, 530–47.

Bulterman, S., A. Van Klink and V. Schutjens (2007), 'Ondernemers en hun bedrijven in de wijk: het cement voor de economische pijler', in J. Van Dijk and V. Schutjens (eds), *De Economische Kracht van de Stad*, Assen: Van Gorcum, pp. 129–44.

Davidsson, P. and B. Honig (2003), 'The role of social and human capital among nascent entrepreneurs', *Journal of Business Venturing*, **18** (3), 301–31.

Davidsson, P., L. Achtenhagen and L. Naldi (2010), 'Small firm growth', *Foundations and Trends in Entrepreneurship*, **6** (2), 69–166.

Dubini, P. (1989), 'The influence of motivations and environment on business start-ups: some hints for public policies', *Journal of Business Venturing*, **4**, 11–26.

Forrest, R. and A. Kearns (2001), 'Social cohesion, social capital and the neighbourhood', *Urban Studies*, **38**, 2125–43.

Garnsey, E. (1998), 'A theory of the early growth of the firm', *Industrial and Corporate Change*, **7**, 523–55.

Glaeser, E., J. Kolko and A. Saiz (2001), 'Consumer city', *Journal of Economic Geography*, **1**, 27–50.

Hackler, D. and H. Mayer (2008), 'Diversity, entrepreneurship, and the urban environment', *Journal of Urban Affairs*, **30** (3), 273–307.

Hox, J. (2002), *Multilevel Analysis; Techniques and Applications*, Mahwah, NJ and London: Lawrence Erlbaum Associates.

Johannisson, B. (2011), 'Towards a practice theory of entrepreneurship', *Small Business Economics*, **35**, 135–50.

Kaniovski, S. and E.M. Peneder (2008), 'Determinants of firm survival: a duration analysis using the generalized gamma distribution', *Empirica*, **35**, 41–58.

Lambooy, J. (2010), 'Knowledge transfers, spillovers and actors: the role of context and social capital', *European Planning Studies*, **18** (6), 873–91.

LISA (2007), *Landelijk Informatiesysteem van Arbeidsplaatsen en Vestigingen*, Enschede: Stichting LISA.

Love, L. and J. Crompton (1999), 'The role of quality of life in business (re)location decisions', *Journal of Business Research*, **44**, 211–22.

Marlet, G. (2010), 'Bedrijf in de buurt', in Planbureau voor de Leefomgeving, *Bedrijvigheid en Leefbaarheid in Stedelijke Woonwijken*, The Hague and Bilthoven: Planbureau voor de Leefomgeving, pp. 107–16.

Marlet, G., M. Bosker and C. Van Woerkens (2008), *De Schaal van de Stad*, Utrecht: Atlas voor Gemeenten.

Musterd, S. and R. Andersson (2006), 'Employment, social mobility and neighbourhood effects: the case of Sweden', *International Journal of Urban and Regional Research*, **30** (1), 120–40.

Ouwehand, A. and M. Van Meijeren (2006), *Economische Initiatieven in Stadswijken; Een Verkennend Onderzoek*, Gouda: Habiforum.

Planbureau voor de Leefomgeving (PBL) (2010), *Bedrijvigheid en Leefbaarheid in Stedelijke Woonwijken*, The Hague and Bilthoven: Planbureau voor de Leefomgeving.

PPM (2005), Politiemonitor Bevolking 2005, Hilversum: Intomart GFK bv.

Ruimtelijk Planbureau (RPB) (2006), *Economische Netwerken in de Regio*, The Hague: Ruimtelijk Planbureau.

Sampson, R.J., S.W. Raudenbusch and F. Earls (1997), 'Neighborhoods and violent crime: a multilevel study of collective efficacy', *Science*, **277** (5328), 918–24.

Santarelli, E. and M. Vivarelli (2007), 'Entrepreneurship and the process of firms' entry, survival and growth', *Industrial and Corporate Change*, **16** (3), 455–88.

Schutjens, V. and W. Steenbeek (2010), 'Buurtbinding van ondernemers. Over lokale betrokkenheid en inzet voor de leefbaarheid', High Potential Programme, ICS/URU, in Planbureau voor de Leefomgeving, *Bedrijvigheid en Leefbaarheid in Stedelijke Woonwijken*, The Hague and Bilthoven: Planbureau voor de Leefomgeving, pp. 117–50.

Schutjens, V. and B. Völker (2010), 'Space and social capital: the degree of locality of entrepreneurs' contacts and their consequences for firm success', *European Planning Studies*, **18** (6), 941–63.

Sorenson, O. (2003), 'Social networks and industrial geography', *Journal of Evolutionary Economics*, **13**, 513–27.

SSNE (2008), Survey of the Social Networks of Entrepreneurs, Utrecht: Utrecht University.

Statistics Netherlands (2006), *Kerncijfers Postcodegebieden, 2004*, Voorburg: CBS.

Steenbeek, W. (2011), *Social and Physical Disorder. How Community, Business Presence and Entrepreneurs Influence Disorder in Dutch Neighborhoods*, Utrecht: ICS.

Storper, M. and A. Venables (2004), 'Buzz: face-to-face contact and the urban economy', *Journal of Economic Geography*, **4** (4), 351–70.

Tamásy, C. (2006), 'Determinants of regional entrepreneurship dynamics in contemporary Germany: a conceptual and empirical analysis', *Regional Studies*, **40** (4), 365–84.

Van Gent, W.P.C., S. Musterd and W.J.M. Ostendorf (2009), 'Bridging the social divide? Reflections on current Dutch neighborhood policy', *Journal of Housing and the Built Environment*, **24**, 357–68.

Völker, B., H. Flap and S. Lindenberg (2007), 'When are neighbourhoods communities? Community in Dutch neighbourhoods', *European Sociological Review*, **23** (1), 99–114.

Welter, F., L. Trettin and U. Neumann (2008), 'Fostering entrepreneurship in distressed urban neighbourhoods', *International Entrepreneurship and Management Journal*, **4**, 109–28.

Wilson, W.J. (1987), *The Declining Significance of Race: the Truly Disadvantaged – the Inner City, the Underclass, and Public Policy*, Chicago: University of Chicago Press.

Wittebrood, K. and M. Permentier (2011), *Wonen, Wijken & Interventies; Krachtwijkenbeleid in Perspectief*, The Hague: Sociaal en Cultureel Planbureau.

4. The role of the entrepreneur in determining growth: a longitudinal analysis of a new venture

Colm O'Gorman

1. INTRODUCTION

New and small firms that grow, particularly those that grow rapidly, make a disproportionally large contribution to regional and national economic growth. In past decades the focus of enterprise policies in many countries was typically on increasing the number of start-ups. However, in recent decades policy makers have become more aware of the impact of start-ups, and have sought interventions that increase the 'quality' of start-ups, that is start-ups that survive and grow (Greene et al. 2008).

This chapter explores new firm growth, and in particular, the role of the entrepreneur in a new venture characterized by organic growth. The motivation for this chapter is to contribute to the debate in the entrepreneurship literature on the determinants of growth. Recently, Greene et al. (2008) argued that growth is determined more by choice of location and of sector, leading them to claim that it is in fact 'chance' that matters in growth. They concluded that researchers must reconsider what factors explain growth (Greene et al. 2008: 242).

Our review both of our own results and of those of other scholars has emphasized that chance plays a key role, if not the key role in the survival and growth of new businesses. Researchers, in our view, have to highlight this, rather than brush it under the carpet by placing their emphasis upon the factors that only modestly influence performance.

We contribute to this debate by using Penrose's *Theory of the Growth of the Firm* to explore the role of the entrepreneur in the growth of a new venture (1959). While not identifying the context of new firm growth, Penrose did identify the growth of small firms as an important application for her theory. Despite the recognized contribution of Penrose to the study of firm growth, as evidenced among other things by the extensive citation of her work, direct applications of Penrose's theory to the study of new firms are rare.

2. LITERATURE REVIEW: THE GROWTH OF NEW VENTURES

Penrose's theory of growth, which was developed inductively from a case study of the Hercules Powder Co., states that growth is the outcome of the interaction between firm resources and market opportunities. Penrose summarizes her arguments as follows (1959: 1):

> Growth is governed by a creative and dynamic interaction between a firm's productive resources and its market opportunities. Available resources limit expansion; unused resources (including technological and entrepreneurial) stimulate and largely determine the direction of expansion. While product demand may exert a predominant short-term influence, over the long term any distinction between 'supply' and 'demand' determinants of growth becomes arbitrary.

Penrose is unequivocal in her explanation of firm growth: growth is the result of the purposive activity of management. In her theory 'supply and demand are intrinsically linked, as planned supply responds to perceived demand' (Pitelis 2002: 3). According to Penrose, growth may be induced by internal factors, such as excess resources, particularly entrepreneurial and managerial services, or external factors, such as productive opportunities. While growth may be induced by external productive opportunities, Penrose does not see these as a given, but rather the outcome of the entrepreneur's perceptions of the environment. She describes demand as 'nothing more or less than his own ideas about what he can sell at various prices with varying degrees of selling effort' (Penrose 1959: 81).

In contrast, within the entrepreneurship literature, there is ambiguity as to the determinants of growth. Some research suggests that founding a new firm in a product-market characterized by high growth is associated with high levels of growth (see for example, Bhide 2000). These results are consistent with the environment determinism arguments of the population ecology perspective (Carroll and Hannan 2000; Hannan and Freeman 1977). This leads to the normative implication that choice of market is more important than choice of strategy (Greene et al. 2008; Storey 1994).

Other research suggests that growth is determined by firm level and individual level factors. Drawing implicitly and explicitly on the resource-based view of the firm, researchers have studied new firm growth from the perspective of factors such as external finance, venture teams, external advisors, and business plans, and from the perspective of firm strategies, which are the manifestation of resources in product-market positions (see for example, Barringer et al. 2005; Eisenhardt and Schoonhoven 1990). Some research suggests that attributes of the entrepreneur, in terms of social capital, the entrepreneur's networks, learning, and the entrepreneur's prior experiences explain new venture growth (see for example, Blundel 2002; Kisfalvi 2002; Shane 2000).

Penrose (1959) also considers the role of the entrepreneur to be important in determining the direction and pace of growth. The entrepreneur provides entrepreneurial services and acquires managerial services for the firm. Through their ongoing activities firms develop entrepreneurial and managerial resources, through the acquisition of new personnel, the adoption of new managerial practices, and the new experiences for existing management. Where new entrepreneurial and managerial resources are developed and are not required for existing activities, these unused productive services become a 'selective force in determining the direction of expansion' (Penrose 1959: 87). However, Penrose (1959) also suggests that in the context of new and small firms, because entrepreneurs may need to expend their entrepreneurial and managerial services on 'current operations', there may be no 'time available for expansion'.

Penrose devoted considerable attention to the entrepreneur in her book (Chapter 3 of her book deals extensively with the entrepreneur). While her explanation includes extensive reference to the entrepreneur, Penrose excludes the characteristics of the entrepreneur from her theory. In her discussion of the entrepreneur she suggests that the essential characteristics of entrepreneurs are: entrepreneurial versatility, that is, the imagination and vision of the entrepreneur; fund-raising ingenuity; ambition, suggesting that some entrepreneurs are focused on 'empire building'; and judgement.

Penrose argues that the entrepreneur performs a different function from the manager. While not offering a definitive list of services of the entrepreneur, examples suggested by Penrose include the following: the introduction and acceptance of new ideas; acquisition of new technology; acquisition of new management; fundamental changes in 'administrative' organization of the firm; raising capital; plans for expansion.

Despite Penrose's unequivocal explanation of growth, there is a notable absence of studies in the entrepreneurship literature that explicitly draw on her theory. This may be due to the general nature of her theory, with Penrose making a 'contribution to everything' (Pitelis 2002: 7). Reflecting on her own work, Penrose commented: 'the testing of the theory set forth here is difficult indeed' (Penrose 1959: 211). She noted that it is difficult to measure growth, and in particular it is difficult to measure a core component of her study 'heterogeneity in entrepreneurial and managerial service'.

The literature on the growth of new ventures draws implicitly and explicitly on Penrose's theory of growth. Penrose (1959) and subsequent work by other authors point to a number of factors that either separately or combined are likely to be important in explaining the growth of a firm. These include the characteristics of the entrepreneur, characteristics of the firm, specifically firm resources and capabilities, and characteristics of the market. Informed by these perspectives we study the growth of a new venture. Empirically, the central question we study is what determines the direction and rate of growth of a new venture. Specifically we study the evolution of, and interactions between, the entrepreneur, resources and market positions to explore the extent that growth is the outcome of entrepreneurial choices or, as Greene et al. (2008) have suggested, due to chance. These ideas are discussed empirically in the context of a longitudinal single case study. The case study is of the start-up and growth of an Irish firm, Cooley Distillery plc, over the period 1986 to 2008.

3.   METHOD

We present a longitudinal, process orientated single case study of the emergence and growth of a new venture in Ireland. This small firm, Cooley Distillery plc, is the only Irish-owned distiller of Irish whiskey. In 2008 Cooley Distillery plc was awarded 'World Distiller of the Year' at the International Wine and Spirits Competition. The publicly owned firm was founded in 1986 by an Irish entrepreneur, Dr John Teeling. Its revenues have grown to €18.7 (US$23.2) million, most of which are from export sales, and it has profits of €3.33 (US$4.12) million. Cooley sells premium specialist whiskeys, brands such as Connemara, Tyrconnell and Kilbeggan, 'retail own label' whiskey to leading European retailers such as Tesco and Sainsbury in the UK and Carrefour in France, and, to a lesser extent 'private own label' whiskey such as the Michael Collins brand sold by Sidney Frank in the US. Products are sold in over fifty countries.

Ex ante, Cooley Distillery plc represented a good choice to study new firm growth for several reasons. First, the firm has experienced growth in terms of revenues, profits and market scope. Second, we had access to a diverse range of data, including data collected or published at various times during the evolution of the firm. We draw on interview data, interactions with the entrepreneur, published annual reports and secondary documents, and on published case studies of Cooley Distillery plc (European Case Clearing House 1997, 2006, 2010). As such we are able to 'triangulate' our data (Kanter 1977).

Analysis follows standard approaches used in qualitative analysis of case data (Miles and Huberman 1994). Our objective is to understand what happened over time and why. We began the process with the written case studies and interview data. From the extensive descriptive account of the evolution of the firm we developed a series of tables that described various aspects of the emergence of the firm. We focused on the founder, the initial founding event, and the growth of the firm over time in terms of markets entered and strategies pursued. The second stage of the analysis was to use Penrose's framework that she used in her study of Hercules Powder Co. to structure and analyse the case data.

The single case study limits the generalizability of our analysis and finding to other new firms. In terms of context a number of factors are worth noting. First, the industry was not experiencing growth at the time of start-up; second, the industry has relatively high barriers to entry; third, the start-up is atypical in terms of the level of resources the entrepreneur was able to attract to the new business; and fourth, the entrepreneur was a serial entrepreneur, and this might have influenced the resources he was able to bring to the new business.

We begin by providing a description of the founding and growth of Cooley Distillery. We then present an explanation for the growth of the firm in terms of two factors: (i) the growth objective of the entrepreneur at founding and (ii) the implications of this objective on the firm in terms of what we refer to as the growth imperative.

4. CASE DESCRIPTION: THE FOUNDING AND GROWTH OF COOLEY DISTILLERY

Cooley Distillery was founded in 1986 by John Teeling. In the autumn of 1986 John Teeling noticed an advert announcing the sale of an alcohol-producing plant in the Cooley Mountains, one hundred kilometres north of Dublin. The plant produced alcohol which was sold for the production of gin and vodkas. The equivalent of over €4 million had been invested in upgrading and modernizing the plant. Teeling believed that the plant could produce whiskey, and that there might be a market opportunity for a new supplier of Irish whiskey. His knowledge of the sector led him to believe that one of the major drinks companies would attempt to acquire the only producer of Irish whiskey in the Republic of Ireland, the Irish Distillers Group (IDG), an event which subsequently came to pass in 1988, and that therefore there would be opportunities for an alternative supplier of Irish whiskey. Teeling and a business associate bought the plant for a nominal €135 000. Teeling commissioned a feasibility study that estimated the total cost of creating a whiskey distillery to be €2.5 million, with a further €1.3 million working capital requirement. Teeling approached Ireland's industrial development agency for support but he failed to get them interested in his project.

Teeling reopened the plant and began producing pure alcohol. While the market for pure alcohol had little long-term potential, Teeling believed that it could support the reopening of the distillery. In addition he identified that a market existed for competitively priced white spirits, for example rums, vodkas and gin. Teeling raised an initial €444 000 for a one-third stake in the venture, bringing on board a few other core investors. The purchase of the distilleries and the construction of a pot still (with low production volumes) and a column still (with high production volumes) distillery were financed by raising €3 million under a special financial incentive called the Business Expansion Scheme (BES), created by the Irish government to promote investment in indigenous industry.

In 1988 Teeling purchased the assets of Locke's Distillery in Kilbeggan, Co Westmeath, Ireland (100 kilometres from Cooley). Locke's is the world's oldest licensed distillery (licensed since 1757). This distillery provided him with extensive warehousing space. During 1987 and 1988 Teeling began to acquire old discontinued brand names, such as John Locke, Locke's 'Old Kilbeggan' whiskey, Old Tyrconnell, Inishowen, Andrew A. Watt, Millars, and the equipment of old Irish distillers, including the Tullamore Dew pot stills.

Within a few years of founding, Cooley Distillery had the ability to produce relatively high volumes of Irish whiskey. However, the firm was constrained in its ability to grow markets due to a lack of financial resources (owing to the large funds required to fund the storage of the whiskey as it matured) and the inexperience of the entrepreneurial and managerial team at developing markets. The need for cash and the availability of a production facility resulted in Cooley Distillery selling bulk Irish whiskey to Irish confectionary firms and selling white spirits such as vodkas, rums and gins (these could be produced relatively easily and could compete on price).

Over time, Cooley Distillery developed a number of whiskey markets. The first market base, in terms of Cooley's evolution, was the 'retail own label' market. This market is significant in mature consumer markets of the Northern Hemisphere. For example, in the early 1990s, in the UK, own-label accounted for 32 per cent of all whiskey sold in supermarkets. In this market Cooley has developed own label brands with selected retailers, principally in the UK and France, such as Tesco, Carrefour and Sainsbury's. By 2008, Cooley Distillery supplied 18 of the top 40 retailers in Europe. Cooley Distillery works with the retailer on product and label design and assists in 'own label' promotions. Over time Cooley has sought to deepen product lines by adding malts and speciality products.

The second, though smaller, market position developed was the sale of 'private own label' whiskey, for example the Michael Collins brand sold by Sidney Frank in the US. The strategy in this market was to identify drinks companies whose name will give status to an 'Irish whiskey'. Cooley sought partners with a long-term commitment to develop the brand and then they enter a long-term supply contract.

The third, and largest market base, is the sale of their branded whiskey worldwide. Cooley targets malts, blended and speciality whiskey to markets where there is an established demand for Irish whiskey products. These include the US, Germany and France. The product position is high margin speciality products. The core brands are Tyrconnell, Kilbeggan, Connemara and Greenore. The strategy was to sell through exclusive deals with distributors, granting exclusive distribution rights based on targeted sales figures. This market position evolved over time. Initially Cooley had sought to compete in many markets, and included a focus on new emerging whiskey markets. However, over time, the new management began to focus on 'mature' whiskey markets and focused on the provision of premium and differentiated products to these markets. This change in focus was possible for several reasons. First, previously unsold whiskey that was still maturing in casks could be sold as a premium aged product (a signal of quality among whiskey drinkers). Second, the firm developed new varieties of whiskey over time.

Since start-up in 1986, Cooley Distillery's annual revenues grew to €18.7m, its assets to €18.4m and its profits to €3m (Table 4.1). Sales grew at an annual compound rate of 7 per cent for the 20-year period of 1988 to 2008, while net assets grew at a 12 per cent compound rate. Cooley has also grown in terms of non-financial indicators of growth, operating from multiple locations in Ireland and selling into 50 countries. Industry growth of Irish whiskey was about 4 per cent per annum for the period 1993 to 2008, which represents more than a doubling of case sales over the period (Table 4.2). Cooley represented an approximate 5 per cent share of total case sales for most of this period, suggesting that growth was largely in line with growth in industry sales.

Table 4.1   Yearly change in turnover and profits

Year	Case sales	Net assets (€)	Sales (€)	Profits (after tax) (€)	Annual change in sales (%)	Return on sales (%)
1988*		2 019 000	855 000	−121 000		
1989		3 611 000	1 910 000	−145 000	123	−8
1990		3 179 000	3 383 000	−475 000	77	−14
1991		3 237 000	4 155 000	47 000	23	1
1992		3 021 000	4 555 000	−189 000	10	−4
1993		2 073 000	4 321 000	−1 007 000	−5	−23
1994	30 000	2 043 000	4 492 000	−30 000	4	−1
1995	75 000	1 873 000	4 096 000	−170 000	−9	−4
1996	110 000	5 734 000	4 392 000	90 000	7	2
1997	120 000	5 876 000	5 154 000	34 000	17	1
1998	150 000	5 845 000	6 537 000	267 000	27	4
1999	160 000		6 892 000	437 000	5	6
2000	185 000		8 117 000	654 000	18	8
2001	175 000		8 393 000	816 000	3	10
2002	185 000		9 135 000	924 000	9	10
2003	190 000	10 018 000	9 544 000	1 120 000	4	12
2004	180 000		10 012 000	1 277 000	5	13
2005	180 000		9 206 000	1 188 000	−8	13
2006	210 000		11 730 000	1 507 000	27	13
2007	206 000		11 585 000	1 401 000	−1	12
2008	416 000	18 392 000	18 713 000	2 997 000	62	16

Note: * 15-month period.

Source: Company annual reports.

5.   CASE ANALYSIS: WHY DID COOLEY DISTILLERY GROW?

An analysis of the data suggests two factors were important to growth in the case. First, the case data suggests that growth was an objective of the founder. The analysis suggests that growth was not a consequence of the founding of the firm, as typically suggested in the literature, but rather, that growth was the cause of the founding of the firm. Second, as suggested by Penrose, the choice of market sector was an outcome of the entrepreneurial resources of the firm, and as such, the entrepreneurial resources of the firm determined the firm's growth. These two factors are now discussed.

Table 4.2   The market for (Irish) whiskey (cases)

Year	Sales of Cooley whiskey	Sales of Jameson brand	Sales of Irish whiskey
1970	n/a*	n/a	2 000 000
–	–	–	–
1980	n/a	n/a	n/a
–	–	–	–
1990	n/a	n/a	2 308 000
1991	n/a	n/a	n/a
1992	n/a	n/a	n/a
1993	n/a	n/a	2 226 000
1994	30 000	n/a	n/a
1995	75 000	833 000	n/a
1996	110 000	1 000 000	n/a
1997	120 000	n/a	n/a
1998	150 000	n/a	n/a
1999	160 000	1 200 000	n/a
2000	185 000	1 300 000	2 700 000
2001	175 000	1 400 000	2 700 000
2002	185 000	1 500 000	n/a
2003	190 000	1 600 000	n/a
2004	180 000	1 700 000**	n/a
2005	180 000	1 900 000***	n/a
2006	210 000	2 100 000	n/a
2007	206 000	2 300 000	n/a
2008	416 000	2 600 000	4 500 000

Notes:
* n/a: not available or not applicable.
** In 2004 Jameson was the world's fastest growing international whiskey brand (International Wine and Spirits Record 2004).
*** Estimate as accounting year changed. Subsequent annual sales refer to year ending June.

Source: Compiled by author from various secondary sources including presentations to investors, annual reports and company websites.

The case data suggests that the objective of the new firm was growth. Penrose argues that the objective of a firm is to grow but that a 'lack of "enterprise" will preclude or substantially retard' growth (1959: 30). The rate and direction of growth of a firm 'depend on the extent to which it is alert to act upon opportunities for profitable investment' but the ability to act on opportunities is not 'a homogenous quality' (1959: 30). While recognizing other objectives, such as 'power, prestige, public approval, or the mere love of the game' Penrose also argues that increasing long-term profits, which is 'equivalent to increasing the long run rate of growth', is the ultimate objective of the firm (1959: 30).

What were the objectives of Cooley Distillery's founders and management? In three important ways the case data suggests that John Teeling's (the founding entrepreneur) ambitions of growth were significant from the outset. Indeed, it could be argued that growth was the motivation for founding the firm, rather than a consequence of firm founding.

First, the stated objective of the firm has been to grow. For example, in 1989, just 18 months after the start-up, Teeling described to his shareholders the objectives for the business as follows: 'Let me put our project in context. The objective of this venture is the creation of a profitable publicly quoted company in the alcoholic beverage industry focused on Irish whiskey production and marketing.' (Annual Report, 30 August 1989).

Recent accounts suggest that growth is still an objective, with Teeling stating 'for this business to work, we have to sell 500,000 cases a year'.

Second, Teeling's perceptions of the opportunities in the whiskey market led him to acquire a distillation plant that would necessitate large sales. Some background context helps explain why Teeling purchased an alcohol distillation plant in 1986. Teeling explains: 'In Spring 1971, two graduate students, one at Harvard, myself, and the other, Willie McCarter, at MIT, were each undertaking independent student projects on Irish whiskey. The results convinced us of the opportunities in Irish whiskey.'

The opportunities identified by Teeling in the 1970s and 1980s were (i) that the Irish whiskey category had underperformed relative to Scottish whisky; (ii) leading international drinks firms would be interested in having an Irish whiskey brand in their portfolio, but this was not possible as one firm, Irish Distillers Group, was the only producer of Irish whiskey; and (iii), in the 1980s when Irish Distillers Group consolidated their distribution channels, that 'delisted' 'international' distributors who had formally distributed Irish Distillers brands would be interested in an alternative supplier of Irish whiskey. According to Teeling: 'In 1986, I looked again at Irish whiskey. I was interested in a financial play on the then listed Irish Distillers Group.'

The objective of such a play would be to break up the firm, selling the established Irish Distillers brands to international drinks firms. However

> nothing came of this but a chance reading of a notice in a newspaper announcing the liquidation of a closed State alcohol plant in Cooley, Co. Louth led to a bid for the facilities being lodged by myself and Donal Kinsella. After we agreed to attempt to 'rescue and resuscitate' the plant we bought the facilities from the State.

A third reason why we believe that Teeling's objective was to grow the firm is that there is evidence, based on an analysis of Teeling's own career, of a personal objective to 'build something', referring to the desire to create a manufacturing export orientated Irish firm. In 2003 Teeling and a fellow director voted a third director off the board because of to his desire to seek an exit for shareholders.

While the above suggests that Teeling's primary objective was to grow the firm, the case data reveals that during its relatively short history there were multiple attempts to sell the firm. There were a total of five possible exit events, though none actually materialized. Why were there so many exit attempts if the objective was to grow the firm? First, an early exit may have been Teeling's unstated objective for the firm. The description provided above of Teeling's perceptions of the opportunities in the Irish whiskey market included that the new firm would be an attractive invest- ment for a leading drinks firm. Second, some of the early exit attempts occurred at a time of crisis, when the new firm was experiencing financial difficulties. Third, the exit attempts may reflect Teeling's loyalty to his early investors. These initial investments were 'locked' into the firm during the 1990s as share prices declined.

The second factor that might explain the growth of Cooley Distillery is the entrepreneurial resources embedded in the firm. Penrose focused par- ticular attention on entrepreneurial and managerial resources as key deter- minants to the direction of growth of the firm. The founding entrepreneur, John Teeling, a graduate of both Wharton and Harvard, is an Irish entre- preneur known for his international interests in mining exploration and his entry into the whiskey distilling business in Ireland (Table 4.3). Teeling is the co-founder and chairman of six London Stock Exchange (AIM) listed natural resources firms. These firms have a market capitalization of about €200 million. Teeling is a 'portfolio' entrepreneur (Westhead et al. 2003), having started a number of exploration companies.

Teeling exhibits elements of the four characteristics Penrose identified as important for entrepreneurs that seek to grow (Table 4.4). Teeling's entre- preneurial versatility, that is, his imagination and vision and his horizons, are evident from his prior ventures and from his consideration of mount- ing a hostile takeover bid of Irish Distillers Group in 1986, just prior to his launch of Cooley Distillery. In a more narrow sense, imagination and versa- tility could refer to the specific product-market focus of the new business. In this sense Teeling specifically set out his vision for the new business in terms of growth. Teeling exhibited extensive fund-raising ingenuity in funding the building of the distillery and the three years' storage of his whiskey. Teeling's ambition is evident in his perceptions that his new firm would in time be an acquisition target of the four largest drinks firms in the world.

Table 4.3   Founder's descriptive data

Characteristics	John Teeling
Year of birth	1946
Father's occupation	Commission agent for insurance Operated a small money lending business
Childhood experiences	Teeling worked with his father from the age of 12 His father died when Teeling was aged 14 Teeling, aged 14, as eldest son, 'took over' his father's business
University Education	Bachelor of Commerce Degree, University College Dublin, Ireland Master of Economic Science, University College Dublin, Ireland Master of Business Administration (MBA), Wharton School of Finance, USA Doctorate of Business Administration, Harvard Business School, USA
Work Experience	Lecturer of business at University College Dublin, Ireland Consultant to the small Irish mining industry (part-time) CEO of Seafield and Glen Abbey (firms he invested in) Chairman of various mining firms CEO of Cooley Distillery plc
Speculation and entrepreneurial activity	Teeling developed an interest in stocks while studying in the US. He began to invest in Irish equities, focusing on companies that had a net asset value greater than their share price. He leveraged his investments through bank debt, and typically pursued a focused strategy. In one investment, Irish Oil and Cake, he was joined by Donal Kinsella. The investment by the two, labelled a 'share raid', generated a lot of publicity in financial circles as it was new to the Irish stock exchange. They exited from this in 1979 at a significant profit.
Entrepreneurial experience	1983: Started first mining/exploration firm: Minquest. 1983–2009: Started 12 mining/exploration firms in total. By 2009, he was co-founder and chairman of six London Stock Exchange (AIM) listed natural resources companies. (Market capitalization of €200m in 2009) 1986: CEO of Cooley Distillery plc, aged 40.

Source: Author's interviews and secondary sources.

Table 4.4   Founder's entrepreneurial attributes

Entrepreneurial characteristics	What might this mean?	John Teeling
Entrepreneurial versatility (imagination and vision of the entrepreneur)	Could refer to the entrepreneur's vision in terms of the specific businesses.	Teeling is characterized by imagination and vision. For example, Teeling saw an opportunity to buy Irish Distillers Group (IDG) in a leveraged buyout, with a planned debt finance of US$176m and equity finance of US$22m.
Fund-raising ingenuity	Evidence of extensive fund raising from external sources and/or extensive resource acquisition during start-up and growth of the business.	Funding this business was one of Teeling's achievements. For example, he made extensive use of a Government incentive scheme, the BES, to fund the storage of whiskey.
	Fund-raising ingenuity might also refer to the development of a profitable business model such that retained earnings fund growth.	He described himself as follows: 'I am in essence a speculator, so the concept of high risk exploration companies fitted well with my former life as a share speculator.'
Ambition	Could refer to the entrepreneur's overall personal ambition. This ambition might be realized through a specific business.	Teeling's ambition(s) are evident from the following: 'I would like to be known as somebody who actually developed a mining business' (Kenny 1991: 358).
	Needs to be distinguished from entrepreneurial versatility.	I had read a lot 'about people who had created things', and I wondered 'about the fact that those who stuck it out are now seen as the great entrepreneurs' (Kenny 1991: 353). 'But, there was also an ulterior motive – could I build a mining and/or oil company? Some of the early ventures have gone on to bigger things. Kenmare is now a €400 million titanium producer in Mozambique; African Gold is a €250 million gold and nickel producer in Zimbabwe; Pan Andean produces oil and gas in the Gulf of Mexico; and West African Diamonds has a small diamond mine in Guinea'.

Table 4.4   (continued)

Entrepreneurial characteristics	What might this mean?	John Teeling
Judgement	Outcomes, in terms of growth or profits or wealth creation, can be evidence of judgement. Judgement might refer to outcomes across a series of initiatives, either within one business, or across a portfolio of businesses.	Teeling's judgement could be questioned in terms of the failed exit attempts. In his own words he questions his decision to move from speculator to owner-manager over his career: 'I should have quit after Minquest, but I now wanted to set up and manage. I should have stayed a speculator. It has been hard to repeat the Minquest success'.
	Also refers to the ability to gather information from external sources. Could possibly be measured in terms of the entrepreneur's networks.	

Source: Author.

While Penrose suggests that some entrepreneurs are focused on 'empire building', this is unclear from the case, as much of his efforts were initially focused on finding a route to exit. Teeling's judgement is evident from the outcomes. He believed that exit possibilities would exist, though none of these did in fact materialize. However, Penrose argues that judgement is not just a function of the entrepreneur as a person but also of his capacity to gather information and to consult with outsiders. There is evidence that the idea for Cooley Distillery and Teeling's entry into the whiskey industry was based on information about this industry that he gathered over time, starting with his time in the US in the early 1970s. However, the management team and the board of directors at Cooley are characterized by relatively little change over the course of the case study. It could be argued that Teeling failed to bring new 'external' perspectives into Cooley.

Teeling also provided the initial management resources at Cooley Distillery. His prior experience was largely in mining activities and financing. He had acted as CEO in several of the firms in which he had acquired shareholdings, but his experience was that 'management' was not his core strength. The decision to begin whiskey production at Cooley meant that Teeling was back operating as a manager. He said in 1991: 'I am now back in management which is where I do not want to be. I'm making decisions on advertising campaigns, employees, wage rates – all the things I don't want to do' (Kenny 1991: 356). 'I have no interest in running things and I don't think I'm a good manager'; 'I am not a people person'; and 'I suffer from the appalling problem that I know that nobody can do the job as well as I can do it. It's not that I believe it, I know it.' (Kenny 1991: 359)

Teeling's experience may have allowed him to attract management resources to the new firm. Teeling's first managerial hire was David Hynes as General Manager (in 1989). Hynes, then aged 33 years, was a chemical engineer with an MBA from Harvard. His experience was in building and operating chemical plants in the USA. His initial role was to develop the distilling capability of Cooley Distillery. James Finn, an accountant, joined Cooley in 1987. He worked with Teeling in his exploration business prior to this. The expertise of this team is focused on the operational and the finance functions. The core managerial skills of the management team at Cooley were focused, in terms of function, on the finance, accounting and operations. These functional skills allowed the management team to build a new distillery and to produce award-winning new Irish whiskeys.

However, the absence of marketing and 'route to market' experience is also evident from the functional experiences of the management team. In terms of sales and marketing Teeling himself provided the initial sales skills, with his 'entrepreneurial drive' opening new markets for Cooley during the period 1994 to 2000. As such, Teeling's entrepreneurial skills may be a determinant of growth, in the sense that they influenced the selection of markets, while at the same time his managerial skills may at times have been a limit to growth.

6. DISCUSSION: GROWTH AS A CAUSE OF VENTURE FOUNDING

Penrose specifically considered entrepreneurial ambition, at the level of the firm, as an important determinant of growth. The case suggests that the entrepreneur had an ambition to grow the business, as expressed by his desire to 'build a firm'. There was also a more specific objective in terms of creating a business that would be an attractive acquisition target for a larger drinks firm. The ambition did not relate to a specific product market position, but was the ambition to create a firm that could distil sufficient Irish whiskey to supply a leading firm with sufficient volumes of Irish whiskey. This suggests that growth was the reason for founding the firm. This is in contrast to the research question that informs much of the research on firm growth, which assumes that growth is a consequence of founding.

In the context of new firms why do some entrepreneurs endow their new businesses with a specific ambition to grow? The entrepreneur's ambitions and aspirations need to be considered in the context of his or her prior experiences and the alternative opportunities the entrepreneur could pursue. The entrepreneur's 'horizon', as indicated by his understanding of the whiskey industry, was based on references to the leading Irish whiskey producer and the major drinks firms. In contrast, others could approach this business with the craft whiskey distillers of Scotland as the reference point. The two major strategic forms in the whiskey industry are large drinks firms producing blended whiskey products and craft producers of typically single malt whiskeys. A third strategic form could be the own label producer, though few firms pursue this strategy. The most notable difference, in terms of the initial resource commitments needed between these organizational forms, is the production process. The entrepreneur's reference point was the larger whiskey producers, and therefore the column still production process with larger production volumes, and therefore the need for larger sales volumes. Considering his career, it would appear, *ex post*, that if the 'distillery opportunity' did not represent a sufficient return, the entrepreneur could pursue other activities. The description of the entrepreneur's career suggests that he had alternative opportunities, particularly in exploration firms, and that on previous occasions he had not pursued specific opportunities. So while searching for specific opportunities, the entrepreneur did evaluate specific opportunities against his own personal objectives, which, at times, included growth. In this case the suggestion was that his 'desire to build' was an important motivation in starting the whiskey distillery. This leads us to suggest that for some entrepreneurs the opportunity for growth may be the reason for founding a new venture, rather than growth being a consequence of the founding.

How did Teeling's growth objective result in growth? The case suggests that an entrepreneurial, financial and operational survival imperative to grow characterized the firm. What were these growth imperatives? The entrepreneurial imperative for growth was the entrepreneur's personal aspirations for the firm. The financial imperative reflects the expectations of the shareholders, including other investors and members of the Board of Directors. The case data highlights how the Board of Directors experienced internal disagreement about the direction of the firm in terms of possible exit routes. The fact of this dissent, and the presence of a shareholder base who had not been rewarded for their investment, created an ongoing need to grow the business as this would create possible exit options for shareholders.

The operational imperative for growth was the development of large, and increasingly valuable, stocks of products and the associated costs of carrying stock. Ongoing distillation meant that the firm continued to have available large volumes of product for sale. The unusual lag between distillation and product availability meant that the firm had to continue to distil to have sufficient product to meet some inspirational level of future demand (which the founding entrepreneur articulated as 500 000 cases per annum).

The growth imperative meant that that the pace of growth, whatever it was in an absolute sense or relative to other firms, was perceived by the entrepreneur, the board, and by shareholders, as insufficient. This ongoing 'problem' or 'failure' led to an ongoing search for solutions. Specifically, the firm addressed the perceived level of poor performance by trying to sell the firm; with efforts to increase sales through new products and new markets; by seeking new resources, the firm expanded its capital over time through increasing debt and retained earnings; and by exploiting existing management resources.

Poor sales and financial difficulties resulted in attempts to sell the firm. The failure of these initial exit opportunities to materialize was associated with a gradual improvement in trading conditions and an easing of the day-to-day financial problems at the firm. The focus of the entrepreneur and the Board of Directors (which included management) shifted towards growing the business, though the possibility of a trade sale and an IPO remains. However, the firm experienced internal disagreement among the Board of Directors and management as to what specific product-market positioning would best exploit the firm's limited resources. In the late 1990s the entrepreneur restructured the management of the firm, which effectively involved the passing of responsibilities from him to the Managing Director, and the replacement of his 'many-products, many-markets' strategy with a more focused strategy (where the firm focused on premium speciality products targeted at 'developed' whiskey markets) as developed by the Managing Director. This internal reorganization of management responsibilities and the resulting change in strategy was a critical step in positioning the firm for growth. Why did this happen?

There are several possible explanations for why the entrepreneur facilitated a change of direction. First, there were managerial resources within the firm who could replace him. So while the management team was small, the firm had within its relatively small team an alternative management option. Second, there were organizational structures that allowed and required organizational goals to be discussed. The existence of an operating Board of Directors meant that organizational goals were discussed. Further reasons why the entrepreneur might have stepped aside from management were: first, he expressed an inherent dislike of management; and second, he had other business interests and opportunities, including his substantial investments and interests in exploration firms.

7. CONCLUSIONS

Is growth determined by choice of location and of sector, and 'chance', as suggested by Greene et al. (2008) or, as Penrose suggests, the outcome of the interaction between resources and markets? In the entrepreneurship literature there is ambiguity about how best to measure (Delmar et al. 2003) and explain (Barringer et al. 2005; Davidsson et al. 2006; Storey 1994; Wiklund et al. 2009) growth in new and small firms. In terms of explaining growth, extant research studies can be broadly classified into those that draw on resource-based explanations, including the entrepreneur, and those that draw on market-based explanations. While these might appear to be dichotomous explanations, Penrose provides a theory that integrates the two perspectives. Research from the strategy literature also suggests that these explanations are complementary (Spanos and Lioukas 2001), with each explaining aspects of firm performance.

Our analysis of the growth of a single firm suggests that the entrepreneur's growth objective at founding, and the resulting resource commitments determined the growth of the firm. This objective of growing the firm appears to be an intrinsic element of the decision to found the firm, rather than, as much of the literature assumes, a consequence of the decision to found the firm. Some entrepreneurs set out to create specific firms. Such a new venture creation process has been described by Sarasvathy as following a causation logic. A causation logic in the venture creation process suggests that entrepreneurs 'take a particular effect as given and focus on selecting between means to create that effect' (Sarasvathy 2001: 245). Baker et al. (2003) describe such processes as design-proceeding-execution. One element of the causation logic is that the entrepreneur may have explicit expectations about the growth of the firm. The case data suggests that these explanations influenced the decision to found the firm and in effect created what we termed a growth imperative.

One aspect of the firm founding that might explain why such a growth objective existed at founding was that the entrepreneur had prior entrepreneurial experience, including starting and managing larger firms. This does not necessarily lead to the argument that a growth expectation in and of itself will lead to growth. Indeed, Davidsson and co-authors have recently argued that a focus on high growth may not be appropriate for entrepreneurs, as it may not lead to high profitability in subsequent periods (Davidsson et al. 2009).

The outcome of the growth objective observed in the case was that there was what we termed a growth imperative. An imperative to grow can lead to resource commitments, and a path dependency, in terms of resources, that allows a firm to exploit opportunities as they emerge overtime. As time evolves, the firm's resource commitment may lead to the discovery or creation of market opportunities that lead to growth. Therefore, following Penrose, the case data suggests that 'purposive activity' of the entrepreneur led to the growth over time. However, Penrose's theory focuses on 'purposive activity' driven by the desire to use excess managerial and entrepreneurial resources as the explanation for growth. In the context of a new firm, excess resources are unlikely to exist (Aldrich 1999; Aldrich and Fiol 1984). Rather than excess entrepreneurial or managerial resources embedded within the firm, the growth imperative may reflect the growth objective and the 'entrepreneurial services' of the founding entrepreneur. The growth imperative observed related to an entrepreneurial imperative to grow, a financial imperative to grow and an organizational imperative to growth. Failure to achieve the expected growth resulted in the development of new products, the search for new markets, and changes in the management of the firm.

This chapter contributes to our understanding of growth in several ways. First, we suggest that the research question that drives much of the literature on growth of new ventures may have an implicit incorrect bias. Extant literature treats growth as a consequence of firm founding, seeking to identify what aspects of the founding process might cause growth. In contrast, based on our case data, we suggest that in some cases the objective of growing may in fact be the cause, and not consequence, of firm creation. Second, we contribute to Penrose's theory of growth by extending it to the context of the new firm. In this context we suggest that excess resources, a core element of Penrose's model, are unlikely to be the initial cause of growth. We suggest that the actions of the entrepreneur can create an imperative for growth, and such an imperative may lead to purposive activity that leads to growth.

Third, we contribute to the debate on the role of chance in explaining new firm growth. Our research suggests that the resource base and market opportunity based view of growth are complementary when applied to firms over extended periods of time. As an entrepreneur develops the firm's resource base, new market opportunities will be discovered or created. At times, the growth in these markets will lead to high growth within the firm. This would suggest to us that over extended periods of time, chance is not the 'key' explanation for growth. This suggests that studying growth over short time frames may produce conflicting results as in any given time period either markets or resources might account for growth. It requires time for resources, including entrepreneurial and managerial resources, to evolve. So while comparing growth rates to those of markets might suggest that firms are 'riding' a growth wave, it ignores how an entrepreneur develops the resources required to 'ride' the wave. As such the researchers of growth need to be aware that over shorter time frames growth may appear to be a consequence of either markets or resources, but that it is the interaction of these factors that may explain growth over longer periods of time.

Fourth, in terms of researching growth, our study suggests that combining units of analysis provides a deeper insight into the process of growth. While Penrose's core focus is on the firm's resources, one unit of analysis, her theory requires consideration of the market, a second unit of analysis. Specifically, in the context of the new firm, Penrose argues that a third unit of analysis, the entrepreneur, needs to be considered. Furthermore, this study suggests that by adopting a multilevel evolutionary perspective it may be possible to develop a framework that explains why it is that some new businesses grow and others do not.

REFERENCES

Aldrich, H.E. (1999), *Organizations Evolving*, London: Sage Publication.
Aldrich, H.E. and C. Fiol (1994), 'Fools rush in? The institutional context of industry creation', *Academy of Management Review*, **19** (4), 645–70.
Baker, T., S. Miner and D.T. Eesley (2003), 'Improvising firms: bricolage, account giving and improvisational competencies in the founding process', *Research Policy*, **32**, 255–76.
Barringer, B., F. Jones and D. Neubaum (2005), 'A quantitative content analysis of the characteristics of rapid-growth firms and their founders', *Journal of Business Venturing*, **20** (5), 663–87.
Bhide, A. (2000), *The Origin and Evolution of New Business*, New York: Oxford University Press.
Blundel, R. (2002), 'Network evolution and the growth of artisanal firms: a tale of two regional cheese makers', *Entrepreneurship & Regional Development*, **14**, 1–30.
Carroll, G. and M. Hannan (2000), *The Demography of Corporations and Industries*, Princeton, NJ: Princeton University Press.
Davidsson, P., F. Delmar and J. Wiklund (2006), *Entrepreneurship and the Growth of Firms*, Cheltenham, UK and Northampton, MA, USA: Edward Elgar Publishing.
Davidsson, P., P. Steffens and J. Fitzsimmons (2009), 'Growing profitable or growing from profits: putting the horse in front of the cart?', *Journal of Business Venturing*, **24** (4), 388–406.
Delmar, F., P. Davidsson and W. Gartner (2003), 'Arriving at the high-growth firm', *Journal of Business Venturing*, **18** (2), 189–216.
Eisenhardt, K. and C. Schoonhoven (1990), 'Organizational growth: linking founding team, strategy, environment, and growth among US semiconductor ventures, 1978–1988', *Administrative Science Quarterly*, **35** (3), 504–29.
European Case Clearing House (1997), 'Cooley Distillery plc.: a new spirit in the world whiskey industry', Cranfield University, Case No.: 397-111-1.
European Case Clearing House (2006), 'Strategy for US market entry (6): Cooley Whiskey', Cranfield University, Case No. 506-062-1.

European Case Clearing House (2010), 'Cooley Distillery plc.: start-up and growth challenges (1986–2009)', Cranfield University, Case No. 810-007-1.

Greene, F., K. Mole and D. Storey (2008), *Three Decades of Enterprise Culture: Entrepreneurship, Economic Regeneration and Public Policy*, Basingstoke: Palgrave Macmillan.

Hannan, M. and J. Freeman (1977), 'The population ecology of organizations', *American Journal of Sociology*, **82**, 929–64.

Kanter, R. (1977), *Men and Women of the Corporation*, New York: Basic Books.

Kenny, I. (1991), *Out on their Own: Conversations with Irish Entrepreneurs*, Dublin: Gill and Macmillan.

Kisfalvi, V. (2002), 'The entrepreneur's character, life issues, and strategy making: a field study', *Journal of Business Venturing*, **17**, 489–518.

Miles, M. and A. Huberman (1994), *Qualitative Data Analysis: An Expanded Sourcebook*, (2nd edn), Thousand Oaks, CA: Sage Publications.

Penrose, E. (1959), *The Theory of the Growth of the Firm*, London: Basil Blackwell (revised and reprinted 1995).

Pitelis, C. (ed.) (2002), *The Growth of the Firm – the Legacy of Edith Penrose*, Oxford: Oxford University Press.

Sarasvathy, S. (2001), 'Causation and effectuation: toward a theoretical shift from economic inevitability to entrepreneurial contingency', *Academy of Management Review*, **26** (2), 243–63.

Shane, S. (2000), 'Prior knowledge and the discovery of entrepreneurial opportunities', *Organization Science*, **11**, 448–69.

Spanos, Y. and S. Lioukas (2001), 'An examination into the causal logic of rent generation: contrasting porter's competitive strategy framework and the resource-based perspective', *Strategic Management Journal*, **22** (10), 907–34.

Storey, D.J. (1994), *Understanding the Small Business Sector*, London: Routledge.

Westhead, P., D. Ucbasaran and M. Wright (2003), 'Differences between private firms owned by novice, serial and portfolio entrepreneurs: implications for policy makers and practitioners', *Regional Studies*, **37** (2), 187–200.

Wiklund, J., H. Patzelt and D. Shepherd (2009), 'Building an integrative model of small business growth', *Small Business Economics*, **32** (4), 351–74.

5. New moderating factors for the pioneer's success

Pedro M. García-Villaverde, María J. Ruiz-Ortega and Gloria Parra-Requena

1. INTRODUCTION

The literature on First Mover Advantages (FMAs) has been very extensive (Finney et al. 2008; Lieberman and Montgomery 1988; Vanderwerf and Mahon 1997, among others) over the last three decades. The difficulties of obtaining and maintaining net advantages from pioneering, especially in contexts of strong dynamism and hostility, have been highlighted (Covin et al. 2000; Suarez and Lanzolla 2007; Zhou, 2006).[1] Furthermore the biases in the development of empirical studies detected by several compilation studies limit the obtaining of concluding results on FMAs (Kerin et al. 1992; Szymanski et al. 1995, amongst others). The marketing approach has developed some of the most relevant contributions in this field of FMAs (Boulding and Christen 2008; Song et al. 1999, among others). However, we must note that the great majority of these studies are focused on one product or one brand as a unit of analysis (Golder and Tellis 1993). Besides, we have not found any empirical study that analyses the moderating effects of new product development (NPD) factors on the success of pioneering. In this line we consider that market intelligence and cross-functional integration linked to the NPD process can have relevant implications for the effectiveness of pioneer orientation, because these factors influence the exploration and exploitation of new products in the market. We consider that the contingent approach of organization theory is a good option to complement the approaches of marketing and strategy (Chandler 1962). From this approach the pioneer's new product performance will be improved by internal commitment to new products introduced in the market, linked to the development of resources and the process of strategy establishment (Wu et al. 2007). We integrate the contingent role of market intelligence and cross-functional integration of the NPD, and internal commitment to the new products on the effectiveness of pioneer orientation on new product performance (Tellis and Golder 1996).

Therefore the aim of this study is to analyse the moderating effect of market intelligence, cross-functional integration and internal commitment on the relationship between pioneering and new product performance. With marketing and organization theory approaches we try to reinforce and complement the FMA literature and link it with the entrepreneurial research. In this sense, we analyse the interactive effects of pioneering with the internal factors linked to new product success.

The chapter is structured as follows. First we offer an introduction to the topic under study and the aim we wish to achieve. In the second section, we explain the theoretical framework and the derived hypotheses. Third we describe the research method, and in section 4 we present the results obtained and a discussion. Finally we illustrate the main conclusions obtained in the study, managerial implications, limitations and future lines of research.

2. LITERATURE REVIEW AND HYPOTHESES DEVELOPMENT

2.1 Pioneering and New Product Performance

The FMA literature highlights the finding that pioneer firms attain higher performance levels (Chen and Chang 2010; Robinson and Fornell 1985). However, doubts about the results obtained for FMAs have been raised in the last two decades, due to inconsistencies in the scales for measuring pioneer orientation, the definition of the pioneer industry selection (bias towards industries with stronger FMAs), the choice of dependent variables, and failure to account for entrants' internal factors (Finney et al. 2008; Lieberman and Montgomery 1998; Vanderwerf and Mahon 1997). Following Suarez and Lanzolla (2007), when firms face dynamic environments in technology and demand, the FMAs are not so evident. We believe that it is necessary to study in depth certain internal factors that can influence the effectiveness of pioneer orientation. In this study we analyse the contingent role of certain internal factors provided by marketing and organization theory.

The strong positive influence of pioneering orientation on firm performance has been demonstrated (Cui and Jiang 2009; Kuivalainen et al. 2007; Urban et al. 1986, among others). Owing to entry barriers that have to be overcome by those firms that enter the market after the pioneer firm (Karakaya 2002), firms that develop a pioneer strategy will have an advantageous cost position with regard to followers (Lieberman and Montgomery 1998). Other advantages are that early entrants can limit the market for the products of competitor firms, can influence systems of consumer preferences and can also have better positioning in the market which will allow them to exploit certain scarce resources not available for late followers (Boulding and Christen 2008; Kerin et al. 1992). In the same line, pioneer firms also have greater access to distribution channels as well as the possibility of developing investments that will allow them to take over technological leadership. This will provide pioneer firms with differentiation advantages with regard to followers and information advantages with consumers (Golder and Tellis 1993). Thus Miller et al. (1989) argue that as a consequence of the above-mentioned advantages pioneer firms obtain greater market shares than followers.

Despite all the mentioned advantages, we can find several studies which propose possible advantages for follower firms (Schilling 2002). These advantages result in disadvantages for pioneer firms, linked to imitation, the 'free rider' effect, the 'vintage effect', lower demand and technological uncertainty after the pioneer enters the market, and the 'incumbent inertia' (Boulding and Christen 2008; Lieberman and Montgomery 1988).

In this study we consider that the promptness of the moment of entry into the market will have a net positive effect on new products' performance. Thus, from the previous arguments, we consider that early entrants have an important opportunity for defining the market, thus obtaining and maintaining competitive advantages in the new products (Di Benedetto and Song 2008). We can propose the first hypothesis:

H1:   Pioneering has a positive effect on new product performance.

2.2   Moderating Internal Factors

2.2.1   Market intelligence and cross-functional integration in the NPD process

From the marketing view it has been analysed how different elements of the new product development process influence new products' success (Song and Montoya-Weiss 2001). We have not found studies that analyse the contingent character of several elements linked to the NPD process on the success of pioneer orientation. In this sense Kodama (1995: 8) highlights that the most relevant capability in the NPD process is the 'ability to convert demand from a vague set of distant wants into well-defined products'. From this approach we consider that market intelligence and cross-functional integration can play a relevant moderator role in the effectiveness of pioneering.

Following Cornish (1997), we can understand market intelligence as the process of acquiring and analysing information in order to understand the market (both existing and potential customer); to determine the current and future needs and preferences, attitudes and behaviour of the market; and to assess changes in the business environment that may affect the size and nature of the market in the future. When a firm has capabilities linked to market knowledge it also has a better understanding of customer requirements and needs, competitive markets and market trends. This knowledge is conducive to the success of the firm (Wren et al. 2000). Thus, there are several studies that show that market intelligence is positively related to organization performance (Juntarung and Ussahawanitchakit 2008; Matsuno et al. 2002). Furthermore, market intelligence will allow pioneer firms to adapt new products better to consumer tastes and preferences, allowing these firms to gain a good reputation amongst consumers, to reduce uncertainty and develop entry barriers. These barriers will allow firms to establish a temporary monopoly position that both favours the obtaining of competitive advantages and offers the chance to influence the development of the market to make these advantages sustainable (Carpenter and Nakamoto 1994). Therefore, these firms will be able to obtain a greater performance for their new products and avoid the imitation of competitors (Kerin et al. 1992; Lieberman and Montgomery 1998). According to the marketing literature, market intelligence is expected to improve a firm's success when the firm develops a pioneer behaviour (Li and Calantone 1998). By means of market intelligence, firms are able to detect the unfilled needs of customers and are expected to respond to that intelligence. Studies like that by Verhees and Meulenberg (2004) highlight that those firms that lag behind in innovativeness in a specific domain are stimulated by customer market intelligence to come up with an innovation because customers are able to express their needs for innovative products, these often being modifications of existing products. Thus, we propose the next hypothesis:

H2: Higher market intelligence in the NPD process improves the effect of pioneering on new product performance.

According to Song and Montoya-Weiss (2001: 65), we can understand cross-functional integration in the NPD context as 'the magnitude of interaction and communication, the level of information sharing, the degree of coordination, and the extent of joint involvement across functions in specific new product development tasks'. We interpret cross-functional integration as a united effort by R&D, manufacture and marketing in NPD, because these three functional units are critical to the success of the NPD process (Song and Xie 2000). Cross-functional integration has been identified in the literature as the key driver of new product success (Olson et al. 1995). This is because it increases constant communication and the amount of information flow in the organization; it also provides flexibility and improvements in the use of the resources by gathering resources and capabilities from different functional areas (Troy et al. 2008).

However, we must highlight some disadvantages of cross-functional integration because diversity can generate more complexity and confusion in the decisions (Sethi 2000) and can be more time-consuming and less efficient than more centralized and bureaucratic processes. Finally the different backgrounds and perspectives on work and goals can cause various conflicts, which increase the costs for firms and reduce new product performance (Olson et al. 1995). Despite these disadvantages the positive relationship between cross-functional integration and new product performance has been well established in previous studies (Song and Xie 2000).

The effectiveness of pioneering can be significantly influenced by cross-functional integration. In this line, Schoenecker and Cooper (1998) suggest that the new products' success that pioneering can generate requires a joint and coordinated effort in R&D, manufacture and marketing. Pioneer firms will obtain first mover advantages if the NPD process is developed with an exchange of information, a fluid communication and an interaction among the main functional units of the firm. This will favour a suitable definition of the characteristics of new products that will facilitate production efficiency and the effectiveness in the response and loyalty of consumers (Thomas 1996). Likewise an early cross-functional integration in the NPD process reduces the number of redesigns and specifications, as well as the time and cost of product development, whilst favouring an improvement of the new products' performance obtained by pioneer firms (Song and Parry 1997b). Therefore, cross-functional integration can fortify the resource position barriers of pioneer firms, which will be difficult for followers to surpass (Makadok 1998). Thus the joint effect of cross-functional integration and the novelty of both the products developed by the firm and the markets in which the firm competes will favour new products' success (Song and Xie, 2000). Drawing upon these arguments, we can propose the next hypothesis:

H3:　Higher cross-functional integration in the NPD process improves the effect of pioneering on new product performance.

2.2.2 Internal commitment to new products

Organization theory tries to explain how the fit between the firm's structure and strategy leads to a greater performance (Chandler 1962). A firm's internal commitment to developed strategies, shown in the development of resources and the implementation of suitable strategies, will favour the obtaining of competitive advantages. Thus, the extent to which there is a strong internal commitment is essential in determining which resources are to be used for the exploitation of new products, which in turn increases the chances of new product success in the market (Tellis and Golder 1996; Wu et al. 2007).

Internal commitment usually lies at the heart of a strategy implementation. Furthermore, from the classical view, internal commitment is considered as the development of tasks and the resource linking that concur with the continuing display of behaviour directed towards goal achievement and other positive outcomes (Swailes 2000).

Furthermore, pioneer firms develop their activity with products and markets that are new and different, and managerial and strategic commitment is needed to access and deploy limited resources (Simon et al. 2002; Tellis and Golder 1996). Therefore, internal commitment is especially critical for the pioneering entry. In this sense, we argue that the performance effect will be significant if pioneer firms are willing to maintain an internal commitment over a longer timeframe, because the interaction of actions and commitments provides a means to economize on the costs of committing to an innovation with an uncertain future value. Therefore, following Wu et al. (2007), high levels of internal commitment should also increase the efficiency of pioneer behaviour, thereby increasing new product performance. In this line, internal commitment is one of the most important ingredients of the right mindset required to become a successful innovative company (Pearson 2002). Due to inertia, an excessive level of internal commitment may result in risk for the effectiveness of a pioneer behaviour (Henderson and Clark 1990). However, we focus on the positive side of a firm's commitment to a given strategic posture, in this case a pioneer posture, because of its logical link with the required strategic persistence just when the firm develops a pioneer behaviour. In this vein a commitment to a pioneer behaviour reflects not only that the firm's resources are focused and engaged but also that the firm tends to develop a pioneer orientation with regard to its new products. Consequently, we hypothesize the following:

H4: Higher internal commitment to new products improves the effect of pioneering on new product performance.

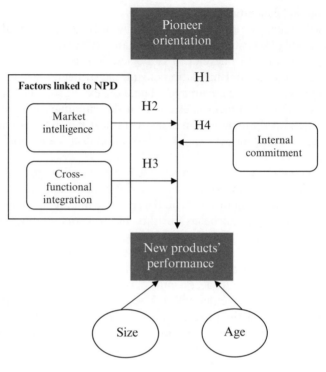

Source: Authors.

Figure 5.1   Contingent model

In Figure 5.1 we present the theoretical model, the direct and moderating effects and the proposed hypotheses. We also include size and age as control variables.

3.   SAMPLE AND METHODS

3.1 Sample

The empirical study focuses on the Information and Communications Technology (ICT) industry in Spain. We used two official databases in order to establish the total number of firms in this sector: SABI and Camerdata. In order to complete the original file and update records, we used the databases of the Spanish Association of the Electronic and Telecommunications Industry and the census of exporters. We have not included those companies that had fewer than 10 employees since, in companies of such a small size, their characteristics differ substantially from the considerations raised in the theoretical argumentation, and hence a minimal operative structure and a specific study are required (Spanos and Lioukas 2001). Moreover we included only non-diversified firms, that is, companies that make at least 70 per cent of their income from their main activity (Rumelt 1974). After eliminating duplicated cases resulting from the use of different information sources, we were left with a database with 1847 companies, to which we sent the questionnaire prepared for this study by mail. We obtained a total of 253 valid questionnaires from CEOs, which constitutes a rate of response of 13.7 per cent, for a confidence level of 95 per cent and a sampling error of 5.7 per cent. We tested for non-response bias and no significant differences were observed between respondent and non-respondents on structural characteristics (Armstrong and Overton 1977).

3.2 Variables[2]

3.2.1 New product performance

Based on Gupta and Govindarajan (1984) and Zahra (1996), this construct has been operationalized considering CEOs' self-reported importance and satisfaction for three items: profitability, sales, and market share of new products (Chronbach's alpha of 0.85). As an approximation to performance sustainability, respondents had to evaluate the three items over the previous three years (Spanos and Lioukas 2001).

3.2.2 Pioneering

This variable reflects firms' propensity to develop a pioneer behaviour, which is not so much the creation of a new product or entry into a specific market, as a way of going about making decisions and taking actions (Covin et al. 2000). Pioneering was measured with a three-item scale previously validated (Covin et al. 2000). This scale is as follows: 'we compete heavily on the basis of being first to the market with new products, we typically precede our major competitors in bringing new products to the market and we offer products that are unique and distinctly different from those of our major competitors' (Chronbach's alpha of 0.71). We have used a five-point Likert scale which, though it supports a bias derived from a subjective valuation of pioneer orientation, eliminates the tendency of the late follower group existing in the PIMS database to self-exclude (Golder and Tellis 1993).

3.2.3　Market intelligence for the NPD

This variable refers to the firm's knowledge of market conditions, and more specifically of consumers, when the firm introduces new products onto the market. The construct includes two items adapted from Song and Parry (1997a): 'during the development of new products, we understood the customer's purchase decision well – the "who, what, when, where and how" of his (or her) purchase behaviour for this selected product and we knew how much the customer would pay for such a new product – his/her price sensitivity' (Cronbach's alpha of 0.87).

3.2.4　Cross-functional integration for the NPD

This variable refers to the coordination among the three functional areas we proposed: R&D, manufacture and marketing. The construct includes three items adapted from Song and Parry (1997a):

> The R&D and manufacture areas are highly coordinated for the development and launch of new products onto the market; the R&D and marketing areas are highly coordinated for the development and launch of new products onto the market; and the manufacture and marketing areas are highly coordinated for the development and launch of new products onto the market (Cronbach's alpha of 0.82).

3.2.5　Internal commitment

This variable refers to the firm's commitment to its products and strategies. The construct includes two items adapted from Tellis and Golder (1996) and Song and Parry (1997b): 'when our products are successful in the market, we direct our technology and strategy exclusively towards promoting and consolidating them, and given the changes in the technology sector we tend to inject more resources and capabilities into the known technology to reinforce our products' (Cronbach's alpha of 0.74).

3.2.6　Control variables

We have included size and age as control variables. *Size* is frequently included in studies to control the effect that it can have on firm performance. Big firms can own more resources to obtain a better position in the market and develop scale economies that will help them achieve a better performance (McEvily and Zaheer 1999). This variable has been included through the natural logarithm of the number of employees (Spanos and Lioukas 2001). *Age* is usually included in the studies in order to control its influence on the firm's performance (Chandler and Hanks 1994).

3.3 Analysis Techniques

We used several statistical techniques to test the hypotheses raised in our research. First in order to verify that there were no multi-collinearity problems between the variables included in the models, we developed a correlation analysis. Then we developed a hierarchical regression analysis to test hypotheses. The hierarchical approach is necessary since an inter-action effect exists if, and only if, the interaction term gives a significant contribution over and above the main-effects-only model (Cohen and Cohen 1983). The means and standard deviations for all variables and a correlation matrix can be observed in Table 5.1. In Table 5.2 we present the value inflation factors (VIFs), all under five, which is well below the benchmark (Hair et al. 1998).

4. RESULTS AND DISCUSSION

On a base model were first entered the variables of size, age, pioneer-ing, cross-functional integration, market intelligence and internal com-mitment[3] (see Table 5.3). This model explains a statistically significant share of the variance of firm performance ($R^2_{adj}= 0.215$). The results obtained in this model show that pioneer orientation ($\beta = 0.276$; $p < 0.001$) and market intelligence ($\beta = 0.278$; $p < 0.001$) have a positive and significant influence on new product performance. It should be high-lighted that our base model has a strong predictive power. Pioneering has a positive and significant influence on firm performance. Therefore, we can accept Hypothesis 1. This result supports the findings of studies that highlight the marked influence of an early entry into the market on the firm's performance (Cui and Jiang 2009; Di Benedetto and Song 2008; Zhou 2006). We have not found a significant influence of cross-functional integration or internal commitment in the new product performance.

As a next step, in the contingent model we include the double interactive effects (market intelligence × pioneering, cross-functional integration × pioneering and internal commitment × pioneering). This model makes a significant contribution over and above the base model ($\Delta R^2_{corr} = 0.27$). In this model, we find once again the positive and significant influence of pioneering ($\beta = 0.288$; $p < 0.001$), and market intelligence ($\beta = 0.290$; $p < 0.001$) on new product performance. With regard to the interactive effects, we have found that cross-functional integration ($\beta = 0.145$; $p < 0.05$) and internal commitment ($\beta = 0.128$; $p < 0.05$) moderate in a positive way the relationship between pioneer orientation and firm performance.

Table 5.1 Correlations and descriptive statistics

	Size	Age	Pioneer-ing	Market Intell.	Cross Funct. Int.	Internal Commitm.	MI × Pion	CFI × Pion	IC × Pion	NP Perform.
Mean	3.97	21.09	3.16	3.84	3.39	2.99	0.19	0.26	0.09	12.28
SD	1.55	20.40	0.86	0.88	1.07	0.73	0.81	1.01	0.59	4.36
Size	1									
Age	-.287**	1								
Pioneering	0.092	0.003	1							
Market Int.	0.105	-0.031	0.255**	1						
Cross F. I.	0.072	-0.039	0.290**	0.405**	1					
Int. Com.	0.068	-0.119	0.152*	0.198**	0.132*	1				
MI × Pioneering	0.038	-0.108	-0.137*	-0.016	-0.072	-0.025	1			
CFI × Pioneering	0.098	-0.072	-0.037	-0.073	-0.068	-0.023	0.548**	1		
IC × Pioneering	0.028	-0.080	-0.138*	-0.028	-0.026	0.172**	0.277**	0.112	1	
NP Performance	0.044	0.054	0.376**	0.379**	0.286**	0.121	-0.058	0.068	0.055	1

Note: * $p < 0.1$; ** $p < 0.05$.

Source: Own study.

Table 5.2   Tolerance and VIF

Variables	Tolerance	VIF
Size	0.815	1.227
Age	0.865	1.156
Pioneering	0.802	1.246
Market intelligence	0.719	1.390
Cross-functional integration	0.745	1.342
Internal commitment	0.876	1.142
Market intelligence × Pioneering	0.602	1.660
Cross-functional integration × Pioneering	0.682	1.466
Internal commitment × Pioneering	0.856	1.168

Table 5.3   Regression analysis

Variables	Base model		Contingent model	
	β	t	β	t
Size	0.001	0.011	−0.065	−1.059
Age	−0.064	−.01045	−0.016	−0.259
Pioneering	0.276	4.467****	0.288	4.637****
Market intelligence	0.278	4.305****	0.290	4.523****
Cross-functional integration	0.071	1.112	0.076	1.187
Internal commitment	0.024	0.397	−0.001	−0.017
Market intelligence × Pioneering			−0.107	−1.502
Cross-functional integration × Pioneering			0.145	2.119**
Internal commitment × Pioneering orientation			0.128	2.079**
Model				
R²		0.236		0.263
R² adjusted		0.215		0.234
Change in R²				0.27***

Note: * p < 0.1; ** p < 0.05; *** p < 0.01; **** p < 0.001.

Source: Own study.

These findings support Hypotheses 3 and 4. By contrast, we have found that market intelligence has a non-significant moderating effect on the relationship between pioneering and firm performance (β = −0.107; ns). Therefore, we cannot accept Hypothesis 2.

The results obtained allow us to add new empirical support to the FMA literature (Di Benedetto and Song 2008). Thus, we demonstrate that pioneering has a direct effect on the new product's performance. Furthermore we also show that the relationship between pioneering and new product performance is moderated by certain complementary factors. The results obtained add new empirical evidence to the studies that found market intelligence to be positively related to firm performance (Kohli and Jaworski 1990; Matsuno et al. 2002). Thus, market intelligence has a positive and significant influence on the new product performance (Juntarung and Ussahawanitchakit 2008). With regard to the moderating role of market intelligence, the results obtained did not match what we expected. The results show that market intelligence moderates in a negative way, but not significantly, the relationship between pioneering and new product performance. A possible explanation for this weak negative effect is that in an industry with high levels of dynamism and hostility, the close link with consumers could lead the firm to guide its NPD towards the preferences and needs of the latter, thereby generating inertia that limits the potential pioneer advantages (Lieberman and Montgomery 1998).

Although cross-functional integration improves the relationship between pioneer behaviour and new product performance, it does not influence firm performance. We consider it is possible for cross-functional integration to generate more complexity and confusion in the NPD (Sethi 2000). However, it is a basic element when pioneer firms develop their activity in environments of high dynamism and hostility, since, through the coordination of the functional areas of R&D, manufacture and marketing, the NPD process favours the obtaining of FMAs. Therefore cross-functional integration reinforces the effect of pioneering on new product performance.

The results obtained show that internal commitment has a negative but not significant influence on new product performance. In this sense, the literature also shows that prior organizational success leads to strategic persistence, that is, a tendency for firms to stick with strategies that have been successful in the past (e.g. Miller and Chen 1994). This can be explained because given the importance of commitment for holding the organization to a particular line of behaviour, it is also likely that new opportunities may be valued less if the firm's existing resources are already engaged in the pursuit of certain opportunities (McGrath and Nerkar 2004). However, the results obtained show that this negative effect is eliminated if the firm develops a pioneer orientation. Thus, internal commitment has a positive and significant moderator effect on the relationship between pioneer orientation and new products' performance.

Therefore, internal commitment allows the firms that develop pioneering to adopt an entrepreneurial attitude, which will prevent new opportunities from being valued inadequately. In this way pioneering would allow firms to take advantage of the benefits traditionally linked to internal commitment and to avoid the possible negative effects (Simon et al. 2002; Wu et al. 2007).

5. CONCLUSIONS

In this study we analyse the moderating effect of the NPD process and internal commitment on the relationship between pioneering and new product performance. This has allowed us to study in depth the promoting role of several internal factors on the advantages derived from a pioneer orientation in a context of high dynamism and hostility. The results obtained add new and enlightening evidence to the literature on FMAs. Thus, the great majority of studies which analyse the indirect effect of pioneer behaviour on firm performance are focused on firm capabilities or competitive tactics. In this sense, it is important to highlight the relevance of analysing the complementary character of the marketing and organization theory for the explanation of firm performance when developing a pioneer orientation.

With regard to the contributions of the study, we consider that the main contribution is that we provide a more complex and complete approach to the internal factors that moderate the relationship between pioneering and new product performance. In this sense this study combines the approaches of marketing (new product development process) and organization theory (internal commitment). This combined analysis allows us a better grasp of the different stages in the NPD developed by pioneer firms. Thus a call was made in the literature to include in the studies on entry timing some variables linked to the NPD process (Song and Parry 1997a; 1997b). Therefore, as highlighted by Tellis and Golder (1996), the inclusion of variables linked to market intelligence, cross-functional integration and internal commitment can allow pioneer firms not only to be the first onto the market, but also to become market leaders. In line with the approaches of Shepherd and Shanley (1998), another contribution is that we have considered pioneering as continuous, spreading from market pioneer to late follower. For this purpose, as opposed to the utilization of self-definition measures, like those established in the PIMS database, we have used a Likert scale which, though it supports a bias derived from a subjective valuation of the entry timing in the market, eliminates the tendency of the late follower group that existed in the PIMS database to self-exclude (Golder and Tellis 1993). Furthermore our measurement of pioneering reflects a firm's propensity to develop a pioneer behaviour, which is not so much the creation of a new product or entry into a specific market, as a way of going about making decisions and *taking* actions. This pioneering approach allows us to connect the FMAs view to entrepreneurship theory. Thus, internal moderating factors, linked to new product development and exploitation, lead us to a configurational view of entrepreneurial orientation, which involves proactiveness, innovativeness, risk-taking and competitive aggressiveness to compete effectively in contexts of high dynamism and hostility (Lumpkin and Dess 1996; Wiklund and Shepherd 2005).

Unlike the limitations of numerous studies that have detected advantages in developing pioneering in mature sectors, traditionally profitable sectors for pioneer companies (Lieberman and Montgomery 1988), we have developed the study in a sector with a strong degree of dynamism and rivalry in which the advantages of pioneer strategy are more dubious, precisely because these advantages are more easily eliminated and for the risk that this strategy implies for companies.

A novel aspect with regard to the majority of studies on FMAs is that our measurement of performance refers to new product performance. Furthermore, our measurement of new product performance includes a profitability item, an aspect greatly demanded in previous studies (Kerin et al. 1992). Vanderwerf and Mahon (1997) highlight that there is a strong tendency to detect FMAs in studies that include market share as a measurement of performance. In this sense, some authors are hesitant on whether the effect of pioneer behaviour on market share can prove the existence of first mover advantages. Finally, not only do the results of our study make a solid contribution to the FMA literature but they also draw the attention of researchers in this field to the pressing need to incorporate the results of other theoretical approaches in determining how other factors internal to the firm itself influence the effectiveness of pioneering, and in what specific areas.

We propose several managerial implications. Thus, pioneer firms should strive to coordinate R&D, manufacture and marketing functional areas in the development and launch of new products, because this cross-functional integration in the NPD is a complementary capability for the success of pioneering. However, they should avoid linking the NPD exclusively to the needs and preferences of customers, because it can generate inertia and limit the success of pioneering. Finally, to ensure the persistence of FMAs, managers should adopt an internal commitment to exploitation in the market for new products. We can extend these recommendations to entrepreneurs. Thus, we encourage them to develop a coherent entrepreneurial orientation, which combines the innovativeness and proactiveness in developing and launching new products with continued aggressive competition to rivals, which can provide high performance of new products.

We assume several limitations of this study that can concern, in part, the extension of the results obtained. We must indicate the cross-sectional and non-longitudinal approach of the study. Nevertheless we think that a longitudinal study would be excessively complex, because of the detailed information required to achieve our research aims. Furthermore, the perceptions of CEOs with regard to the main aspects of this study would not necessarily coincide exactly with objective reality, which might lead to possible limitations in the results obtained. In agreement with the approaches of Spanos and Lioukas (2001), we think that managerial perceptions are very important in shaping the extension of the company's strategic behaviour. In this respect, we can justify the use of these subjective measures of performance.

We propose several lines of future study. A possible line would be to extend this study to other sectors of industrial activity, as well as to service sector companies. We consider it to be of great importance to prepare an in-depth study, from a configurational approach, of the internal coherence of pioneering by means of the inclusion of new factors. We also recommend the development of a dynamic analysis, in which the evolution of factors modifying the effect of pioneering on firm performance is analysed, as well as an in-depth study of the sustainability of competitive advantages. According to Durand and Coeurderoy (2001), the development of a longitudinal study would allow us to use multiple clocks to evaluate the influence of several variables, such as the age of industry, pioneering and short-term and long-term performance.

NOTES

1. There are strong links between FMAs and entrepreneurship literature because of the shared need to compare windows of opportunity to gain competitive advantage and the liabilities of newness (Shepherd and Shanley 1998). Thus several studies highlight the role of pioneering in the new venture success (Durand and Coeurderoy 2001; García-Villaverde and Ruiz-Ortega 2011; Shepherd and Shanley 1998). Furthermore pioneering is strongly connected with several dimensions of entrepreneurial orientation, that is proactivity, innovativeness, risk-taking or competitive aggressiveness (Covin et al. 2000; Lumpkin and Dess 1996).
2. We test the potential common method bias for the use of self-report questionnaires for a single respondent.
3. All the variables included in the regression analysis had been previously typified.

REFERENCES

Armstrong, J.S. and T. Overton (1977), 'Estimating nonresponse bias in mail surveys', *Journal of Marketing Research*, **14**, 396–402.

Boulding, W. and M. Christen (2008), 'Disentangling pioneering cost advantages and disadvantages', *Marketing Science*, **27** (4), 699–716.

Carpenter, G.S. and K. Nakamoto (1994), 'Reflections on consumer preference formation and pioneering advantage', *Journal of Marketing Research*, **31**, 570–73.

Chandler, A.D. (1962), *Strategy and Structure: Chapters in the History of the Industrial Enterprise*, Cambridge, MA: MIT Press.

Chandler, G. and S.H. Hanks (1994), 'Market attractiveness, resource-based capabilities; venture strategies and venture performance', *Journal of Business Venturing*, **9** (4), 331–49.

Chen, H. and W. Chang (2010), 'The essence of the competence concept: adopting an organization's sustained competitive advantage viewpoint', *Journal of Management and Organization*, **16** (5), 690–712.

Cohen, J. and P. Cohen (1983), *Applied Multiple Regression/Correlation Analysis for the Behavioural Sciences*, 2nd edn, Hillsdale, NJ: Lawrence Erlbaum Associates.

Cornish, S.L. (1997), 'Product innovation and the spatial dynamics of market intelligence: does proximity to markets matter?', *Economic Geography*, **73** (2), 143–65.

Covin, J.G., D.P. Slevin and M.B. Heeley (2000), 'Pioneers and followers: competitive tactics, environment, and firm growth', *Journal of Business Venturing*, **15**, 175–210.

Cui, L. and F. Jiang (2009), 'FDI entry mode choice of Chinese firms: a strategic behaviour perspective', *Journal of World Business*, **44** (4), 434–44.

Di Benedetto, A. and M. Song (2008), 'Managerial perceptions of global pioneering advantage: theoretical framework and empirical evidence in the US and Korea', *Industrial Marketing Management*, **37** (7), 863–72.

Durand, R. and R. Coeurderoy (2001), 'Age, order of entry, strategic orientation, and organizational performance', *Journal of Business Venturing*, **16**, 471–94.

Finney, R.Z., J.E. Lueg and N.D. Campbell (2008), 'Market pioneers, late movers, and the resource-based view (RBV): a conceptual model', *Journal of Business Research*, **61**, 925–32.

García-Villaverde, P.M. and M.J. Ruiz-Ortega (2011), 'Ways to improve pioneer new ventures' performance in the ICT industry', *Telecommunications Policy*, **35**, 20–35.

Golder, P.N. and G.J. Tellis (1993), 'Pioneer advantage: marketing logic or marketing legend?', *Journal of Marketing Research*, **30**, 158–70.

Gupta, A.K. and V. Govindarajan (1984), 'Business unit strategy, managerial characteristics, and business unit effectiveness at strategy implementation', *Academy of Management Journal*, **27** (1), 25–41.

Hair, J.F., R.E. Anderson, R.L. Tatham and W.C. Black (1998), *Multivariate Data Analysis*, 5th edn, Englewood Cliffs, NJ: Prentice Hall.

Henderson, R.M. and K.B. Clark (1990), 'Architectural innovation: the reconfiguration of existing product technologies and the failure of established firms', *Administrative Science Quarterly*, **35**, 9–30.

Juntarung, N. and P. Ussahawanitchakit (2008), 'Knowledge management capability, market intelligence, and performance: an empirical investigation of electronic businesses in Thailand', *International Journal of Business Research*, **8** (3), 69–80.

Karakaya, F. (2002), 'Barriers to entry in industrial markets', *Journal of Business and Industrial Marketing*, **17** (5), 379–88.

Kerin, R., R.R. Varadarajan and R. Peterson (1992), 'First-mover advantage: a synthesis, conceptual framework, and research propositions', *Journal of Marketing*, **56**, 33–52.

Kodama, F. (1995), *Emerging Patterns of Innovation: Sources of Japan's Technological Edge*, Boston, MA: Harvard Business School Press.

Kohli, A.K. and B.J. Jaworski (1990), 'Market orientation: the construct, research proposition, and managerial implications', *Journal of Marketing*, **54** (2), 1–18.

Kuivalainen, O., S. Sundqvist and P. Servais (2007), 'Firm's degree of born-globalness, international entrepreneurial orientation and export performance', *Journal of World Business*, **42** (3), 253–67.

Li, T. and R.J. Calantone (1998), 'The impact of market knowledge competence on new product advantage: conceptualization and empirical examination', *Journal of Marketing*, **62**, 13–29.

Lieberman, M.B. and D.B. Montgomery (1988), 'First mover advantages', *Strategic Management Journal*, Summer Special Issue, **9**, 41–58.

Lieberman, M.B. and D.B. Montgomery (1998), 'First-mover (dis)advantages: retrospective and link with the resource-based view', *Strategic Management Journal*, **19**, 1111–25.

Lumpkin, G.T. and G.G. Dess (1996), 'Clarifying the entrepreneurial orientation construct and linking it to performance', *Academy of Management Review*, **21**, 135–72.

Makadok, R. (1998), 'Can first-mover and early-mover advantages be sustained in an industry with low barriers to entry/imitation?', *Strategic Management Journal*, **19** (7), 683–96.

Matsuno, K., J.T. Mentzer and A. Özsomer (2002), 'The effects of entrepreneurial proclivity and market orientation on business performance', *Journal of Marketing*, **66**, 18–32.

McEvily, B. and A. Zaheer (1999), 'Bridging ties: a source of firm heterogeneity in competitive capabilities', *Strategic Management Journal*, **20**, 1133–56.

McGrath, R.G. and A. Nerkar (2004), 'Real options reasoning and a new look at the R&D investment strategies of pharmaceutical firms', *Strategic Management Journal*, **25** (1), 1–21.

Miller, A., W.B. Gartner and R. Wilson (1989), 'Entry order, market share, and competitive advantage: a study of their relationships in new corporate ventures', *Journal of Business Venturing*, **4**, 197–209.

Miller, D. and M.J. Chen (1994), 'Sources and consequences of competitive inertia: a study of the US airline industry', *Administrative Science Quarterly*, **39** (1), 1–23.

Olson, E.M., O.C. Walker Jr and R.B. Ruekert (1995), 'Organizing for effective new product development: the moderating role of product innovativeness', *Journal of Marketing*, **59** (1), 48–62.

Pearson, A.E. (2002), 'Tough-minded ways to get innovative', *Harvard Business Review*, **80** (8), 117–25.

Robinson, W.T. and C. Fornell (1985), 'The sources of market pioneer advantages in consumer goods industries', *Journal of Marketing Research*, **222**, 305–17.

Rumelt, R.P. (1974), *Strategy, Structure and Economic Performance*, Boston, MA: Harvard University Press.

Schilling, M.A. (2002), 'Technology success and failure in winner-take-all markets: the impact of learning orientation, timing and network externalities', *Academy of Management Journal*, **45** (2), 387–98.

Schoenecker, T.S. and A.C. Cooper (1998), 'The role of firm resources and organizational attributes in determining entry timing: a cross-industry study', *Strategic Management Journal*, **19**, 1127–43.

Sethi, R. (2000), 'Superordinate identity in cross-functional product development teams: its antecedents and effect on new product performance', *Journal of the Academy of Marketing Science*, **28** (3), 330–44.

Shepherd, D.A. and M. Shanley (1998), *New Venture Strategy. Timing, Environment Uncertainty, and Performance*, London: Sage Publications.

Simon, M., B. Elango, S. Houghton and S. Savelli (2002), 'The successful product pioneer: maintaining commitment while adapting to change', *Journal of Small Business Management*, **40** (3), 187–203.

Song, X.M. and M. Montoya-Weiss (2001), 'An examination of the effect of perceived technological uncertainty on Japanese new product development', *Academy of Management Journal*, **44**, 61–80.

Song, X.M. and M. Parry (1997a), 'The determinants of Japanese new product successes', *Journal of Marketing Research*, **34**, 64–76.

Song, X.M. and M. Parry (1997b), 'A cross-national comparative study of new product development processes: Japan and the United States', *Journal of Marketing*, **61** (2), 1–18.

Song, X.M. and J. Xie (2000), 'Does innovativeness moderate the relationship between cross-functional integration and product performance?', *Journal of International Marketing*, **8** (4), 61–89.

Song, X.M., A. Di Benedetto and Y.L. Zhao (1999), 'Pioneering advantages in manufacturing and service industries: empirical evidence from nine countries', *Strategic Management Journal*, **20** (9), 811–36.

Spanos, Y.E. and S. Lioukas (2001), 'An examination into the causal logic of rent generation: contrasting Porter's competitive strategy framework and the resource based perspective', *Strategic Management Journal*, **22**, 907–34.

Suarez, F. and G. Lanzolla (2007), 'The role of environmental dynamics in building a first mover advantage theory', *Academy of Management Review*, **32** (2), 377–92.

Swailes, S. (2000), 'Goals, creativity and achievement: commitment in contemporary organizations', *Creativity and Innovation Management*, **9** (3), 185–94.

Szymanski, D., L. Troy and S. Bhradwaj (1995), 'Order of entry and business performance: an empirical synthesis and re-examination', *Journal of Marketing*, **59** (4), 17–33.

Tellis, G.J. and P.N. Golder (1996), 'First to market, first to fail? The real causes of enduring market leadership', *Sloan Management Review*, **37** (2), 65–75.

Thomas, L.A. (1996), 'Brand capital and entry order', *Journal of Economics and Management Strategy*, **5** (1), 107–29.

Troy, L.C., T. Hirunyawipada and A.K. Paswan (2008), 'Cross-functional integration and new product success: an empirical investigation of the findings', *Journal of Marketing*, **72**, 132–46.

Urban, G.L., T. Carter, S. Gaskin and Z. Mucha (1986), 'Market share rewards to pioneering brands: an empirical analysis and strategic implications', *Management Science*, **32** (6), 645–59.

Vanderwerf, P. and J.F. Mahon (1997), 'Meta-analysis of the impact of research methods on findings of first-mover advantages', *Management Science*, **43**, 1510–19.

Verhees, J.H.M. and M.T. Meulenberg (2004), 'Market innovation, innovativeness, product innovation, and performance in small firms', *Journal of Small Business Management*, **42** (2), 134–54.

Wiklund, J. and D. Shepherd (2005), 'Entrepreneurial orientation and small business performance: a configurational approach', *Journal of Business Venturing*, **20**, 71–91.

Wren, B.M., W.E. Souder and D. Berkowitz (2000), 'Market orientation and new product development in global industrial firms', *Industrial Marketing Management*, **29** (6), 601–11.

Wu, H.L., B.W. Lin and C.J. Chen (2007), 'Contingency view on technological differentiation and firm performance: evidence in an economic downturn', *R&D Management*, **37** (1), 75–88.

Zahra, S.A. (1996) 'Technology strategy and new venture performance: a study of corporate-sponsored and independent biotechnology ventures', *Journal of Business Venturing*, **11**, 289–321.

Zhou, K.Z. (2006), 'Innovation, imitation, and new product performance: the case of China', *Industrial Marketing Management*, **35**, 394–402.

6. The use of financial bootstrapping in small and medium-sized ventures and the impact on venture growth

Eddy Laveren, David Helleboogh and Nadine Lybaert

1. INTRODUCTION

It is well documented that the availability of financial resources is one of the challenges of new venture creation (Cassar 2004; Steier 2003). It is difficult and expensive for new ventures to find outside capital from banks and investors because of the high information asymmetries (Huyghebaert and Van de Gucht 2007; Parker 2002), the absence of a financial or operating history (Huyghebaert and Van de Gucht 2007), the lack of collateral (Parker 2002), and the higher *ex ante* failure risk compared to existing ventures (Chaganti et al. 1995; Huyghebaert and Van de Gucht 2007). This could lead to a lack of finance which may hamper the venture's growth. In order to overcome these challenges, it is necessary and desirable that founders are aware of methods that minimize the need for financing by securing resources at little or no cost, and by creatively acquiring resources without using bank financing or equity. This collective set of methods is called financial bootstrapping and refers to financing methods other than traditional debt and equity financing from financial institutions and investors (Bhide 1992; Carter and Van Auken 2005; Freear et al. 1995; Landström and Winborg 1995).

Despite the fact that the use of some bootstrap methods in actual practice is widespread (Van Auken 2005; Winborg and Landström 2001), there is a lack of research focusing on developing an understanding of financial bootstrapping use within new ventures (Brophy 1997; Ebben and Johnson 2006; Lahm and Little 2005). In the pioneering study on financial bootstrapping of Winborg and Landström (2001) different bootstrapping methods are identified and classified into four financial bootstrapping types. Up till now, there is little understanding about whether the founder's human capital is related to the use of (any of) these financial bootstrapping types. Chandler and Hanks (1998) and Ebben and Johnson (2006) underline the importance of this gap in the literature and urge future research to look into the impact of individual characteristics of founders on the adopted bootstrapping types. For this purpose, as a first research goal of this study, we analyse which human capital characteristics of the owner-manager have an impact on the use of financial bootstrapping. Although prior research has made reference to a possible relationship between the use of bootstrapping and subsequent venture growth, the lack of direct empirical research on this relationship is also recognized to be a gap in the literature (Chandler and Hanks 1998; Ebben and Johnson 2006). Therefore, the second research goal of this study is to assess whether and to pinpoint which financial bootstrapping types affect the venture's growth.

This chapter is structured as follows. First, we start with a literature review, resulting in the formulation of hypotheses. Next, we provide information about the research methodology. In the next section, we present the results, followed by an elaboration on some robustness tests. Finally, we conclude with a discussion of the findings.

2.   LITERATURE REVIEW AND DEVELOPMENT OF HYPOTHESES

Financial bootstrapping may be defined as a collection of methods used to minimize the amount of outside debt and equity financing needed from banks and investors (Ebben and Johnson 2006; Winborg and Landström 2001). Based on the pioneering study on financial bootstrapping of Winborg and Landström (2001), there are at least four types of method that can be used to bootstrap ventures: (1) customer-related methods (being methods to improve cash flow from customers, such as speeding up invoicing, obtaining advance payments or granting cash discount); (2) owner-related financing and resources (being methods such as the use of credit cards or loans from the founder's family or friends); (3) joint-utilization of resources with other ventures (being actions such as hiring temporary staff or outsourcing); and (4) delaying payments (being methods to improve cash flow by making payments at a later date, such as leasing of equipment, postponing payments of value-added tax, or delaying payments to suppliers).

Ebben and Johnson (2006) underline the importance of studying financial bootstrapping on the basis of these four different bootstrapping types. The authors also indicate that different types of bootstrapping are utilized at different periods in the life cycle of a small firm. Owner-related and joint-utilization techniques are primarily used early in the life of a venture and their use will decrease over time. Conversely, in line with the resource-dependency theory, the use of customer-related and delaying-payments techniques are initially low and will increase over time. When a new venture becomes more important to its customers and suppliers over time, it gains leverage in those relationships with which it wants to negotiate payment terms (Ebben and Johnson 2006). Overall, studying bootstrapping on the basis of these different bootstrapping types enables us to gain a better understanding of why some antecedents (and consequences) of bootstrapping methods are more prevalent than others.

2.1   Human Capital and Financial Bootstrapping

Within new ventures, the human capital of the founder can be considered as a key determinant of venture performance (Brown and Kirchhoff 1997; Chandler and Jansen 1992; Stoner 1987) as the concentration of decision-making power is typically very high (Shepherd et al. 2000). Human capital refers to the knowledge that is not easily appropriable and that yields competitive advantages (Barney 1991). It comprises an extensive range of variables, including traits (such as age and gender), general human capital (including education, management experience and work experience in the same sector), and founder-specific human capital (such as parental and partner's self-employment background) (Baum et al. 2001; Cliff 1998; Sapienza and Grimm 1997; Ucbasaran et al. 2006; Watson et al. 2003).

Chandler and Hanks' (1998) analysis shows that, on average, firms with high levels of founder human capital and low levels of initial financial capital perform similarly to firms that have low levels of founder human capital and high levels of financial capital. In this sense, their findings are hopeful for many new ventures which typically face difficulties in collecting financial capital from banks and investors (Berger and Udell 1995; Huyghebaert and Van de Gucht 2007; Parker 2002), since they can compensate the low financial capital with high levels of human capital. The underlying assumption here is that the level of human capital is a prerequisite for using financial bootstrapping techniques. Also a number of studies indicate that the founder's human capital is probably associated with the different financial bootstrapping types since they suggest that it will be difficult to get customers to pay quickly (Aaronson et al. 2004; Long et al. 1993), to postpone payments to suppliers (McMillan and Woodruff 1999), to have easy access to external financing (Ebben and Johnson 2006; Shane and Cable 2002) or to cooperate with third parties (Bradley 1994; Harrington 1994) before these stakeholders are convinced of the founder's human capital.

The question regarding whether the founder's human capital promotes or constrains the use of financial bootstrapping has not yet been explicitly addressed. In this respect, two opposing theoretical views prevail. On the one hand, in line with the resource-based theory (Barney 1991; Wernerfelt 1984), a positive relationship between human capital and financial bootstrapping can be expected. As this theory argues that financing decisions are closely related to the founder's human capital (Barney 1991; Wernerfelt 1984), higher human capital levels lead to a better knowledge of financial bootstrapping techniques, resulting in a higher use of these techniques. On the other hand, human capital theory (Becker 1975) suggests that the founder's human capital is negatively associated with the extent to which the financial bootstrapping types are used. In fact, human capital theory argues that founders with high human capital levels are more likely to generate higher incomes, and hence are able to contribute more to the start-up's initial financial capital (Åstebro and Bernhardt 2005; Xu 1998). Moreover, a high level of human capital helps to attract more financial capital from banks and investors due to an increased negotiation capacity and expertise (Dorf and Byers 2005; Van Auken 2001) or due to a signalling or reputation effect (Blumberg and Letterie 2008). The higher the obtained financial capital, the lower the financial bootstrapping use will be (Winborg and Landström 2001). In line with the majority of the authors who mainly suggests a negative relationship, the following hypotheses are formulated:

H1a: The founder's human capital is negatively associated with the use of customer-related bootstrap financing.

H1b: The founder's human capital is negatively associated with the use of owner-related bootstrap financing.

H1c: The founder's human capital is negatively associated with the use of joint-utilization bootstrap financing.

H1d: The founder's human capital is negatively associated with the use of delaying payments bootstrap financing.

2.2   Financial Bootstrapping and Venture Growth

The resource-dependency theory suggests that a venture can only create limited added value on assets for which it is dependent upon other ventures. Accordingly, the venture will strategically react in order to reduce the dependency on others for this asset, which will increase the venture's survival chances and growth (Pfeffer and Salancik 1978). Moreover, in line with the pecking order theory (Myers 1984), prior research suggests that growth is predominantly financed with internally generated funds (Carpenter and Petersen 2002; Winborg and Landström 2001). Since financial bootstrapping generates financing by using methods that minimize the amount of outside debt and equity financing needed from banks and investors, it should also have an impact on the venture's growth rate.

Although empirical research into the bootstrapping–growth relationship is almost non-existent, there are strong theoretical arguments suggesting a positive relationship with venture growth. For example, Van Auken (2005) poses that bootstrapping is a way to obtain finance often without collateral and to keep working capital in the cashbox, which could provide the founder with more cash to grow the venture. Freear et al. (1995) indicate that founders who learn to bootstrap their venture effectively gain legitimacy in the eyes of the stakeholders, which could be beneficial for the venture's growth. Authors like Bhide (1992) and Lahm and Little (2005) suggest that bootstrappers may have an advantage over other individuals who are able and willing to belong to more resource-rich environments in terms of being forced to run their venture more inventively, which could improve the growth chances of the venture. Also Timmons (1999) states that ventures can create a competitive advantage by using financial bootstrapping since it signals an efficient attitude throughout the venture. In line with these arguments, a positive influence of bootstrapping on growth can be expected. However, we are aware that Lahm and Little (2005) contend that founders may spend too much time in performing bootstrap tasks that are worth less than other tasks that are fundamental to their businesses or that bootstrappers may tend to cut corners too close in areas such as, for example, number of days accounts receivable or accounts payable, which could affect their good relationship with these stakeholders.

We expect that not all bootstrapping types have an impact on the new venture's growth. As mentioned, Ebben and Johnson (2006) find that the owner-related and joint-utilization techniques are primarily used early in the life cycle of a venture and that their use will decrease over time, whereas – in line with the resource-dependency theory – the use of customer-related and delaying-payments techniques is initially low and will increase over time. As de novo ventures constitute the research population of this study, the following hypotheses are formulated with regard to the techniques used early in the venture's life cycle:

H2a: The extent to which owner-related bootstrapping is used is positively associated with venture growth.

H2b: The extent to which joint-utilization bootstrapping is used is positively associated with venture growth.

3. RESEARCH METHODOLOGY

3.1 Data Collection Process

A large-scale mail survey was sent out in September 2006 to the founders of 3480 randomly selected Belgian ventures out of a total population of 23 045 companies which were founded in 2002 and 2003. After two rounds, responses of 558 ventures were collected, which represents a response rate of 16.03 per cent. Firm size (employment, assets), industry and location (province) were compared between these respondents and the original sample (3480 ventures), but no significant differences could be found. We also compared respondents of the first round of our questionnaire with the respondents of the follow-up questionnaire, and no statistically significant response bias was detected either.

As in this study only small and medium-sized ventures are considered, 93 large ventures with more than 250 employees were omitted from our sample. Moreover, 97 re-registrations were excluded from the data since they were the continuation of an existing venture. Re-registrations of existing ventures can occur if the venture changes its legal form. This resulted in a final sample of 368 ventures. Their profile is described in Table 6.1.

Financial statement information about these ventures was collected from publicly available archival data (Bel-First database). However, many variables used in this study come from the same source of self-report data, that is the owner who filled in the questionnaire. Most self-report data in this study is based on demographic and factual data that is objective and verifiable, and not subject to any prediction, interpretation, or evaluation. As argued by Podsakoff et al. (Podsakoff and Organ 1986; Podsakoff et al. 2003), this kind of data is considerably less subject to common method bias. Moreover, we empirically tested whether this bias is present by using Harman's one-factor test. The basic assumption of Harman's (1967) test is that if a substantial amount of common method variance exists in the data, either a single factor will emerge or one general factor will account for the majority of the covariance among the variables. According to this test, an exploratory factor analysis was performed on all the questionnaire items in our study (Hair et al. 2006). This analysis did not yield on overarching factor, but nine separate ones (where the first factor accounted only for 11.5 per cent), suggesting the absence of common method bias.

Table 6.1   Profile of the respondents

Characteristics	
Number of firms	368
Human capital characteristics	
Gender: Male	326 (88.6%)
Female	42 (11.4%)
Age: < 30	74 (20.3%)
30–40	180 (48.9%)
41–50	84 (22.8%)
> 50	27 (7.3%)
Level of education (minimum bachelor's degree)	190 (51.6%)
Self-employed parents	184 (50.1%)
Self-employed life partner	72 (20%)
Management experience (average)	7.5 years (SD: 8.58)
Work experience in the same sector (average)	11.2 years (SD: 8.63)
Prior venture ownership experience	208 (56.5%)
Venture characteristics	
Industry: Services	121 (32.9%)
Manufacturing	43 (11.7%)
Construction	81 (22.0%)
Trade	123 (33.4%)
Legal form: Limited liability (BVBA)	322 (87.5%)
Limited by shares (NV)	46 (12.5%)
Credit constraints (on a scale from −3 to +3)	−.84 (SD: 1.906)
Average employment in FTE (2006)	4.7 FTE (SD: 7.44)
Mean total assets (2006)	441 543 Euro (SD: 679 965)
Average debt ratio (2003)	71.3% (SD: 135.3%)
Employment growth (2005–2007)	132% (SD: 395%)
Average use of bootstrapping (2003–2005):	
Customer-related	Seldom
Owner-related	Sometimes
Joint-utilization	Sometimes
Delaying-payments	Seldom

Source: Authors.

3.2   Variables

3.2.1   Dependent variables

In the questionnaire, founders are asked to indicate the extent to which they made use of different bootstrapping methods over the time span 2003–2005 on a 5-point Likert scale ranging from 'never', 'seldom', 'sometimes', 'often' to 'always'. To verify the grouping of the separate bootstrapping

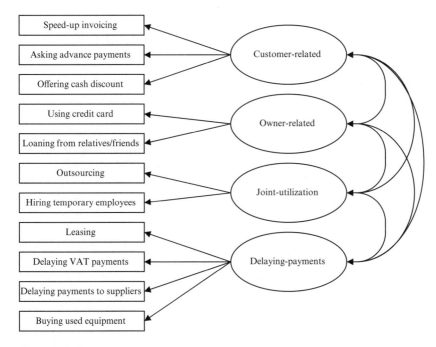

Source: Authors.

Figure 6.1   *Confirmatory factor analysis of bootstrapping types*

methods out of the questionnaire into the four types proposed by Winborg and Landström (2001) and Ebben and Johnson (2006), a confirmatory factor analysis (CFA) is performed on the survey responses. Based on the cut-off values suggested by Kline (1998) and Hair et al. (2006) (Chi-square not significant; CMIN/DF < 2, CFI > 0.95, RMSEA < 0.05), we can conclude that this model, which is presented in Figure 6.1, provides a good model fit (Chi-square = 44.239 [p = .091]; CMIN/DF = 1.341; CFI = 0.958; RMSEA = 0.032). Therefore, we conclude that we can group the separate bootstrapping methods into the four cluster types with reasonable confidence. In line with other bootstrapping studies such as Carter and Van Auken (2005), the bootstrapping types are calculated based on summated scales.

In order to analyse the impact of bootstrapping on growth, employment growth is used as the dependent variable. Employment growth and turnover growth are the most widely used growth measures in empirical growth research (Delmar 1997). However, Belgian SMEs are not obliged to make their sales figures publicly available, whereas employment growth is a widely available indicator for all of the firms of interest. The employment growth rate is captured by calculating the average employment growth from 2005 to 2007.

3.2.2 Independent variables

Corresponding to the work of Baum et al. (2001), Van Praag (2003), Bosma et al. (2004), Brush et al. (2004) and Alsos et al. (2006), human capital comprises an extensive range of variables. These include: education (dummy that takes the value 0 for founders with a lower education than a bachelor's degree and 1 for founders who attained at least a bachelor's degree at the moment of start-up); management experience (number of years of management experience at the moment of start-up); work experience in the same sector (number of years of working experience in the same sector at the moment of start-up); self-employed parents (dummy that takes the value 0 for founders without self-employed parents and 1 for founders with self-employed parents); self-employed partner (dummy that takes the value 0 for founders without a self-employed partner and 1 for founders with a self-employed partner); novice/habitual dummy (dummy that takes the value 0 for novice founders with no prior venture ownership experience and the value 1 for habitual founders with prior venture ownership experience); gender (dummy that takes the value 0 for male and 1 for female founders); and age (age of the founder at the moment of start-up).

3.2.3 Control variables

Since the use of financial bootstrapping differs according to the new venture's industry, credit constraints, size and debt level (Carter and Van Auken 2005; Harrison et al. 2004), these variables are included in the regressions. We control for industry by including three dummy variables (manufacturing, construction and trade sector), whereas the services sector is used as a reference category. The credit constraints variable measures how the business owner perceives to what extent the venture has experienced problems in attracting external financing during the start-up process (based on a 7-point Likert scale ranging from -3 (not at all) to $+3$ (to a very high extent)). Size is included by means of the natural logarithm of the average total assets. The venture's total debt ratio is defined as the average ratio of total debt to total assets. With regard to Hypotheses 1a, 1b, 1c and 1d, size and debt ratio are calculated at the moment of start-up, whereas in the growth regression (Hypotheses 2a and 2b) these measures are calculated over the time span 2003–2005. In line with Huyghebaert and Van de Gucht (2007) we also introduce legal form as a control variable in the growth regression. Compared to the private companies with limited liability (BVBA), the companies limited by shares (NV) face higher equity requirements at the moment of start-up and are also considered to be more prestigious, which enables a new venture to gain legitimacy leading to a higher survival rate and growth (Donckels 1993).

Pearson correlations of the variables in this study are shown in Table 6.2.

3.3   Testing Procedures

In order to analyse how the founder's human capital is associated with the use of financial bootstrapping, we apply ordered logit models as they are the most commonly used models for ordinal outcomes in the social sciences, introduced by McKelvey and Zavoina (1975). The ordinal logistic regressions are run in SPSS. These regressions yield cumulative odds ratios, where the cumulative odds can be interpreted as the odds of being in a particular category or a higher one (of the dependent variable) versus being in lower ones.

In order to analyse the influence of bootstrapping on growth, an OLS regression analysis is used. The model we estimate considers the impact of bootstrapping techniques in period $t-1$ (time span 2003–2005) on growth in period t (growth from 2005 to 2007) to minimize reverse causation.

4.   EMPIRICAL RESULTS

4.1   Human Capital and Financial Bootstrapping

The results of the ordinal logistic regressions testing the impact of the founder's human capital on the different financial bootstrapping types are presented in Table 6.3. Each regression model includes the extent to which the founder makes use of a specific financial bootstrapping type as dependent variable. All regressions are significant with R^2 ranging between .075 and .132.

With respect to the *customer-related* bootstrapping methods, the presence of self-employed parents and a female gender are associated with a lower use of these techniques. Therefore, we believe that Hypothesis 1a is not rejected. Regarding self-employed parents, the odds ratio is .539. We can say, then, that the odds for founders with self-employed parents of being in a higher rather than a lower category of customer-related bootstrapping usage are 46.1 per cent lower ([odds−1] × 100) compared to founders without self-employed parents. So founders with

Table 6.2   Pearson correlations of the variables

Variables	1	2	3	4	5	6	7
1 Employment growth							
2 Gender	−0.04						
3 Age	−0.06	−0.06					
4 Education	−0.02*	−0.04	0.07				
5 Self-employed parents	0.08	−0.16**	−0.04	−0.01			
6 Self-employed partner	0.07	−0.16**	0.10	−0.03	0.21**		
7 Work experience	−0.10	−0.12*	0.48**	−0.13	−0.07	0.00	
8 Management experience	−0.10	−0.07	0.57**	0.09	−0.20**	−0.04	0.45**
9 Novice/habitual dummy	−0.11	−0.05	0.25**	−0.01	0.01	−0.11	0.22**
10 Credit constraints	0.02	−0.06	−0.06	−0.09	0.12*	0.05	0.04
11 Size	0.02	0.00	0.04	0.10	−0.14*	−0.03	0.07
12 Manufacturing sector	0.04	−0.01	−0.00	−0.11	0.02	0.00	−0.01
13 Construction sector	−0.05	−0.08	−0.07	−0.19**	0.01	0.11	0.13
14 Trade sector	−0.07	0.05	0.12*	0.11	−0.15*	−0.01	0.00
15 Delaying-payment	−0.09	−0.09	−0.05	0.03	0.04	0.07	−0.03
16 Joint-utilization	−0.11	0.05	−0.16*	0.05	0.04	−0.01	−0.08
17 Owner-related	0.08	0.00	−0.20**	0.11	0.03	−0.07	−0.23**
18 Customer-related	−0.09	−0.12*	−0.07	0.01	0.18**	0.02	0.01

Note: * $p < .05$; ** $p < .01$.

Source: Authors.

self-employed parents appear to be less risk-averse with respect to their company and to possess an entrepreneurial culture (Uusitalo 2001), which leads these founders to attach higher value to strengthen long-term customer relationships than to reduce the short-term credit risk of their venture by using customer-based techniques (Paul and Wilson 2007). Regarding gender, the odds ratio is .538. This indicates that the odds that female founders use more customer-related bootstrapping are .538 times smaller (or 46.2 per cent lower) than the odds that male founders use more customer-related bootstrapping. A possible rationale is that female founders are less interested in purely monetary gain, whereas male founders may demonstrate a greater preference for immediate economic return (Brush et al. 2006).

Regarding the use of *owner-related* bootstrapping techniques, work experience has a significant negative impact. The odds ratio for work experience is .961, meaning that the odds of using more owner-related bootstrapping are 3.9 per cent lower ([.961−1] × 100) for each extra year of work experience in the same sector. Since it indicates that the work experience is negatively associated with the use of owner-related boot-strapping methods, Hypothesis 1b is not rejected. A possible rationale for

8	9	10	11	12	13	14	15	16	17
0.36**									
−0.01	0.14*								
0.14*	0.12*	−0.07							
−0.07	−0.03	−0.06	0.17**						
−0.09	−0.04	0.08	−0.11*	−0.20**					
0.11	−0.01	−0.06	0.07	−0.28**	−0.37**				
−0.02	0.12	0.33**	0.07	0.06	−0.06	0.02			
−0.02	0.02	0.09	0.13*	0.12*	−0.01	0.03	0.32**		
−0.12*	−0.05	−0.04	0.08	−0.02	−0.19**	0.01	0.21**	0.30**	
−0.04	0.03	0.01	0.07	0.06	0.01	0.07	0.20**	0.15*	0.16*

this relationship is that the use of owner-related bootstrapping is inversely related to the extent to which a new venture is able to gain easy access to financing from banks and investors (Ebben and Johnson 2006). The underlying assumption is that founders are not risk takers with respect to their personal wealth (Brockhaus 1980; Cooper et al. 1988), and therefore they are unlikely to place their personal wealth (or the wealth of their family or friends) at risk via the use of owner-related bootstrapping methods (Ebben and Johnson 2006). Since founders with work experience in the same sector obtain closer ties to banks and investors of that sector, they find it easier to attract bank financing (Berger and Udell 1995; Colombo and Grilli 2005) and to receive external funds from investors (Shane and Cable 2002). Further, the control variable size of the venture (odds ratio = 1.269) is positively related to the use of owner-related bootstrapping. A possible explanation can be found in the fact that the use of these techniques is dependent on the risk level for the founder's personal wealth (or the wealth of the owner's family and friends) (Ebben and Johnson 2006). Since prior studies have found that the probability of survival increases with the size of the new venture at the moment of entry (Acs and Audretsch 1989; Audretsch et al. 1999; Nurmi 2006), it is likely

Table 6.3   Ordinal logistic regression results (dependent variable: the use of a financial bootstrapping type)

	Financial bootstrapping types					
	Customer-related			Owner-related		
	B	SE	Exp(B)	B	SE	Exp(B)
Gender	−0.620*	0.345	0.538	−0.639	0.346	0.528
Age	−0.218	0.158	0.804	−0.096	0.160	0.908
Education	0.030	0.211	10.030	0.158	0.214	1.171
Self-empl. parents	−0.617***	0.219	0.539	−0.114	0.220	0.892
Self-empl. partner	0.467	0.278	1.595	0.265	0.281	1.303
Work experience	0.003	0.015	1.003	−0.040***	0.015	0.961
Manag. experience	0.019	0.016	1.019	0.004	0.017	1.004
Nov/hab dummy	0.069	0.220	1.071	0.027	0.224	1.027
Credit constraints	0.054	0.054	1.055	0.026	0.055	1.026
Manufact. sector	0.851**	0.359	2.342	−0.515	0.364	0.598
Construct. sector	0.663**	0.292	1.941	−0.844***	0.298	0.429
Trade sector	0.475*	0.255	1.608	−0.207	0.258	0.813
Debt ratio	−0.006	0.009	0.994	0.004	0.009	1.004
Size	0.150	0.110	1.161	0.238**	0.112	1.269
Model Chi square	23.499**			38.402***		
Nagelkerke R^2	0.075			0.122		
N	303			304		

Note: B: unstandardized coefficient; SE: standard error; Exp(B): odds ratio; * $p < .10$; ** $p < .05$; *** $p < .01$.

Source: Authors.

that large start-ups will be associated with a higher use of owner-related bootstrapping compared to small start-ups.

The results about *joint-utilization* bootstrapping methods show that the age of the founder is negatively associated, whereas management experience is positively associated with the use of these techniques. We therefore reject Hypothesis 1c. On the one hand, the odds ratio of the age variable (odds ratio = .684) tells us that older founders are more likely to use less joint-utilization bootstrapping. A possible explanation is that older founders not only tend to be more financially self-reliant, but they also prefer in-house control of their venture (Carroll et al. 2000). On the other hand, the odds ratio of management experience (odds ratio = 1.028) tells us that each extra year of management experience increases the odds by 1.028 times of using more joint-utilization bootstrapping. Thus, years of management experience is positively associated with joint-utilization

| Financial bootstrapping types | | | | | |
| Joint-utilization | | | Delaying-payment | | |
B	SE	Exp(B)	B	SE	Exp(B)
0.167	0.340	1.182	−0.379	0.333	0.685
−0.380**	0.160	0.684	−0.011	0.157	0.989
0.337	0.213	1.401	0.068	0.210	1.070
−0.131	0.218	0.877	−0.155	0.217	0.856
0.108	0.278	1.114	−0.110	0.276	0.896
−0.008	0.015	0.992	0.003	0.015	1.003
0.028*	0.017	1.028	−0.015	0.016	0.985
0.289	0.222	1.335	0.166	0.220	1.180
0.128**	0.055	1.137	0.323***	0.057	1.381
1.107***	0.365	3.025	0.369	0.358	1.446
0.534*	0.294	1.706	−0.384	0.291	0.681
0.279	0.256	1.321	0.001	0.253	1.001
−0.009	0.009	0.991	0.002	0.009	1.002
0.219**	0.111	1.245	0.029	0.109	1.029
	30.158***			42.593***	
	0.097			0.132	
	304			305	

bootstrapping. As an explanation for this positive influence, prior studies indicate that founders with management experience are more familiar with delegating and evaluating third parties with whom the venture wants to cooperate (Bradley 1994; Harrington 1994). With respect to the control variable size, the odds ratio (odds ratio = 1.245) indicates that a large venture size increases the propensity to use joint-utilization techniques such as outsourcing and hiring temporary employees. In this respect, Besanko et al. (1996) state that larger ventures may also have more bargaining power with vendors and employment agencies, rendering more favourable conditions for outsourcing and temporary employment. As such, joint-utilization bootstrapping becomes a more attractive option. This is in line with Ono and Stango (2005) who find that larger SMEs are more likely to outsource, although this relationship is reversed for large, established companies.

The results about *delaying-payments* bootstrapping methods provide evidence that their use is not influenced by any human capital characteristic of the founders. Thus, we reject Hypothesis 1d. Regarding the control variable credit constraints, the odds ratio of 1.381 tells us that each one-level increase in credit constraints elevates the odds by 1.381 of using more delaying-payments bootstrapping. This is in line with Huyghebaert (2006) who finds that start-ups use more delaying-payments methods such as trade credit when credit constraints are high.

Overall, none of the ordinal logistic regressions provide evidence that the founder's education has a significant impact on the use of financial bootstrapping techniques. This result is in line with Mamis (1992) and Lahm and Little (2005) who suggest that today's academic textbooks used in college and university courses seldom provide in-depth coverage of bootstrapping.

4.2   Financial Bootstrapping and Venture Growth

The regression findings on Hypotheses 2a and 2b are presented in Table 6.4. The results provide evidence that the use of joint-utilization and owner-related bootstrapping types has a significant influence on the venture's employment growth. However, owner-related bootstrapping has a

Table 6.4   OLS regression results (dependent variable: employment growth)

Independent variables	B	SE
Constant	1.237	3.676
Customer-related	−0.598	0.763
Owner-related	2.266**	0.980
Joint-utilization	−2.277**	0.944
Delaying-payments	−1.019	1.303
Manufacturing sector	1.416	2.275
Construction sector	−1.220	1.887
Trade sector	−2.237	1.827
Legal form	2.148*	1.353
Size	0.130*	0.068
Debt ratio	0.093	0.065
F	1.969**	
R^2	0.167	
Adjusted R^2	0.082	
N	109	

Note: B: unstandardized coefficient; SE: standard error; * $p < .10$; ** $p < .05$.

Source: Authors.

positive impact (Hypothesis 2a is not rejected), whereas joint-utilization bootstrapping has a negative impact on employment growth (Hypothesis 2b is rejected).

The findings with regard to the positive impact of owner-related bootstrapping on growth are in line with Leland and Pyle (1977) and Carter and Van Auken (1990) who suggest that the founder, his/her friends and family may have a better knowledge of the personal characteristics and of the quality of the venture that are unobservable to a bank. Taking into account that founders are unlikely to place their personal wealth (or the wealth of their family or friends) at risk (Brockhaus 1980; Cooper et al. 1988; Ebben and Johnson 2006), more owner-related financing will be used only if they expect future cash flows and growth to be high. Additionally, founders might be more committed and motivated to grow their venture when owner-related financing is involved. A possible explanation regarding the negative influence of joint-utilization bootstrapping is that these methods, such as outsourcing and hiring temporary employees, are inherently aimed at obtaining an asset without incurring the asset's full costs and at keeping the number of employees low.

With regard to the control variables, we find a positive association between the corporation type and growth. This is in accordance with Donckels (1993) who notes that a venture with a 'NV corporation type' is considered to be more prestigious, and as such it indicates the venture's ambition to grow (Bruneel et al. 2009). Further a positive relationship between the venture's initial size and employment growth is registered. For mature firms, firm size and growth rate are generally found to be negatively related – in other words: larger firms have lower growth rates (Evans 1987; Wagner 1995). However, with respect to start-ups, a positive relationship between size and growth is recorded (Phillips and Kirchhoff 1989; Wagner 1992). This is explained by the fact that start-ups that are larger gain more legitimacy in the eyes of their stakeholders and are able to employ more skilful employees and acquire more efficient production facilities.

5.   ROBUSTNESS TESTS

This section presents some tests in order to assess the robustness of the research findings. First, we re-estimate the analyses including the variable 'type of education'. This variable distinguishes between economic, technical and other type of education. The OLS regression analyses show that this variable does not have a significant impact on the use of bootstrapping techniques.

Secondly, a potential multicollinearity problem might be present due to the high correlation between the age variable and the management experience and working experience variables. Although the correlation coefficients between these variables are all below the .600 cut-off level, we also calculated Variance Inflation Factors and condition indexes. Hair et al. (2006) mention in their book that a calculated figure above 10 for Variance Inflation Factors or a calculated figure above 30 for condition indexes imply that there is a multicollinearity problem. Because the obtained results are all below the cut-off level of 10 and 30 respectively, we may conclude that there is no multicollinearity between the variables. Although there is no multicollinearity problem, we replicate our analyses by excluding age from our regressions. The estimates, however, again provide support to all the results from the previous regressions.

Thirdly, total assets growth and added value growth are used as an alternative growth measure in order to assess the relationship between the different bootstrapping types and venture growth. Similar findings are obtained.

Fourthly, instead of using sector dummies, we re-estimate the growth regressions by using an industry-adjusted growth measure. To control for the influence of the sector, the average growth rate for each of the sectors comprised in our dataset is determined. Next, from each venture's growth rate the corresponding sector mean growth rate is subtracted. The estimates provide support to the results from the growth regression with sector dummies.

Finally, we check whether our findings are still robust when using the Birch-index. The Birch-index is a growth measure developed by Birch (1987) and takes into account size differences between ventures when calculating the growth rate. He created an unbiased measure of growth by the multiplicative combination of percentage growth with a 'correction factor' (that is, absolute growth). The indicator can be said to be unbiased due to the fact that percentage growth typically declines with firm size, whereas for absolute growth the reverse holds. The estimates confirm the results of the growth regressions without the Birch correction factor.

6. DISCUSSION AND CONCLUDING REMARKS

With this study we contribute to the general knowledge of bootstrap financing within new ventures. More specifically, we throw light on two gaps in the literature by analysing the relationship between the founder's human capital and financial bootstrapping and by assessing the effect of financial bootstrapping on venture growth.

With respect to the relationship between the founder's human capital and financial bootstrapping, we reveal that the use of financial bootstrapping types is overall negatively associated with the founder's human capital, which is in line with the human capital theory. Firstly, female founders and founders with self-employed parents make less use of customer-related bootstrapping. Secondly, the founder's work experience in the same sector is negatively related to the use of owner-related bootstrapping techniques. Thirdly, the founder's age is negatively associated with the use of joint-utilization methods such as outsourcing or hiring temporary employees. These results can provide some guidance to consultants and accountants to offer tailored advice on bootstrap financing according to the founder's particular background. For firm owners, this study provides some direction as to where to look internally for financial resources.

As a second general conclusion of this study we highlight that financial bootstrapping impacts venture growth. This is in line with the resource-dependency theory (Pfeffer and Salancik 1978). More specifically, we reveal that joint-utilization bootstrapping is negatively related to employment growth, whereas owner-related bootstrapping is positively related to this growth measure. These findings imply that it is important for owners to know that the different bootstrapping types do not appear to relate consistently to venture growth in the same way, since some bootstrapping types ameliorate, while other bootstrapping types deteriorate their venture's growth. Such knowledge about non-traditional sources of financing may be especially valuable in times of economic crisis, when credit constraints are typically high.

ACKNOWLEDGEMENT

We thank the National Bank of Belgium for its financial support.

REFERENCES

Aaronson, D., R. Bostic, P. Huck and R. Townsened (2004), 'Supplier relationships and small business use of trade credit', *Journal of Urban Economics*, **55**, 46–67.
Acs, Z.J. and D.B. Audretsch (1989), 'Births and firm size', *Southern Economic Journal*, **56**, 467–75.
Alsos, G.A., E.J. Isaksen and E. Ljunggren (2006), 'New venture financing and subsequent business growth in men- and women-led businesses', *Entrepreneurship Theory and Practice*, September, 667–86.
Åstebro, T. and I. Bernhardt (2005), 'The winner's curse of human capital', *Small Business Economics*, **24** (1), 63–78.

Audretsch, D.B., E. Santarelli and M. Vivarelli (1999), 'Start up size and industrial dynamics: some evidence from Italian manufacturing', *International Journal of Industrial Organization*, **17**, 965–83.

Barney, J. (1991), 'Firm resources and sustained competitive advantage', *Journal of Management*, **17**, 99–129.

Baum, J.R., E.A. Locke and K.G. Smith (2001), 'A multidimensional model of venture growth', *Academy of Management Journal*, **44**, 292–303.

Becker, G.S. (1975), *Human Capital*, New York: National Bureau of Economic Research.

Berger, A. and G. Udell (1995), 'Relationship lending and lines of credit in small firm finance', *Journal of Business*, **68**, 351–81.

Besanko, D., D. Dranove and M. Shanley (1996), *The Economy of Strategy*, New York, Chichester and Toronto: Wiley.

Bhide, A. (1992), 'Bootstrap finance: the art of start-ups', *Harvard Business Review*, **70**, 109–17.

Birch, D.L. (1987), *Job Creation in America*, New York: Free Press.

Blumberg, B. and W. Letterie (2008), 'Business starters and credit rationing', *Small Business Economics*, **30** (2), 187–200.

Bosma, N., M. van Praag, R. Thurik and G. de Wit (2004), 'The value of human and social capital investments for the business performance of startups', *Small Business Economics*, **23**, 227–36.

Bradley, P. (1994), 'Cozy up, but stay tough', *Purchasing*, 17 March, 47–51.

Brockhaus, R. (1980), 'Risk-taking propensity of entrepreneurs', *Academy of Management Journal*, **23**, 509–20.

Brophy, D. (1997), 'Financing the growth of entrepreneurial firms', in D.L. Sexton and R.W. Smilor (eds), *Entrepreneurship 2000*, Chicago, IL: Upstart Publishing, pp. 5–27.

Brown, T. and B. Kirchhoff (1997), 'The effects of resource availability and entrepreneurial orientation on firm growth', in P. Reynolds, W. Bygrave and N. Carter (eds), *Frontiers of Entrepreneurship Research*, Wellesley, MA: Babson College, pp. 32–46.

Bruneel, J., B. Clarysse and M. Wright (2009), 'Linking entrepreneurial strategy and firm growth', Working paper Ghent University, 2009/571.

Brush, C.G., N.M. Carter, E.J. Gatewood, P.G. Greene and M.M. Hart (2004), *Gatekeepers of Venture Growth*, Kansas City, MI: Kauffman Foundation.

Brush, C.G., N.M. Carter, E.J. Gatewood, P.G. Greene and M.M. Hart (2006), *Growth-Oriented Women Entrepreneurs and their Businesses: A Global Research Perspective*, Cheltenham, UK and Northampton, MA, USA: Edward Elgar Publishing.

Carpenter, R.E. and B.C. Petersen (2002), 'Is the growth of small firms constrained by internal finance?', *The Review of Economics and Statistics*, **84** (2), 298–309.

Carroll, R., D. Holtz-Eakin, M. Rider and H.S. Rosen (2000), 'Income taxes and entrepreneurs' use of labor', *Journal of Labor Economics*, **18** (2), 324–51.

Carter, R.B. and H.E. Van Auken (1990), 'Personal equity investment and small business financial difficulties', *Entrepreneurship Theory and Practice*, **15**, 51–60.

Carter, R.B. and H.E. Van Auken (2005), 'Bootstrap financing and owners' perceptions of their business constraints and opportunities', *Entrepreneurship and Regional Development*, **17**, 129–44.

Cassar, G. (2004), 'The financing of business start-ups', *Journal of Business Venturing*, **19**, 261–83.

Chaganti, R., D. DeCarolis and D. Deeds (1995), 'Predictors of capital structures in small ventures', *Entrepreneurship Theory and Practice*, **20**, 7–18.

Chandler, G.N. and S.H. Hanks (1998), 'An examination of the substitutability of founders human and financial capital in emerging business ventures', *Journal of Business Venturing*, **13**, 353–69.

Chandler, G.N. and E. Jansen (1992), 'The founder's self-assessed competence and venture performance', *Journal of Business Venturing*, **7** (3), 223–37.

Cliff, J.E. (1998), 'Does one size fit all? Exploring the relationship between attitudes towards growth, gender, and business size', *Journal of Business Venturing*, **13**, 523–42.

Colombo, M.G. and L. Grilli (2005), 'Founders' human capital and the growth of new technology-based firms: a competence-based view', *Research Policy*, **34**, 795–816.

Cooper, A., W. Dunkelberg and C. Woo (1988), 'Entrepreneurs' perceived chances for success', *Journal of Business Venturing*, **3**, 97–108.

Delmar, F. (1997), 'Measuring growth: methodological considerations and empirical results', in R. Donckels and A. Miettinen (eds), *Entrepreneurship and SME Research: On its Way to the Next Millennium*, Aldershot: Ashgate, pp. 199–216.

Donckels, R. (1993), *KMO's ten Voeten uit. Van Onderzoek tot Actie*, Roeselare: Roularta Books.

Dorf, R.C. and T.H. Byers (2005), *Technology Ventures: from Idea to Enterprise*, New York: McGraw-Hill.

Ebben, J. and A. Johnson (2006), 'Bootstrapping in small firms: an empirical analysis of change over time', *Journal of Business Venturing*, **21**, 851–65.

Evans, D.S. (1987), 'Tests of alternative theories of firm growth', *Journal of Political Economy*, **95** (4), 657–74.

Freear, J., J.E. Sohl and W.E. Wetzel (1995), 'Angels: personal investors in the venture capital market', *Entrepreneurship and Regional Development*, **7**, 85–94.

Hair, J.F., W.C. Black, B.J. Babin, R.E. Anderson and R.L. Tatham (2006), *Multivariate Data Analysis*, Englewood Cliff, NJ: Prentice-Hall.

Harman, H.H. (1967), *Modern Factor Analysis*, Chicago, IL: University of Chicago Press.

Harrington, L. (1994), 'Van Lines change their stripes', *Transportation and Distribution*, December, p. 29.

Harrison, R.T., C.M. Mason and P. Girling (2004), 'Financial bootstrapping and venture development in the software industry', *Entrepreneurship and Regional Development*, **16**, 307–33.

Huyghebaert, N. (2006), 'On the determinants and dynamics of trade credit use: empirical evidence from business start-ups', *Journal of Business Finance and Accounting*, **33** (1), 305–28.

Huyghebaert, N. and L.M. Van de Gucht (2007), 'The determinants of financial structure: new insights from business start-ups', *European Financial Management*, **13** (1), 101–33.

Kline, R.B. (1998), *Principles and Practice of Structural Equation Modelling*, New York: The Guilford Press.

Lahm, R.J. and H.T. Little (2005), 'Bootstrapping business start-ups: entrepreneurship literature, textbooks, and teaching practices versus current business practices?', *Journal of Entrepreneurship Education*, **8**, 61–73.

Landström, H. and J. Winborg (1995), 'Small business managers' attitudes to use of financial resources', in W. Bygrave, B. Bird, S. Birley, N. Churchill,

F. Hoy, R. Keeley and W. Wetzel (eds), *Frontiers of Entrepreneurship Research*, Wellesley, MA: Babson College, pp. 172–86.

Leland, H. and D. Pyle (1977), 'Information asymmetries, financial structure and financial intermediation', *Journal of Finance*, **32**, 371–87.

Long, M., I. Malitz and A. Ravid (1993), 'Trade credit, quality guarantees, and product marketability', *Financial Management*, **22**, 117–27.

Mamis, R.A. (1992), 'The secrets of bootstrapping: 18 ways to grow or survive by substituting imagination, know-how, or effort for capital', *Inc. Magazine*, available at http://www.inc.com/magazine/19920901/4287.html.

McKelvey, R.D. and W. Zavoina (1975), 'A statistical model for the analysis of ordinal level dependent variables', *Journal of Mathematical Sociology*, **4**, 103–20.

McMillan, J. and C. Woodruff (1999), 'Interfirm relationships and informal credit in Vietnam', *Quarterly Journal of Economics*, February.

Myers, S. (1984), 'The capital structure puzzle', *Journal of Finance*, **39**, 575–92.

Nurmi, S. (2006), 'Sectoral differences in plant start-up size in the Finnish economy', *Small Business Economics*, **26**, 39–59.

Ono, Y. and V. Stango (2005), 'Outsourcing, firm size, and product complexity: Evidence from credit unions', Federal Reserve Bank of Chicago, Working paper 01, pp. 2–11.

Parker, S.C. (2002), 'Do banks ration credit to new enterprises? And should governments intervene?', President's lecture delivered at the annual general meeting of the Scottish Economic Society 4–5 September 2001, *Scottish Journal of Political Economy*, **49** (2), 162–95.

Paul, S. and N. Wilson (2007), 'The determinants of trade credit demand: survey evidence and empirical analysis', *Journal of Accounting, Business and Management*, **14**, 96–116.

Pfeffer, J. and G. Salancik (1978), *The External Control of Organizations*, New York: Harper and Row.

Phillips, B.D. and B.A. Kirchhoff (1989), 'Formation, growth, and survival: small firm dynamics in the US economy', *Small Business Economics*, **1**, 65–74.

Podsakoff, P. and D. Organ (1986), 'Self-reports in organizational research: problems and prospects', *Journal of Management*, **12**, 531–44.

Podsakoff, P., S. MacKenzie, J. Lee and N. Podsakoff (2003), 'Common method biases in behavioral research: a critical review of the literature and recommended remedies', *Journal of Applied Psychology*, **88** (5), 879–903.

Sapienza, H.J. and C.M. Grimm (1997), 'Founder characteristics, start-up process, and strategy-structure variables as predictors of shortline railroad performance', *Entrepreneurship Theory and Practice*, **22** (1), 5–24.

Shane, S. and D. Cable (2002), 'Network ties, reputation, and the financing of new ventures', *Management Science*, **48**, 364–81.

Shepherd, D.A., E.J. Douglas and M. Shanley (2000), 'New venture survival: ignorance, external shocks, and risk reduction strategies', *Journal of Business Venturing*, **15**, 393–410.

Steier, L. (2003), 'Variants of agency contracts in family-financed ventures as a continuum of familial altruistic and market rationalities', *Journal of Business Venturing*, **18**, 597–618.

Stoner, C.R. (1987), 'Distinctive competence and competitive advantage', *Journal of Small Business Management*, **25** (2), 33–9.

Timmons, J.A. (1999), *New Venture Creation: Entrepreneurship for the 21st Century*, Singapore: McGrawHill.

Ucbasaran, D., P. Westhead and M. Wright (2006), *Habitual Entrepreneurs*, Cheltenham, UK and Northampton, MA, USA: Edward Elgar Publishing.

Uusitalo, R. (2001), 'Homo entreprenaurus?', *Applied Economics*, **33**, 1631–8.

Van Auken, H. (2001), 'Financing small technology-based companies: the relationship between familiarity with capital and ability to price and negotiate investments', *Journal of Small Business Management*, **39** (3), 240–58.

Van Auken, H. (2005), 'Differences in the use of bootstrap financing among technology-based versus nontechnology-based firms', *Journal of Small Business Management*, **43** (1), 93–103.

Van Praag, M. (2003), 'Business survival and success of young small business owners: an empirical analysis', *Small Business Economics*, **21** (1), 1–17.

Wagner, J. (1992), 'Firm size, firm growth, and persistence of chance: testing Gibrat's law with establishment data from Lower Saxony, 1978–1989', *Small Business Economics*, **4** (2), 125–31.

Wagner, J. (1995), 'Exports, firm size, and firm dynamics', *Small Business Economics*, **7** (1), 29–39.

Watson, W., W.H. Steward and A. BarNir (2003), 'The effects on human capital, organizational demography, and interpersonal processes on venture partner perceptions of firm profit and growth', *Journal of Business Venturing*, **18**, 145–64.

Wernerfelt, B. (1984), 'The resource-based view of the firm', *Strategic Management Journal*, **5** (2), 171–80.

Winborg, J. and H. Landström (2001), 'Financial bootstrapping in small businesses: examining small business managers' resource acquisition behaviors', *Journal of Business Venturing*, **16** (3), 235–54.

Xu, B. (1998), 'A reestimation of the Evans–Jovanovic entrepreneurial choice model', *Economics Letters*, **58**, 91–5.

7. Knowledge acquisition through strategic networks: the case of franchising

Maryse Brand, Evelien Croonen and Roger Leenders

1. INTRODUCTION

In business format franchise relationships, a franchisor owns a 'business format' – including a uniform identity toward customers and extensive internal procedures – and replicates it by allowing small business owners (that is, franchisees) to use it in return for fees (Kaufmann and Eroglu 1998). The franchise relationship is embedded in a franchise chain consisting of the franchisor and its franchised and possible company-owned units that all operate under more or less the same business format. In the last decades, business format franchising has become an increasingly popular strategy for entrepreneurial wealth creation in different industries in various parts of the world (Welsh et al. 2006). In the US, franchising accounts for 46 per cent of the restaurant industry sales, 55 per cent in speciality food retailing and 71 per cent in printing and copying (Combs et al. 2009). In Europe the situation is similar; in the Netherlands, for example, franchising has a market share of 80 per cent in food retailing and 71 per cent in non-food retailing (Van Essen and Pleijster 2009).

In recent years, different authors have used a knowledge or organizational learning perspective regarding business format franchising (for example, Darr et al. 1995; Ingram and Baum 1997; Jensen and Szulanski 2007; Kalnins and Mayer 2004; Sorenson and Sørensen 2001; Szulanski and Jensen 2006; 2008; Winter and Szulanski, 2001). These studies point out that franchisors typically codify their knowledge and distribute standardized routines in the form of a defined business format to their franchisees. Additionally, these studies assume that franchisors and franchisees have different types of knowledge (see Kalnins and Mayer 2004; Windsperger 2004; Winter and Szulanski 2001). The franchisor mainly has knowledge on the franchise chain level. In terms of Winter and Szulanski the 'replicator' has knowledge of which attributes of the business format are replicable and worth replicating, how these attributes are created, and the characteristics of environments in which they are worth replicating. As a result, the knowledge provided by the franchisor will not be perfect for any one location, but it should be generic enough to be valuable to franchisees at all locations. In contrast, franchisees have knowledge that is idiosyncratic to their own units and local markets, and that is mostly non-codified as opposed to codified (see Kalnins and Mayer 2004; Knott 2003). These authors refer to this knowledge as 'tacit knowledge', but that would mean that it is not possible to codify the knowledge. In our opinion, part of the franchisee's local knowledge may really be tacit (for example, knowledge regarding building a good atmosphere on the unit's work floor) and therefore non-codified, whereas other types of local franchisee knowledge may be very easy to codify (for example, how to place pepperoni on a pizza), but they are not codified because the knowledge remains at the franchise unit and thus there is no need for codification. In the remainder of this chapter, we refer to this type of knowledge as the franchisee's local knowledge.

Previous studies adopting a knowledge or organizational learning perspective have focused on a variety of research questions, such as the question of whether chains or units within chains benefit more from the standardized, chain-level experience and knowledge of their franchisors or from the franchisees' local knowledge (for example, Kalnins and Mayer 2004; Jensen and Szulanski 2007; Szulanski and Jensen 2008). Such studies have produced mixed results. Another relevant research question in the franchising and organizational learning literature has been how specific types of units within chains (i.e. single-unit franchises, multi-unit franchises, or company-owned units) influence organizational learning and hence chain performance (for example, Darr et al. 1995; Sorenson and Sørensen 2001). These studies typically assume that, compared to company managers, franchisees have more *room* to use their local knowledge in running their units due to the fact that they own the assets and are the residual claimants of their units and their monitoring is less stringent and systematic than the monitoring of company managers (Makadok and Coff 2009, Yin and Zajac 2004). Company managers are monitored and controlled closely by means of field audits, mystery shoppers, and automated management knowledge systems and are therefore much more inclined to stick to a format's routines and operations than franchisees (Bradach 1998; Sorenson and Sørensen 2001; Yin and Zajac 2004). Next to more room for local adaptation, franchisees also have a higher *inclination* than company managers to use their local knowledge and to engage in demand-generating and/or cost-reducing activities due to their asset ownership and residual claimant status (Makadok and Coff 2009; Michael 2002; Yin and Zajac 2004). In other words, franchisees will be inclined to engage in entrepreneurial or 'exploration' activities to use their knowledge of the local circumstances to achieve a fit with these circumstances and hence to improve store performance (Ingram and Baum 1997; Sorenson and Sørensen 2001).

We thus argue that franchisees have both the room and the inclination to use their local knowledge to adapt the business format to their own local circumstances and thus to behave entrepreneurially. This approach is supported by various studies arguing that franchise systems should be regarded as an entrepreneurial context in which franchisees are responsible for local entrepreneurial behaviour (for example, Gassenheimer et al. 1996; Kaufmann and Dant 1998; Ketchen et al. 2011; Spinelli and Birley 1996). There are also some studies that have looked at the relationship between franchisee entrepreneurial behaviour and franchisee performance. Phan et al. (1996) found that franchisees' entrepreneurial growth strategies impact franchisees' financial performance. Fenwick and Strombom (1998) found a positive effect of franchisees' entrepreneurial orientation on franchisees' sales growth, but a negative effect of franchisees' entrepreneurial competence on franchisees' return on total assets. Finally, Dada et al. (2011) found that franchisee networks positively affect entrepreneurial behaviour.

In their strive to attain an optimal local fit, franchisees will be inclined to behave entrepreneurially and try to increase the amount and quality of their local knowledge. Since the franchisor has knowledge on the chain level and as a result less knowledge on the franchisee's local level, an important question is how franchisees acquire the local knowledge that is needed to run their units in their specific locations and how this influences the franchisees' unit performance. Since it is often argued that organizations can learn from the experience of others and that interactions between firms are required for transferring non-codified knowledge (for example, Darr et al. 1995; Ingram and Baum 1997), we adopt a network perspective in order to understand how franchisees use their own network to acquire their local knowledge.

Authors adopting a network perspective often argue that a firm's network provides access to resources, such as (non-codified) knowledge or financial resources, and hence influences the firm's development and performance (for literature reviews on network research see Borgatti and Foster 2003; Hoang and Antoncic 2003; Slotte-Kock and Coviello 2009). In recent years, this perspective has also been adopted in the context of SMEs and entrepreneurial firms (Elfring and Hulsink 2003; Greve and Salaff 2003; Hite 2005; Lechner et al. 2006; Watson 2007); however, it has never been adopted to gain insight into the influence of franchisee networks on the performance of their units. A franchising context is different from a regular SME context because franchisees are already part of a very specific network; namely their franchise chain. The question is to what extent and how franchisees use this 'internal' network and other more 'external' networks to acquire the local knowledge needed to adapt to their franchise units' local circumstances and how this affects their performance. According to Combs et al. (2004) performance of franchised units is a very relevant research theme that has received relatively little attention (some exceptions are Morrison 1997 and Fenwick and Strombom 1998). This is odd since franchisees form an important ingredient in the success of a franchise chain (Michael and Combs 2008). Combs et al. (2004) have even specifically referred to the importance of studying the influence of a franchisee's ability to network on this franchisee's unit performance.

In sum, this chapter combines a knowledge and network perspective to look at local knowledge acquisition by franchisees, who will be inclined to demonstrate entrepreneurial behaviour to achieve an optimal local fit and improve their unit's performance. Since this is a very new research area, we build on existing network literature and franchising literature to develop propositions regarding the influence of franchisees' networks on their units' performance that can be tested in future research. Next, we also develop guidelines for applying such an empirical test.

The structure of this chapter is as follows. First, we distinguish different forms of franchisee local knowledge, we introduce the network perspective and we identify the major types of partners present in typical franchisee networks. In section 4 we develop propositions regarding how the franchisee's network behaviour influences the effectiveness of knowledge transfer, and ultimately the performance of its units. Methodological guidelines on future tests of the developed propositions are developed in section 5. Finally, conclusions and implications will be presented.

2. LOCAL KNOWLEDGE

2.1 Local Knowledge and Franchisee Performance

Franchisors provide franchisees with general knowledge embedded in procedures, guidelines and action programmes. Franchisors typically also support franchisees by providing training programmes, aiming at professional development of both the franchisees and their employees. However, to be able to run the local unit effectively, the franchisee also needs access to information about the local environment of the unit (legal developments, customer preferences, competition, labour market developments) and about the management of the specific unit (local HRM policies, local marketing activities). We have defined this type of knowledge as local knowledge. Since the 1990s, the idea that knowledge is a primary source of competitive advantage of firms has been firmly embedded in (strategic) management thinking (see Lubit 2001; Spender and Grant 1996). Possessing or having access to relevant knowledge is related to improved firm performance, such as higher innovation levels and reduced costs (Van Wijk et al. 2008; Yli-Renko et al. 2001). The actual relevance of specific types of local knowledge is highly situation specific. For example, in industries that are highly affected by local regulation, having access to and being able to network with city officials is very relevant indeed, otherwise it is not. Similarly, if a franchisee is located in a geographical area relatively unknown to the franchisor (in another part of the country, abroad, or in a location with a very specific type of customer, such as tourists) having access to local knowledge will be a major condition for the franchisee to be successful.

We argue that franchisees that possess or have access to up-to-date local knowledge have a competitive advantage that is reflected in superior firm performance. This argument is supported by earlier research both in a franchise and in a more generic (marketing) context. Several studies argue that franchisees can achieve a higher strategic or operational fit with their local environments by so-called local adaptation, which is based on the effective use of local knowledge (see Fenwick and Strombom 1998; Kaufmann and Eroglu 1998). More specifically, Brand and Croonen (2010) demonstrated that within a large Dutch dual system (i.e. a chain comprising both company owned and franchised units), local HRM policies of franchised units were more effective than the HRM policies of company owned units. The argument is that local knowledge about the labour market and the needs of the specific team of employees working in the franchised unit is a main cause of this superior performance. Within the marketing domain, micro marketing studies within retail chains have demonstrated that the adaptation of, for example, prices, promotion, and assortment to local circumstances has a considerable positive impact on unit sales (Campo et al. 2000; Campo and Gijsbrechts 2004). Again, a prerequisite for such local adaptation is up-to-date local knowledge, in this situation about local customer preferences and the competitive situation.

2.2 Types of Franchisee Local Knowledge

The literature makes a distinction between 'general' networks, in which general information about day-to-day operations is exchanged, and specific networks. An innovation network, for example, is the specific network of ties that provides knowledge to the focal firm on developing innovative capabilities and/or on concrete innovation opportunities (see Cross and Prusak 2002). Specific networks also have specific performance outcomes. The effectiveness of an innovation network, for example, can be measured by the number of new product introductions or other innovation measures.

Franchisee local knowledge is also still a rather general classification. There are two main types of local knowledge that are particularly relevant in franchise situations. The first one is 'local market knowledge'. This refers to knowledge about the local market needs, the competitive situation, and the marketing instruments that can be used locally next to the marketing instruments as imposed by the franchisor. These marketing instruments include: the assortment (i.e. the products and services offered), unit presentation (i.e. interior and exterior), promotion activities, and price levels. It depends on the franchise chain's standardization level (see Kneppers-Heijnert 1988; Vrolijk 2002) how much freedom franchisees have in conducting local marketing activities, for example in offering new products and services or in adopting new promotion activities. However, it is not uncommon for franchise systems to allow their franchisees to develop local tailor-made marketing activities, although usually these are developed in addition to the system-wide marketing activities executed by the franchisor. Suitable performance measures for local marketing networks would be, for example, sales, customer satisfaction and customer loyalty.

The second type of franchisee local knowledge is 'managerial knowledge'. This refers to the franchisee's knowledge regarding the management and operation of its local unit(s). These activities are not directly visible for customers, but they can have very important indirect effects on customer satisfaction. The most important areas of the franchisee's managerial knowledge that can have indirect effects on customers are knowledge regarding human resource management (HRM) and operations management. HRM is regularly identified as a critical driver of business success in retailing and service industries (McLean 2006; Miller 2006), and in these industries business format franchising is a very important strategy (Combs and Ketchen 2003; Welsh et al. 2006). Brand and Croonen (2010) point out that HR practices are only scantly incorporated in the franchise agreement and/or handbook and that franchisees have a relatively large degree of freedom in conducting their local HRM activities. The importance of HRM in retailing sectors and the large degree of freedom for franchisees in using their own knowledge regarding HRM makes it a very relevant type of franchisee managerial knowledge. The operations management component of franchisee local managerial knowledge refers to the procedures involved in the local production of the goods and/or services and the procurement methods that allow the unit to acquire the inputs needed to carry out those procedures (see Winter and Szulanski 2001). The relevant procedures and procurement methods depend on the industry and/or franchise chain under study. For example, in a pizza fast food chain these procedures may entail a pepperoni placement procedure or a procedure regarding the boxing of pizzas (Darr et al. 1995), whereas in a clothing retail chain these procedures may entail procedures for fitting clothes or keeping inventories. These examples are not so much related to acquiring a local fit, but to professionalization of the unit's management. In other situations, however, local operations can be relevant to achieve a local fit. An example is a restaurant that has to have a high quality reliable local network of fresh produce suppliers. Suitable performance measures for managerial knowledge networks would include employee satisfaction, voluntary turnover, labour productivity (for HRM related knowledge) and purchasing prices, out-of stocks, or customer complaints (for knowledge on purchasing and operation procedures).

3. A NETWORK PERSPECTIVE IN A FRANCHISE CONTEXT

3.1 Introduction to the Network Perspective

In the field of sociology, there is a long-standing tradition of studying individuals as actors relating to others within their social environment. During the last decades, this social network theory has spread to adjacent fields of study such as strategy and entrepreneurship in the business domain. In the course of time, the focus on social relations of individuals has gradually broadened to also include non-social relationships (for example, firm partnerships, collaborative relationships within teams) and relationships between groups of individuals (for example, organizations). This development has also led to a stream of research referring to network theory in general instead of social network theory. The rising interest in (social) networks led to the development of a specific type of empirical research, the so-called (social) network analysis which describes and quantitatively analyses actors (or 'nodes') and ties between actors within a network.

Already in 1986, Aldrich and Zimmer argued that entrepreneurs are embedded in social networks that play a critical role in the entrepreneurial process. A number of studies document that entrepreneurs consistently use networks to get ideas and gather information (for example, Birley 1985;

Table 7.1　Main network components

Components	Explanation
Network content	Interpersonal and interorganizational relationships viewed as media to gain access to resources held by other actors • Access to capital • Access to information and advice (intangible resources) • Reputation or signalling function
Network governance mechanisms	Governance mechanisms that undergird and coordinate network exchange • Trust • Implicit and open-ended contracts supported by social mechanisms
Network structure	Pattern of relationships within networks, consisting of direct and indirect ties. • Amount of resources an actor can access (network size) • Quality of the resource transfer • Diversity of resources

Source:　Derived from Hoang and Antoncic (2003) and Jack (2005).

Smeltzer et al. 1991). Not all firms possess comparable levels of knowledge-rich networks, and firms differ in the levels of benefit they draw from their ties. Specifically, firms' networks vary in terms of pattern of ties (i.e. structure) and the variation in the mix of contacts in firms' networks (i.e. nodal diversity) (Galaskiewicz and Zaheer 1999; McEvily and Zaheer 1999). Similarly, Miller (1996) suggests that a firm's strategic success is a function of the intensity, extensiveness and continuity of a firm's interactions. Hoang and Antoncic (2003) made an excellent review of network-based research in entrepreneurship. In this review, they propose three essential components of networks that emerge as key elements in models studying networks. Table 7.1 summarizes these components. In a franchise context, the elements of this framework have different roles than in general contexts. We will briefly discuss important issues and implications for studying such networks.

First, Hoang and Antoncic (2003) make a distinction between interpersonal and interorganizational relationships. They also state that there is little theoretical distinction between networks of individuals and networks of firms. This implies that in a specific situation, the researcher should make a considered decision about the unit of analysis: the franchisee or the franchised unit. In some situations, the franchisee and the unit largely overlap, for example in cases where there are only few employees who have relatively small or only operational tasks. As regards the type of resource that is typically sought for in a franchise context, we would argue that that is only marginally different from non-franchise entrepreneurs. By being members of a franchise system, franchisees usually already have easier access to capital (by franchisor arrangements) and specific types of information and advice (franchisor services). However, as we argued above, for specific types of information and advice (i.e. local knowledge), other network relationships within or outside the franchise system may be very relevant. The reputation or signalling function of specific network relationships is probably less relevant in franchise contexts than in other situations. Being members of a franchise network has a signalling function in itself (towards customers, suppliers and other relevant parties), so franchisees do not run into major problems related to liabilities of newness or smallness. Therefore, it is probably not very common for individual franchisees to look for additional reputation enhancing relationships.

Regarding prevailing network governance mechanisms, trust and implicit contracts will be relevant just as in other situations. There is a growing body of literature on trust in franchise relationships (Croonen 2010) which mainly focuses on trust between franchisees on the one hand and the franchisor on the other. Trust among franchisees is of course important as well, especially since shirking and free-riding (Bradach 1998) will damage the consistent image for customers. In general, being members of the same franchise system with a shared vision will provide a basic level of trust among the network members. Trust is also influenced by the primariness of contact (Hoang and Antoncic 2003); in a franchise context that would mean that franchisees who see each other as friends, or who even have family ties, will start with a relatively high level of trust and will be in a position to exchange knowledge easily amongst themselves. Finally, regarding network structure, a franchise system provides the researcher with a natural boundary for the formal network under study. At the same time, there is an informal network that will only partly overlap with the formal network; some franchisees of the same chain will never meet or have any direct contacts, while any individual franchisee also has relationships outside the franchise system. The accessibility of actors within the franchise system will be relatively high (by telephone, Intranet, or during organized meetings), the diversity of resources (for example local knowledge) will be relatively low, depending on the geographical and other variation among franchisees.

In this chapter, we propose to start modestly by studying the structure of relationships maintained by individual franchisees: the franchisees' so-called 'ego-networks'. We define a franchisee's ego-network as the structure of the franchisee's (termed 'ego' or 'focal franchisee') relationships with other organizations (termed 'alters'). Although they are also potentially important, for clarity of exposition we do not include the relationships among the franchisee's alters. In sum, we take the networks of relationships that individual franchisees maintain as our focus and discuss how they influence the performance of their units. Our core argument is that, in a world in which relationships and the management of relationships are increasingly essential, and where franchisees manage a business in idiosyncratic contexts in which local knowledge is essential, the franchisee's network ties are central in understanding why some franchisees outperform their colleagues.

No single type of tie represents 'the' network that firms maintain. Various types of relationship may be relevant in building an explanation of behaviour and structure. Although the variety of inter-firm relations is potentially inexhaustible, Kenis and Knoke (2002) contend that most may be classified under five broad substantive headings: knowledge transmissions, resource exchanges, power relations, boundary penetration, and sentimental attachments. Although various network relationships may be essential for understanding franchisee behaviour, we have argued that the franchisees' networks for obtaining local knowledge (i.e. market knowledge and managerial knowledge as we discussed in the previous section) are especially relevant because they determine the opportunities for the franchisee to obtain superior performance through a better local fit.

3.2 Types of Franchisee Network Partners or Knowledge Sources

A general classification that is made in strategy, innovation and entrepreneurship literature is between external and internal sources of knowledge. Laursen and Salter (2006) point out that external knowledge sources (i.e. network partners) are very heterogeneous as regards, for example, the type and relevance of knowledge provided. Therefore it is important to first understand the different types of network partners that franchisees may have and to discuss how interactions with them may influence a franchisee's local knowledge base. We distinguish the following potential network partners or knowledge sources that can provide an individual franchisee with local knowledge:

- Knowledge sources within the chain (*within-chain network*): the franchisor, franchisees from the same chain, and managers of company-owned units in the chain (if present).

- Knowledge sources outside the chain (*outside-chain network*): customers, local (small) business owners, supportive organizations
  (banks/accountants/consultants), family and friends.

We distinguish the following three knowledge sources for franchisees
within a franchise chain.

3.2.1 The franchisor

A first important knowledge provider in any franchise network is of
course the franchisor. Actually, the knowledge transfer of the franchisor
to franchisees is an important element of the definition of business format
franchising as we know it. However, as pointed out in the introduction,
the knowledge provided by franchisors is typically knowledge at the
franchise chain level. As a result, the franchisor is a less obvious source of
local knowledge. On the other hand, the franchisor will usually be willing
to aid in transferring successful local franchisee practices throughout the
franchise chain, since this will probably improve the franchise chain's
performance (Bradach 1997; 1998; Darr et al. 1995; Kalnins and Mayer
2004). In this chapter we will limit ourselves to the franchisor's role of providing local knowledge to individual franchisees, without looking at the
actual source of this knowledge. The processes of learning and knowledge
acquisition by the franchisor and the system-wide adaptations that result
from these processes have been discussed by other scholars (for example,
Bradach 1998; Winter and Szulanski 2001).

3.2.2 Franchisees from the same chain

The franchise literature so far has paid very little attention to franchisee
interactions in general and more specifically to knowledge sharing among
franchisees from the same chain (although some studies have briefly
pointed at the relevance in one or two sentences, such as Sorenson and
Sørensen 2001 and Kalnins and Mayer 2004). Only the studies of Darr
et al. (1995) and Darr and Kurtzberg (2000) have specifically focused on
knowledge acquisition and transfer among units within a large pizza chain.
Within this context, they found knowledge to transfer across units owned
by the same franchisee ('multi-unit franchises') but not across units owned
by different franchisees. In the US fast food industry multi-unit franchising is prevalent, but in other countries (for example, the Netherlands) the
largest part of franchised units is still owned by single-unit franchisees.
Additionally, many franchisors have 'institutionalized' instruments for
knowledge sharing among franchisees within their franchise chains, for
example by means of meetings of the Franchise Advisory Council (FAC)
or an Intranet database of ideas. Since these instruments provide all

franchisees with the same opportunity for knowledge sharing and acquiring, we do not take them into account and focus on non-institutionalized franchisees' networking behaviour. However, the use of institutionalized instruments may serve as a relevant control variable in empirical studies.

Franchisees from the same chain can very well be relevant knowledge sources because they operate in the same industry with the same business format. As Sorenson and Sørensen (2001) put it, units can transfer knowledge most successfully when they operate from the same knowledge base. In particular, franchisees that operate in a geographical area that is close to the focal franchisee can provide valuable knowledge since they operate in an area in which local circumstances are likely to be similar. This knowledge transfer between franchisees can be purposeful and interactive (for example during a personal meeting), or more passive and unidirectional (for example visiting a colleague's unit and observing what is happening there).

There may also be barriers that inhibit franchisee interactions and sharing of local knowledge. First of all, Sorenson and Sørensen (2001) have pointed at the costs of knowledge sharing among franchisees. As discussed in the introduction, franchisees have incentives to engage in demand-generating and/or cost-reducing activities due to their asset ownership and residual claimant status (for example, Michael 2002). Transfer of knowledge across units owned by different franchisees will involve costs that some franchisees are not willing to incur because of their cost-minimization incentives. A second barrier to knowledge transfers between franchisees may be competition between franchisees ('within-chain competition'). Franchisees may not actively transfer local knowledge to other franchisees for fear of encroachment and future competition. This effect will especially be present for franchisees that operate geographically close to each other (for example, due to relatively small exclusive territories), and when customers are willing to travel in order to visit another unit within the same chain. Actually, there is a tension involved here. Franchisees that are geographically close to each other can learn a lot from each other due to their similar local circumstances and their proximity, which enables personal communication and interactions and thus the transfer of non-codified knowledge; however, in specific situations, their proximity may also cause issues of competition that hinders knowledge sharing. The final barrier to franchisee knowledge sharing is 'peer surveillance'. This peer surveillance is likely to be present in highly standardized franchise chains. In order to preserve the image of the chain as a whole, franchisees will monitor each other. A franchisee's local adaptations to the business format may be noticed by other franchisees who may think this will damage the reputation of the chain as a whole. These other franchisees may make an appeal to the 'offender' or notify the franchisor, who in turn may impose sanctions. To prevent such measures, franchisees may be reluctant to share their own local knowledge with their colleagues.

3.2.3 Managers of company-owned units from the same chain (if present)

Many franchise chains are so-called plural chains, consisting of both franchised and company-owned units (see for example Bradach 1998; Bürkle and Posselt 2008; Dant et al. 2008). Similar to our arguments about the potential knowledge transfer from one franchisee to another, there is a possibility of knowledge transfer between unit managers of company-owned units and franchisees, especially those who are geographically close. Company managers and franchisees have many similar problems and issues to deal with in their stores. However, there are also some fundamental differences (see Sorenson and Sørensen 2001). For instance, franchisees are independent business owners and have a broader array of responsibilities than company managers. In contrast with company managers, for example, franchisees do their own human resource management, investment decision making, local marketing, and (part of) supplier selection. As pointed out in the introduction, franchisees and company managers also have different types of incentives, which makes knowledge transfer less valuable. Company managers might also be less inclined to share information with franchisees, because the benefits of receiving knowledge themselves are relatively low. Most company managers will focus on information and instructions from the franchisor with which they have a hierarchical relationship.

From our own earlier empirical work, we know that many plural chains have totally separated managing relationships with company-owned and franchised units. For example, they have separated service departments at the franchisor's organization, have their own meetings and separate training programmes.

We distinguish the following knowledge sources in the franchisee's 'outside-chain network':

3.2.4 Customers

(Potential) customers are the major information source on local market preferences for all firms. Strategic decision makers are responsible for acquiring this type of information, which in franchise chains will usually be organized on the chain level. In some circumstances, however, individual customers can also be part of the focal franchisee's network as we study it. Many franchise chains operate on B-to-B markets which are often characterized by a limited number of customers with much expertise on the product or services to be purchased and repeated voluminous demand

(Ford 2002). In such circumstances, quite intensive buyer–seller relationships may develop in which knowledge is exchanged on many issues including operations, technology and logistics. In many other situations, especially B-to-C markets, however, individual consumers will probably not be part of the franchisee's network.

3.2.5 Supporting organizations

Independent franchisees may have their own business relationships with supporting organizations such as accountants, consultants and/or banks. Existing small business literature especially highlights the importance of the accountant who is often a trusted, highly regarded information source and functions as a general business consultant (Gooderham et al. 2004). Regarding the added value of the (subsidized) business support sector, small firms are usually a lot less positive (Storey 1994; Shaw 2006).

3.2.6 Local (small) business owners

Work by Premaratne (2001) and Shaw (2006) suggests that informal sources may provide small businesses with a higher and more stable flow of information and advice than formal supporting organizations. Other (small) business owners are one such informal source. In particular, if these other owners are active in a similar industry and/or in the same geographic region, they will be able to provide relevant knowledge on, for example, local market developments and local governmental regulations. Contacts with such colleagues can be established through local business networks or on an individual basis.

3.2.7 Friends and family

Several studies (for example, Lechner et al. 2006) have shown that friends and family are relevant in the start-up phase of entrepreneurial firms because the resources they can supply are mainly financial rather than knowledge-based. The study of Shaw (2006), however, suggests that friends and family who own a business themselves are the most important party providing advice in a small business network.

4. DEVELOPMENT OF PROPOSITIONS

The focus of this chapter is on knowledge acquisition by franchisees through their network. By combining a knowledge and network perspective, we argued that franchisees have the task to collect local knowledge in order to adapt their operations to their specific local situation, become more competitive, and ultimately perform better. We are specifically interested in the patterns of direct relationships between individual franchisees (the actors) and other actors within or outside the franchise system. Referring to the network components introduced in section 2, we focus on the structure of the informal network of franchisees.

The structure of a network is typically captured by three dimensions: the amount of resources an actor can access, the quality of the resource transfer, and the diversity of resources. In this section we will briefly discuss these three dimensions and elaborate on the concept of network costs. Next, we propose five franchisee network characteristics that we deem particularly fit for capturing these dimensions. Simultaneously, we develop two hypotheses on how these characteristics influence the transfer of local knowledge to franchisees and hence the performance of their units.

A variety of measures have been utilized to characterize the differential positions of actors in the network (see Hoang and Antoncic 2003; Van Wijk et al. 2008). The most intuitive and popular measure is size, defined as the number of direct links between the focal actor and other actors. The larger the number of ties ('tie volume'), the larger the extent to which resources can be accessed. A second measure of network position is centrality; a centralized position determines the extent to which the actor is able to locate beneficial information and share it within the network (Burt 1992). Owing to the difficulty of measuring network centrality, it has generally been less studied than network size. Size and centrality together determine the *amount of resources* the actor can access.

In addition to the amount of ties, the nature of the ties plays an important role in two ways. First, the closeness of the contact determines the ease and *quality of the knowledge transfer* between partners. Closeness is a measure of tie strength, which in turn is influenced by the frequency and nature of contacts, and the similarity or shared vision of actors (Hoang and Antoncic 2003; Jack 2005). Second, the quality and amount of knowledge available through the network depends upon the combination of ties that the actor has, or, to be more specific, the *diversity of resources* the actor has access to. There are two well-known network concepts related to this diversity: diversity in tie strength (Granovetter 1973) and diversity in ties leading to bridging structural holes (Burt 1992). As regards tie strength, Granovetter argued that weak ties are more important for accessing relevant resources because they typically involve partners that are heterogeneous in a variety of characteristics, thus enhancing the probability of accessing new knowledge for the partners. Later, Uzzi (1996) found that a balanced network of strong and weak ties is most beneficial to a firm. This empirical finding can be explained by the opposite effects of tie strength. On the one hand, strong ties enhance knowledge transfer through the closeness of the tie, but on the other hand, a combination of many strong ties diminishes the variety and newness of the knowledge. Therefore, it is important to make a clear distinction between these two aspects of tie strength. A final network characteristic determining the exposure to novel knowledge is the capacity of ties to bridge structural holes. This capacity can be assessed by network density (a measure of interconnectedness of the actors' contacts) or by the heterogeneity of the actor's ties in linking to actors that belong to different groups possessing different types of relevant knowledge or other resources (Hoang and Antoncic 2003).

Until now we have mainly talked about the benefits of networking. Although much of the literature ignores this economic truth, knowledge transfer and networking come at a cost (Sorenson and Sørensen 2001). The main costs are maintenance costs of external ties (Balkundi and Harrison 2006; Hansen et al. 2001) including, for example, management time, coordination costs and communication costs. It is to be expected that the marginal benefits of new knowledge diminish as the amount of available knowledge has become 'large enough'; at a certain point in time more new knowledge can no longer be absorbed by the firm (see van Wijk et al. 2008). At the same time, the costs of maintaining the ties to access this knowledge remain more or less stable. This means that we would expect a curvilinear relationship between the amount and diversity of ties on the one hand and the outcomes or performance of the network on the other. A similar relationship was identified by Balkundi et al. (2007) who found that diverse thinking within a team showed a curvilinear relationship with team performance. High diversity within the network had positive effects, until the team encountered the effects of isolated thinking and a lack of integration, and performance began to decline.

4.1 Proposition A: Network Strength

Network strength is an overarching qualification describing the nature and quality of the actor's ties. The more intense and close the ties between actors are, the more easily knowledge is exchanged and the higher the quality of this knowledge transfer (see Table 7.1). We distinguish three structural characteristics contributing to network strength: partner similarity, tie intensity and tie longevity.

Partner *similarity* in the context of this study is defined as the extent to which two partners in a network are similar to each other with respect to the core characteristics that facilitate effective knowledge transfer (see Darr and Kurtzberg 2000). Research has shown that knowledge transfer is more likely between individuals who display similar attitudes as well as between firms that have encountered similar problems in the past (Ounjian and Bryan 1987) and that have had similar experiences (Burkhardt and

Brass 1990; Cohen and Levinthal 1990). Darr and Kurtzberg (2000) look at knowledge transfer within a UK-based pizza chain. They argue that partner similarity facilitates knowledge transfer within the franchise chain since similar firms can better understand each other and thus are more capable of sharing relevant knowledge effectively. Darr and Kurtzberg (2000) distinguish between three types of partner similarity: geographical, strategic and customer similarity. Their empirical results indicated that in this particular context, strategic similarity was the most important factor. Building on this, we argue that a focal franchisee's partner similarity has a positive influence on knowledge transfer and hence the franchisee's unit performance. The *intensity* of ties in a knowledge ego-network is important with respect to the depth of the knowledge exchanged. As ties become more intense, the frequency and information richness of the knowledge transfer between two parties is likely to increase (Windsperger and Gorovaia 2010). This is especially true if strong ties allow firms to work more closely together and to engage in joint development and joint operations. Moreover, intense ties facilitate the transfer of non-codified knowledge between network partners. Allowing another 'into one's kitchen' makes it easier for network partners to provide others with knowledge closely aimed at each other's specific knowledge-need. We expect that such strong ties are specifically fruitful for sharing franchisee local managerial knowledge regarding HRM and operations. For example, two restaurant franchisees may advise each other on improving their planning efficiency, identifying high quality local produce suppliers, or exchange specialized staff. Finally, ties in an ego-network may have higher or lower *longevity*. As ties between two parties exist over time, the trust between them is likely to increase (Gulati 1995). As trust deepens, network partners may become likely to share more valuable and reliable knowledge. Such deepening trust also makes them more likely to share sensitive and non-codified knowledge. With increased depth of trust, it is increasingly unlikely that a party will spill received sensitive knowledge to outsiders. In addition, as with intensive ties, long-existing ties are less likely to dissolve. The longer that ties have existed up to the current moment, the more likely it is they will extend into the future (Leenders 1995). The advantage of enduring ties is that they provide the firm with a continued knowledge source that is likely to last into the foreseeable future. On the other hand, it also hinders the focal franchisee in dissolving a defective and unproductive tie in favour of starting a new one with another organization. The security and effectiveness of long-lasting ineffective relationships thus come at the cost of strongly decreased knowledge and flexibility. However, if the focal franchisee identifies a tie as effective and long-standing, knowledge transfer between the partners will be affected positively.

These arguments lead to the following proposition:

Proposition A: Stronger ties, characterized by similarity, intensity, and longevity, will be positively related to franchisee performance.

4.2   Proposition B: Network Size and Diversity

Network size, or tie *volume*, refers to the number of relationships maintained by the focal franchisee. The speed with which knowledge may be transmitted to or from the focal franchisee varies directly with the volume of the focal franchisee's ties. Similarly, tie volume affects the volume of knowledge that the focal franchisee can receive or transmit (see Van Wijk et al. 2008). The more partners the focal franchisee has relationships with, the more knowledge it potentially has access to. A very low-volume ego-network implies that messages are likely to find their way to the other firms in the environment only slowly, and vice versa. Knowledge on and from parties not included in the focal franchisee's ego-network will reach the focal franchisee more slowly, or not at all. In addition, since the knowledge has to travel through other organizations first, it is likely to become altered along the way. The focal franchisee can therefore not assume the correctness of such received second-hand knowledge. Since a low-volume ego-network may strongly restrict the focal franchisee's knowledge base, this may negatively affect the franchisee's performance.

The *diversity* of ties refers to the diversity in network partners. If a clothing retail franchisee only has relationships with other clothes shops, its ego-network diversity is minimal. Network diversity increases considerably if it also has ties with fashion-related companies such as shops selling gifts and accessories, and music stores, in addition to ties to a wide variety of suppliers, trade associations, and so on. A wide variety of network ties endows the franchisee with access to a wide variety of knowledge. Organizations that occupy a similar position in the same industry or organizational field are likely to possess similar knowledge and identify and interpret signals from the environment comparably. Alternatively, organizations in a different industry or that occupy a position different from the focal franchisee within the same industry are likely to have access to different pockets of knowledge and to have diverse ways of decoding and interpreting messages from the (expanded) general environment. As a result, the focal franchisee has access to a much wider base of knowledge and ways to interpret such knowledge. While diversity of knowledge does not necessarily imply high knowledge quality, a high-diversity ego-network does offer the focal franchisee more alternatives to improve its operations and choices. As we argued above, it is necessary to include the *costs of networking* in our analysis (Sorenson and Sørensen 2001). Excessive networking is likely to be counterproductive (Burt 1992;

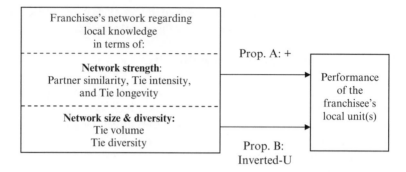

Source: Authors.

Figure 7.1   Conceptual model including propositions

Laursen and Salter 2006; Watson 2007). A high-volume network requires 'high maintenance' (that is, a lot of time, energy and thus resources), and franchisees still need to have time and energy to run their businesses (see Miller 1996). Beyond some limit it is likely that the marginal benefit from further networking will be more than offset by the negative impact of the franchisee's lack of available time to attend to important internal business affairs. Similarly, the disadvantage of diversity is that it requires the focal franchisee to invest considerable resources in building and maintaining relationships with diverse partners and in decoding the knowledge received from such varied sources. Again, beyond some limit it is likely that the marginal benefit from further networking will be more than offset by the costs in time and other valuable resources.

These considerations result in the following proposition (see Figure 7.1):

Proposition B: High maintenance ties, characterized by tie volume and tie diversity will be curvilinear related to franchisee performance in the form of an inverted U-shape.

5.   GUIDELINES FOR FUTURE EMPIRICAL APPLICATIONS

In this chapter we developed an approach to studying knowledge acquisition within franchise networks and proposed two hypotheses about the relationship between the franchisee network structure and unit performance. In this section, we will discuss some methodological issues that can guide future studies aiming at empirical tests of these propositions.

5.1 Empirical Setting and Data Collection

As discussed in the introduction of this chapter, specific characteristics of the franchise chain may influence the quality and level of local knowledge available. Each franchise chain has specific institutionalized instruments (such as FACs, meetings, committees, Intranet systems) and a certain level of knowledge provided by the franchisor (local sales data, benchmarks). In order to isolate the effects proposed in our conceptual model, it would be preferable to perform the empirical study within one franchise chain. This way, the study also controls for other potentially important influences on franchisee performance (see Darr and Kurtzberg 2000). The study of one specific chain also provides the opportunity to work closely with the franchisor. Our experience in several earlier studies is that such collaboration provides useful background information on the franchise system, stimulates a high response level, and provides opportunities for acquiring objective performance data through the franchisor (for example, sales data on unit level).

In order to take full advantage of the rich tradition of quantitative network analysis, it is necessary to collect detailed network data. The sociometric approach is to let respondents fill in a table or roster in which they can indicate the alters (potential network members) with whom they exchange knowledge. The respondents also answer questions about the nature and frequency of these knowledge transfers. Depending on the size and boundaries of the network, researchers let the respondents indicate themselves which five or ten network ties are most important for knowledge acquisition. The data are only collected for these ties. It is also possible to provide the respondent with a full list of all potential network members, and to ask the respondents to fill in data on all or a subset of the potential ties (see Seevers et al. 2010).

At this point in the design of the empirical study, it is also very relevant to ensure that the data collection is in line with the unit of analysis of the study. Network studies can look at firms or individuals being actors within a specific network. The unit of analysis determines both the respondents (only the franchisee, also other key employees) and the exact formulation of questions within the questionnaire. In some situations, the franchisee will have such a dominant position within the firm, that it is empirically impossible to distinguish between the two levels of analysis.

Networks are complex, especially if one looks at both direct and indirect ties. We suggest future empirical studies to start with studies of the structure of direct relationships maintained by individual franchisees: the franchisees' so-called 'ego-networks'. Considering the type of partners, our first interest would focus on the knowledge transfer among franchisees, that is the internal network. As pointed out, franchising literature generally acknowledges the knowledge transfer from franchisor to franchisees. However, extant franchise literature pays very little attention to knowledge sharing among franchisees from the same chain. Franchisees from the same chain can be very relevant knowledge sources because they operate in the same industry with the same business format. As Sorenson and Sørensen (2001) put it, units can transfer knowledge most successfully when they operate from the same knowledge base.

Networks are also specific; franchisees probably turn to different people when they want information on marketing issues, HRM issues, or legal issues. Therefore it is important to define a specific network and a corresponding specific type of local knowledge to be studied empirically. Our priority would be to study the most relevant aspects of local knowledge as discussed earlier in this chapter, that is local market knowledge, local operational knowledge, or local HRM knowledge. It is also important to develop one or more performance variables that fit the specific type of knowledge studied.

An important issue in cross-sectional studies is the fact that data on independent and dependent variables are collected from the same individuals. In order to prevent this common method bias, one can take different measures in questionnaire design, and post hoc statistical analyses are available to check for this bias (Podsakoff et al. 2003). It is much better, however, to prevent this problem by collecting performance data from a second source. In this case, the franchisor is a very useful source of such objective and complete information. Our experience is that it is possible to develop such collaborations with franchisors.

A final consideration regarding data collection is whether to collect it face-to-face or to use mail- or Internet-based questionnaires. Since the complexity of the topic is high and part of the information may be regarded as sensitive, we would prefer to collect the data during face-to-face interviews. An additional advantage of such interviews is that they provide the opportunity to gather qualitative contextual data that may help to assess and interpret the findings from the quantitative analysis.

5.2   Measurement and Analysis

In this section we propose possible measures for the variables that are included in our propositions. For these specific measures we build on a questionnaire design in which respondents can provide up to five important internal and five important external ties. The respondent is asked to provide information about its own strategic intent (sales growth, cost reduction, or both, which are awarded scores of, for example, 3, 1 or 2 respectively). For each tie, the respondent is asked to give: type of contact (franchisor, franchisee, manager company unit, customer, other business owner, supporting organization, family, other), the age of the relationship, and the strategic intent of the alter. The data can be used to derive the following measures:

- *Tie volume*: this is a straightforward measure used very often in network studies (cf. Hoang and Antoncic 2003) and consists of the number of ties mentioned by the respondent (ranging from 0 to 5 for the internal network and 0 to 5 for the external network).
- *Tie diversity*: this heterogeneity-based measure consists of the number of different types of knowledge sources (as defined in section 3) with which the actor has ties. These knowledge sources are meaningful groups of actors created by the researcher. In section 3 we distinguish between seven knowledge sources, so 7 would be the maximum value of this variable.
- *Tie similarity 1*: especially when studying the internal network, it is possible to use a measure of strategic similarity by taking the average difference of the actor's and alter's score on strategic intent (Darr and Kurtzberg 2000).
- *Tie similarity 2*: a simpler measure of tie similarity is the share of highly similar alters (in this case other franchisees, or perhaps even other franchisees with the same strategic intent as the actor) within the total number of ties mentioned by the respondent.
- *Tie longevity*: this is a measure of the period that the actor and alter are already connected within the network; it consists of the average number of years of existence of the ties mentioned (Leenders 1995).
- *Tie intensity 1*: the more frequently actors exchange knowledge, the higher the intensity of the tie. Granovetter (1973) classified two contacts or more per week as a high frequency. However, due to modern communication media it is possible that it is necessary to shift that boundary to a higher frequency. Tie intensity in this measure consists of the average frequency of contact between actor and alter as reported by the respondent (Hoang and Antoncic 2003; Jack 2005).
- *Tie intensity 2*: another aspect of tie intensity is the type of contact determining the information richness of the knowledge transfer (Windsperger and Gorovaia 2010). The more personal and face-to-face the interactions are, the higher the intensity of the tie. We propose to measure this as the average closeness of the contact

between actor and alter, with closeness ranging from telephone, email or SMS contact to formal face-to-face contact, to actual spending time together in the work place sharing relevant local knowledge.

Since we propose to conduct the study within one franchise chain, the number of controls needed is relatively limited. We propose to include the following control variables (see Seevers et al. 2010; Van Wijk et al. 2008): experience of franchisee within this franchise system (*experience*); *unit size* in full-time equivalents (in the case of a multi-unit: unit in which owner is present most frequently); number of units owned (*multi-unit*).

Regarding the dependent variable (performance of the franchise units), we propose to combine subjective performance data using Likert scales with, if possible, objective performance data obtained from the franchisor. Useful subjective performance measures would be: overall performance; sales/turnover; profit; and measures regarding the specific network under study, for example customer satisfaction and customer loyalty in the case of a local market knowledge network. The performance data to be provided by the franchisor depend on the type of data the franchisor collects. Unit sales should always be available. Unit profits are often more difficult because franchisees are legally independent and not obliged to provide these figures to their franchisor. Many franchisors also have data on variables such as number of customers, average amount of purchase, costs of personnel, and so on.

6.   CONCLUSION AND IMPLICATIONS FOR FUTURE RESEARCH

In this chapter we argue that the acquisition of local knowledge by franchisees influences the performance of their units. Taking an entrepreneurship perspective, we argued that applying local knowledge improves the competitive position of the franchisee and ultimately positively affects the franchisee's performance. Since franchisee knowledge is often non-codified and location specific in nature, a network perspective focusing on personal information exchange seems appropriate. Franchisees are by definition part of a formal network with a large number of relatively homogeneous partners (i.e. the franchise chain) which enhances the chances of effective knowledge transfer among them. But, as we explained, individual franchisees within a franchise network have a larger group of natural network partners with which to exchange information, consisting of several parties within and outside the franchise chain. There has been some research on knowledge acquisition by SMEs within networks, but an understanding of this process in franchise chains is still lacking. This gap in the literature is especially surprising since franchise networks seem to be a particularly interesting setting to study this phenomenon. This is first, because franchisee knowledge exchange seems to be valuable and effective, and second, because franchise networks have a natural leader, the franchisor, who knowingly or unknowingly influences franchisee networking, and who benefits at the same time from effective networking within his chain.

As we indicated earlier, the type of study described in this chapter contributes to the identified gap in the franchise and network literature. In this chapter we have formulated propositions in which the franchisee's networking behaviour is an independent variable explaining franchisee performance, which is a major approach in the literature (see Rodan and Galunic 2004; Sparrowe et al. 2001), but franchisee networking behaviour can also be a relevant dependent variable in itself. Whatever the exact focus of the study, we strongly believe that studies regarding franchisee network behaviour can provide highly relevant results for practitioners. Franchisors put a lot of effort and resources in designing and maintaining contractual, hierarchical and informal relationships within their system and in improving the learning capacity of the system as a whole. Better insight in knowledge transfer from within and outside the chain towards the franchisees can help in improving the system's structure and processes. The franchisor has much influence on which franchisees meet each other (and other members of the system such as franchisor representatives and managers of company-owned units), how frequently, and under what circumstances. Franchisors also influence within-chain competition by defining and assigning exclusive territories and developing accompanying procedures; the resulting nature and level of competition affects knowledge transfer as well. It would be very nice if all these resources invested were not wasted.

REFERENCES

Aldrich, H. and C. Zimmer (1986), 'Entrepreneurship through social networks', in D.L. Sexton and R.W. Smilor (eds), *The Art and Science of Entrepreneurship*, Cambridge, MA: Ballinger, pp. 3–23.

Balkundi, P. and D.A. Harrison (2006), 'Ties, leaders, and time in teams: strong inference about network structure's effects on team viability and performance', *Academy of Management Journal*, **49** (1), 49–68.

Balkundi, P., M. Kilduff, Z.I. Barsness and J.H. Michael (2007), 'Demographic antecedents and performance consequences of structural holes in work teams', *Journal of Organizational Behavior*, **28**, 241–60.

Birley, S. (1985), 'The role of networks in the entrepreneurial process', *Journal of Business Venturing*, **1**, 107–17.

Borgatti, S.P. and P.C. Foster (2003), 'The network paradigm in organizational research: a review and typology', *Journal of Management*, **29** (6), 991–1013.

Bradach, J.L. (1997), 'Using the plural form in the management of restaurant chains', *Administrative Science Quarterly*, **42** (2), 276–303.

Bradach, J.L. (1998), *Franchise Organizations*, Boston, MA: Harvard Business School Press.

Brand, M.J. and E.P.M. Croonen (2010), 'Franchised and small; the most beautiful of all; HRM and performance in plural systems', *Journal of Small Business Management*, **48** (4), 605–26.

Burkhardt, M.E. and D.J. Brass (1990), 'Changing patterns or patterns of change: the effects of a change in technology on social network structure and power', *Administrative Science Quarterly*, **35**, 105–27.

Bürkle, T. and T. Posselt (2008), 'Franchising as a plural system: a risk-based explanation', *Journal of Retailing*, **84** (1), 39–47.

Burt, R.S. (1992), *Structural Holes: the Social Structure of Competition*, New York: Academic Press.

Campo, K.E. and E. Gijsbrechts (2004), 'Should retailers adjust their micro-marketing strategies to type of outlet? An application to location-based store space allocation in limited and full-service grocery stores', *Journal of Retailing and Consumer Services*, **11**, 369–83.

Campo, K.E., E. Gijsbrechts, T. Gossens and A. Verhetsel (2000), 'The impact of location factors on the attractiveness and optimal space shares of product categories', *International Journal of Research in Marketing*, **17**, 255–79.

Cohen, M.D. and D.A. Levinthal (1990), 'Absorptive capacity: a new perspective on learning and innovation', *Administrative Science Quarterly*, **35**, 128–52.

Combs, J.G. and D.J. Ketchen (2003), 'Why do firms use franchising as an entrepreneurial strategy?: A meta-analysis', *Journal of Management*, **29** (3), 443–65.

Combs, J.G., S.C. Michael and G.J. Castrogiovanni (2004), 'Franchising: a review and avenues to greater theoretical diversity', *Journal of Management*, **30** (6), 907–31.

Combs, J.G., S.C. Michael and G.J. Castrogiovanni (2009), 'Institutional influences on the choice of organizational form: the case of franchising', *Journal of Management*, **35** (5), 1268–90.

Croonen, E.P.M. (2010), 'Trust and fairness during strategic change processes in franchise systems', *Journal of Business Ethics*, **95** (2), 191–209.

Cross, R. and L. Prusak (2002), 'The people who make organizations go or stop', *Harvard Business Review*, **80** (6), 104–12.

Dada, O., A. Watson and D. Kirby (2011), 'Toward a model of franchisee entrepreneurship', *International Small Business Journal*, published online before print on 7 January.

Dant, R.P. (2008), 'A futuristic research agenda for the field of franchising', *Journal of Small Business Management*, **46** (1), 91–8.

Darr, E.D. and T.R. Kurtzberg (2000), 'An investigation of partner similarity dimensions on knowledge transfer', *Organizational Behavior and Human Decision Processes*, **82** (1), 28–44.

Darr, E.D., L. Argote and D. Epple (1995), 'The acquisition, transfer, and depreciation of knowledge in service organizations: productivity in franchises', *Management Science*, **41** (11), 1750–62.

Elfring, T. and W. Hulsink (2003), 'Networks in entrepreneurship: the case of high-technology firms', *Small Business Economics*, **21**, 409–22.

Fenwick, G.D. and M. Strombom (1998), 'The determinants of franchisee performance: an empirical investigation', *International Small Business Journal*, **16** (4), 28–46.

Ford, D. (2002), *Understanding Business Marketing and Purchasing: an Interaction Approach*, 3rd edn, Andover: Cengage Learning EMEA.

Galaskiewicz, J. and A. Zaheer (1999), 'Networks of competitive advantage', in S.B. Andrews and D. Knoke (eds), *Networks In and Around Organizations*, Stamford, CT: JAI Press, pp. 237–61.

Gassenheimer, J.B., D.B. Baucus and M.S. Baucus (1996), 'Cooperative arrangements among entrepreneurs: an analysis of opportunism and communication in franchise structures', *Journal of Business Research*, **36** (1), 67–79.

Gooderham, P., A. Tobiassen, E. Døving and O. Nordhaug (2004), 'Accountants as sources of business advice for small firms', *International Small Business Journal*, **22** (1), 5–22.

Granovetter, M.S. (1973), 'The strength of weak ties', *American Journal of Sociology*, **78**, 1360–68.

Greve, A. and J.W. Salaff (2003), 'Social networks and entrepreneurship', *Entrepreneurship Theory & Practice*, **28** (1), 1–22.

Gulati, R. (1995), 'Does familiarity breed trust? The implications of repeated ties of contractual choices in alliances', *Academy of Management Journal*, **38**, 85–112.

Hansen, M., J. Podolny and J. Pfeffer (2001), 'So many ties, so little time: a task contingency perspective on corporate social capital in organizations', in S. Gabbay and R. Leenders (eds), *Social Capital or Organizations*, Research in the Sociology of Organizations, vol. **18**, Emerald Group Publishing, pp. 21–57.

Hite, J.M. (2005), 'Evolutionary processes and paths of relationally embedded network ties in emerging entrepreneurial firms', *Entrepreneurship Theory & Practice*, **29** (1), 113–44.

Hoang, H. and B. Antoncic (2003), 'Network-based research in entrepreneurship: a critical review', *Journal of Business Venturing*, **18** (2), 165–87.

Ingram, P. and J.A.C. Baum (1997), 'Opportunity and constraint: organizations' learning from the operating and competitive experience of industries', *Strategic Management Journal*, **18**, 75–98.

Jack, S.L. (2005), 'The role, use and activation of strong and weak network ties: a qualitative analysis', *Journal of Management Studies*, **42** (6), 1233–59.

Jensen, R.J. and G. Szulanski (2007), 'Template use and the effectiveness of knowledge transfer', *Management Science*, **53** (11), 1716–30.

Kalnins, A. and K.J. Mayer (2004), 'Franchising, ownership, and experience: a study of pizza restaurant survival', *Management Science*, **50** (12), 1716–28.

Kaufmann, P.J. and R.P. Dant (1998), 'Franchising and the domain of entrepreneurship research', *Journal of Business Venturing*, **14** (1), 5–16.

Kaufmann, P.J. and S. Eroglu (1998), 'Standardization and adaptation in business format franchising', *Journal of Business Venturing*, **14** (1), 69–85.

Kenis, P. and D. Knoke (2002), 'How organizational field networks shape inter-organizational tie-formation rates', *Academy of Management Review*, **27** (2), 275–93.

Ketchen, D.J., J.C. Short and J.G. Combs (2011), 'Is franchising entrepreneurship? Yes, no, and maybe so', *Entrepreneurship Theory & Practice*, **35** (3), 583–93.

Kneppers-Heijnert, E.M. (1988), *Een Economische en Juridische Analyse van Franchising tegen de Achtergrond van een Property Rights- en Transactiekostenbenadering*, dissertation, University of Groningen, Groningen: Van Denderen.

Knott, A.M (2003), 'The organizational routines factor market paradox', *Strategic Management Journal*, **24** (10), 929–43.

Laursen, K. and A. Salter (2006), 'Open for innovation: the role of openness in explaining innovation performance among UK manufacturing firms', *Strategic Management Journal*, **27** (2), 131–50.

Lechner, C., M. Dowling and I. Welpe (2006), 'Firm networks and firm development: the role of the relational mix', *Journal of Business Venturing*, **21** (4), 514–40.

Leenders, R.Th.A.J. (1995), *Structure and Influence*, Amsterdam: Tesla Thesis Publishers.

Lubit, R. (2001), 'Tacit knowledge and knowledge management: the keys to sustainable competitive advantage', *Organizational Dynamics*, **29** (4), 164–78.

Makadok, R. and R. Coff (2009), 'Both market and hierarchy: an incentive-system theory of hybrid governance forms', *Academy of Management Review*, **34** (2), 297–319.

McEvily, B. and A. Zaheer (1999), 'Bridging ties: a source of firm heterogeneity in competitive capabilities', *Strategic Management Journal*, **20** (12), 1133–58.

McLean, M. (2006), 'Evaluating the importance and performance of the human resources function: an examination of a medium-sized Scottish retailer', *Journal of Retailing and Consumer Services*, **13** (2), 143–56.

Michael, S.C. (2002), 'Can a franchise chain coordinate?', *Journal of Business Venturing*, **17** (4), 325–41.

Michael, S.C. and J.G. Combs (2008), 'Entrepreneurial failure: the case of franchisees', *Journal of Small Business Management*, **46** (1), 73–90.

Miller, D. (1996), 'The embeddedness of corporate strategy: isomorphism vs. differentiation', *Advances in Strategic Management*, **13**, 283–91.

Miller, D. (2006), 'Strategic human resource management in department stores: an historical perspective', *Journal of Retailing and Consumer Services*, **13** (2), 99–109.

Morrison, K.A. (1997), 'How franchise job satisfaction and personality affects performance, organizational commitment, franchisor relations, and intention to remain', *Journal of Small Business Management*, **35** (3), 39–67.

Ounjian, M.L. and C.E. Bryan (1987), 'A study of the factors which affect technology transfer in a multilocation multibusiness unit corporation', *IEEE Transactions on Engineering Management*, **34**, 194–201.

Phan, P.H., J.E. Butler and S.H. Lee (1996), 'Crossing mother: entrepreneur–franchisees' attempts to reduce franchisor influence', *Journal of Business Venturing*, **11** (5), 379–402.

Podsakoff, P.M., S.B. MacKenzie and J.Y. Lee (2003), 'Common method bias in behavioral research: a critical review of the literature and recommended remedies', *Journal of Applied Psychology*, **88** (5), 879–903.

Premaratne, S.P. (2001), 'Networks, resources and small business growth: the experience in Sri Lanka', *Journal of Small Business Management*, **39** (4), 363–71.

Rodan, S. and C. Galunic (2004), 'More than network structure: how knowledge heterogeneity influences managerial performance and innovativeness', *Strategic Management Journal*, **25** (6), 541–62.

Seevers, M.Y., S.J. Skinner and R. Dahlstrom (2010), 'Performance implications of a retail purchasing network: the role of social capital', *Journal of Retailing*, **86** (4), 310–21.

Shaw, E. (2006), 'Small firm networking: an insight into contents and motivating factors', *International Small Business Journal*, **24** (1), 5–29.

Slotte-Kock, S. and N. Coviello (2009), 'Entrepreneurship research on network processes: a review and ways forward', *Entrepreneurship Theory & Practice*, **34** (1), 1–27.

Smeltzer, L.R., B.L. Van Hook and R.W. Hunt (1991), 'Analysis and use of advisors as information sources in venture startups', *Journal of Small Business Management*, **29** (3), 10–20.

Sorenson, O. and J.B. Sørensen (2001), 'Research note: finding the right mix: franchising, organizational learning, and chain performance', *Strategic Management Journal*, **22** (6/7), 713–24.

Sparrowe, T.T., R.C. Liden, S.J. Wayne and M.L. Kraimer (2001), 'Social networks and the performance of individuals and groups', *Academy of Management Journal*, **44** (2), 316–25.

Spender, J.-C. and R.M. Grant (1996), 'Knowledge and the firm: overview', *Strategic Management Journal*, **17** (Special Issue), 5–9.

Spinelli, S. and S. Birley (1996), 'Toward a theory of conflict in the franchise system', *Journal of Business Venturing*, **11** (5), 329–42.

Storey, D.J. (1994), *Understanding the Small Business Sector*, London: Routledge.

Szulanski, G. and R. Jensen (2006), 'Presumptive adaptation and the effectiveness of knowledge transfer', *Strategic Management Journal*, **27** (10), 937–57.

Szulanski, G. and R. Jensen (2008), 'Growing through copying: the negative consequences of innovation on franchise network growth', *Research Policy*, **37** (10), 1732–41.

Uzzi, B. (1996), 'The sources and consequences of embeddedness for the economic performance of organizations: the network effect', *American Sociology Review*, **61**, 674–98.

Van Essen, C. and F. Pleijster (2009), *Franchiseketens: Marktaandeel en Continuïteit*, Zoetermeer: Economisch Instituut voor het Midden- en Kleinbedrijf (EIM).

Van Wijk, R., J.P. Jansen and M.A. Lyles (2008), 'Inter- and intra-organizational knowledge transfer: a meta-analytic review and assessment of its antecedents and consequences', *Journal of Management Studies*, **45** (4), 830–53.

Vrolijk, H. (2002), *Efficiënte Contracten? Institutioneel-economische Beschouwingen over Franchising*, PhD dissertation, University of Nijmegen, The Netherlands.

Watson, J. (2007), 'Modeling the relationship between networking and firm performance', *Journal of Business Venturing*, **22** (6), 852–74.

Welsh, D.H.B., I. Alon and C.M. Falbe (2006), 'An examination of international retail franchising in emerging markets', *Journal of Small Business Management*, **44** (1), 130–49.

Windsperger, J. (2004), 'Centralization of franchising networks: evidence from the Austrian franchise sector', *Journal of Business Research*, **57** (12), 1361–9.

Windsperger, J. and N. Gorovaia (2010), 'Knowledge attributes and the choice of knowledge transfer mechanisms in networks: the case of franchising', *Journal of Management & Governance*, published online 20 January 2010.

Winter, S. and G. Szulanski (2001), 'Replication as strategy', *Organization Science*, **12** (6), 730–43.

Yin, X. and E.J. Zajac (2004), 'The strategy/governance structure fit relationship: theory and evidence in franchising arrangements', *Strategic Management Journal*, **25** (4), 365–83.

Yli-Renko, H., E. Autio and H. Sapienza (2001), 'Social capital, knowledge acquisition, and knowledge exploitation in young technology-based firms', *Strategic Management Journal*, **22** (6/7), 587–613.

8. Openness and innovativeness within science-based entrepreneurial firms

**Einar Rasmussen and
Tommy Høyvarde Clausen**

1. INTRODUCTION

Many studies have demonstrated the potential value of academic research and basic science discoveries for technological change and economic growth (Cohen et al. 2002). However, the process of converting scientific knowledge into new products and services is extremely difficult (Fleming and Sorenson 2004). The knowledge of universities is often 'less targeted' to firms' particular needs and concerns and therefore difficult for firms to assimilate and apply (Cohen and Levinthal 1990). Increasing attention has been paid to the role of science-based entrepreneurial firms (SBEFs) in converting scientific findings into commercial products and services. New ventures are often commercializing more innovative and radical technologies than incumbents (Chesbrough and Rosenbloom 2002) and empirical studies assert that new technology-based firms have an active role in the development and dissemination of technology (Autio and Yli-Renko 1998). Accordingly, governments and universities increasingly rely on the creation of SBEFs as a mechanism to commercialize knowledge and inventions from universities and other public research institutions (Wright et al. 2007).

SBEFs face the same challenge as established firms in converting scientific knowledge into products and services with a commercial value, but from a different point of departure. SBEFs originates within the non-commercial university setting and face challenges of adopting to the requirements of the commercial setting (Rasmussen et al. 2011; Vohora et al. 2004). Moreover, SBEFs often develop embryonic technologies with an uncertain market potential (Jensen and Thursby 2001). As a result, SBEFs have a strong scientific foundation, but typically lack commercial expertise. Although SBEFs are a special 'breed' of start-up firms, they nevertheless need to assemble resources for their firm, like most other start-ups.

In this chapter we examine the contributions from external actors to SBEFs in overcoming the challenge of converting scientific inventions into commercial applications. While the relationship between networking and innovation is well established in the literature (Pittaway et al. 2004), less is known about the types of external knowledge provided from external actors in different contexts. Our aim is to explore how SBEFs benefit from contributions from a diverse set of external actors, rather than exploring why and how firms maintain their external relationships. Thus, our analysis is framed within the open innovation (OI) model, rather than a network perspective. The OI model focuses on external technology sourcing as input to firm innovation (Chesbrough et al. 2006). Laursen and Salter (2004) define openness as 'the number of different sources of external knowledge that each firm draws upon in its innovative activities'. Most studies on OI have looked at the sourcing or acquisition of technological knowledge (Dahlander and Gann 2010), while SBEFs typically need a broad range of different knowledge and resources (Rasmussen et al. 2011).

Academic entrepreneurs need to build an organization around the technology that they aim to commercialize (Rasmussen et al. 2011), they need to gain trust and legitimacy from external stakeholders (Delmar and Shane 2004), and they need to get access to external knowledge about how to turn basic science into commercial products and technology (Vohora et al. 2004). With few initial resources, the majority of academic entrepreneurs need to assemble these resources externally to the start-up firm. This chapter adds to the literature by conceptualizing openness as consisting of three dimensions that separately and together are related to the innovativeness of SBEFs: external sourcing of (1) technology; (2) organization building; and (3) legitimacy. The following research question is asked: whether and to what extent is openness related to the innovativeness of SBEFs?

This study merges the OI model in management with key insights from the entrepreneurship literature to develop an OI model applicable for the new venture context. By including contributions to organization building and legitimacy we complement prior studies that have focused solely on the impact of external technology sourcing on subsequent innovative performance (Dahlander and Gann 2010). In addition, most OI studies have been conducted within large established firms (Chesbrough et al. 2006). Few studies have explored the relevance of the OI model for start-up firms, SBEFs in particular.

In the next section we build on the innovation literature and the entrepreneurship literature to develop theoretically driven hypotheses regarding the role of external actors for technology development in SBEFs. Next we present our methodology and survey data of Norwegian SBEFs. Then the empirical results from our study are presented. Finally, discussions and implications are provided.

2. THEORY AND HYPOTHESES

While SBEFs may differ from other nascent ventures by pursuing a novel scientific innovation, they are similar in the sense that they need to develop a weak initial resource base (Brush et al. 2001). With few resources but their own experience, founders of emerging firms need to assemble such resources externally (Aldrich 1999). The process of transforming scientific findings and knowledge into a commercially viable business needs to span both organizational and technological boundaries (Rosenkopf and Nerkar 2001). Moreover, the integration of internal and external resources is found to be important for technology commercialization (Zahra and Nielsen 2002). Thus, the ability of nascent ventures to develop commercial applications from scientific knowledge depends on their capacity to search for and use external knowledge in developing their innovations. This challenge is central to the OI model which focuses upon external sourcing of technology within established firms.

We adopt an entrepreneurial perspective on the OI model within the context of academic entrepreneurship. Entrepreneurship research has shown that the value of external resources is not limited to technology. Entrepreneurs need to build an organization around the technology that they aim to commercialize (Aldrich 1999), they need to gain trust and legitimacy from external stakeholders (Delmar and Shane 2004), and (in line with the OI model) they need to get access to external knowledge about how to turn basic science into commercial products and technology (Vohora et al. 2004). We therefore argue that openness is far more than just external technology sourcing for SBEFs.

2.1 External Actors and Firm Innovation

Although the literature on how new ventures link technology to market is scant, the literature on innovation and product development in established technology ventures has extensively studied the factors leading to innovativeness (Kotabe and Swan 1995). Considerable attention has been devoted to the role of external actors in explaining innovation performance and new venture growth (Cohen and Levinthal 1990; Von Hippel 1988). Strategic alliances are found to increase the innovation performance in both new high-technology ventures (Li and Atuahene-Gima 2001) and product development in established firms (Kotabe and Swan 1995).

External resource providers play an important role for the establishment of new ventures (Hanlon and Saunders 2007). In the context of SMEs, several studies have revealed that firms using external information have higher innovation performance than firms that do not (Freel 2003).

There is plenty of evidence that firms acquire knowledge and technology from a myriad of different sources such as customers, suppliers, manufacturers, competitors, and universities (Tether 2002; Von Hippel 1988). The academic entrepreneurship literature has pointed at the importance of many different actors for the formation and performance of SBEFs including the academic inventors and their networks, universities and their technology transfer offices (TTOs), industry partners, private investors, incubators, science parks, government support programmes, and students (Rasmussen and Borch 2010). We propose that SBEFs that to a large extent receive contributions from external actors will create more innovative new products and services. In the following section we will key into the resource gaps faced by nascent SBEFs to further specify the resource needs.

2.2   Resource Gaps of SBEFs

SBEFs need to develop and acquire firm-specific resources and capabilities that enable them to overcome the obstacles of transforming scientific findings into technological innovations. A central part of our argument is that the usefulness of external actors is particularly relevant for SBEF because these firms face the challenge of converting research results into products or services with commercial value that typically requires a significant amount of resources. It is also found that SBEFs are significantly more externally oriented compared to other small innovative firms (de Jong and Marsili 2006). Compared to low- and medium-technology firms, high-technology firms developing university inventions may face particular challenges due to the embryonic nature of the technologies (Jensen and Thursby 2001). We want to explore whether some external actors provide more important contributions than others to close the resource gaps faced by SBEFs. Following a resource-based perspective, we propose that SBEFs face three distinct resource gaps that may be resolved by contributions from external actors.

First, SBEFs need to develop their initial idea and technology into a product or service that can be sold in the marketplace (Rasmussen et al. 2011). For instance, Shane (2000) showed how one single university invention formed the basis of eight different business ideas depending on the situation and prior experience of the entrepreneurs. Due to the specificity of the academic context, SBEFs may find it difficult to communicate with external partners about the specialities of the technology they aim to commercialize. Although interaction with users and customers is supposed to benefit new technology-based firms (Yli-Renko et al. 2001), the technologies that many SBEFs develop do not necessarily have an existing or emerging market to address, and therefore no user to consult. Thus, it is likely that SBEFs would benefit from contributions from a variety of external actors to further develop their research-based technology into an innovative product or service.

H1: SBEFs having a high extent of contributions to technology development from several external actors are more innovative than SBEFs having a low extent of contributions to technology development from external actors.

Second, every new venture faces the challenge of building a new organization. Academic entrepreneurs often have limited business experience (Mosey and Wright 2007) and the creation of a new organization to commercialize the technological innovation might be an even greater challenge than developing the technological aspects. This relates to key managerial tasks such as recruitment, marketing and financing. For instance, prior relations to venture capitalists are positively associated with the performance of SBEFs (Shane and Stuart 2002). Thus, for SBEFs, resources from various external actors may be important in the development of an organization that can pursue the technological innovation.

H2: SBEFs having a high extent of contribution to organization building from several external actors are more innovative than SBEFs having a low extent of contributions to organization building from external actors.

Third, unlike the context of established firms, SBEFs have a very limited prior history and accumulated firm-specific knowledge. New ventures face a liability of newness and need to build legitimacy to sustain their operation (Delmar and Shane 2004). Legitimacy is an instrumental resource necessary to acquire other resources from the environment (Zimmerman and Zeitz 2002). SBEFs are typically lacking a track record and need to search actively for legitimacy to be perceived as proper among resource providers. Thus, it is likely that a number of external actors can contribute to increase the legitimacy of SBEFs and thereby improve the chances of developing new innovations.

H3: SBEFs having a high extent of contributions to legitimacy from several external actors are more innovative than SBEFs having a low extent of contributions to legitimacy from external actors.

3. METHOD

To answer the three hypotheses, we collected survey data from SBEFs and used regression analysis (OLS) to analyse the relationship between the three dimensions of openness and the innovativeness of SBEFs. Factor analysis is used to assess the validity of the composite measures of innovativeness and openness.

3.1 Research Context

We conducted a survey of Norwegian SBEFs. Norway can be seen as a typical Western European context regarding entrepreneurial activity and university system. New ventures in Norway face high costs and a small domestic market but good access to technological infrastructure, and personnel with higher education degrees. All universities in Norway are public, but face increasing competition for research funds and expectations for generating external income. Norwegian universities have only recently become formally involved in spin-off formation. Until 2003, the intellectual property (IP) of academic research was owned by the individual academic inventor. Following a legislative change, universities started to hold this ownership instead, which led to the establishment of technology transfer offices (TTOs), increased awareness of commercialization within the institutions, and increased public spending to facilitate commercialization of research. This development resembles the development taking place in many other countries and is well suited to unravelling the role of various external actors to the commercialization process within SBEFs.

3.2 Sample

We sent a questionnaire to the CEO of all SBEFs from public research institutions in Norway established in the period 2003–2008. This sample was identified through the government support programme FORNY, which provides funding to all universities, major research institutes, TTOs and Science Parks in Norway. A major goal of this programme is to increase the number of SBEFs through early stage support of these ventures. As FORNY provides several support mechanisms and grants, it is likely that very few SBEFs, if any, have been established without being in contact with this programme. In total, 158 SBEFs had been established in the period. We were able to obtain contact information for 138 of these firms, while the remaining 20 firms are probably out of business. We received 84 responses, a response rate of 61 per cent. The responding firms were significantly younger than non-responding firms. This may partly be explained by the survey's focus on the early development of the firms, which may be perceived as less relevant for the older firms. We tested for differences concerning industrial sector, size of the firms in terms of invested capital, total sale, or number of employees. No significant differences between responding and non-responding firms were found.

The age of the firms ranged from one to six years and most of these firms were rather small. Thus, we assumed that the CEO of each firm was well informed about the history of the company, which was confirmed by a control question revealing that 76 per cent of the respondents were also the founder of the business.

3.3   Definition and Measurement of Variables

3.3.1   Dependent variable: innovativeness

Our dependent variable is measured by using an established construct for innovativeness (Fang 2008). The construct highlights that a key function of innovation is to challenge existing technology and push the technological frontier forward and consists of five items. The respondents were asked to rate the degree to which the technology/product the SBEF had developed in the last two years, or had under development, was 'very novel for our industry', 'challenging to existing ideas in our industry', 'offering new ideas to our industry', 'creative', and 'capable of generating ideas for other products'. The respondents could rate their agreement for each item on a 7-point Likert scale (1 = completely disagree, 7 = completely agree). The innovation construct is used as a summary scale. A factor analysis verified that all the items in the construct loaded on the same factor with a Cronbach's alpha score of 0.87, which indicates a strong internal reliability.

3.3.2   Independent variables: contributions from external actors

To measure how different external actors contributed to the external sourcing of knowledge, we asked a separate set of questions related to each of the three hypotheses regarding (1) technology development; (2) organization building; and (3) legitimacy. While earlier studies of the role of external actors have relied on measures counting the number of external sources (de Jong and Marsili 2006; Rickne 2006), we measured the contributions from a specified set of external actors. Earlier studies on knowledge sources in the innovation process have revealed the importance of sources such as conferences, meetings, journals and fairs (for example the CIS surveys). We selected only definite organizations or actors representing the original source of the knowledge, not a channel of knowledge transfer. The following 11 actors were identified: industry partners (IND); the university TTO

Table 8.1 Descriptive statistics

Variables	N	Minimum	Maximum	Mean	Std. Deviation
Innovation	82	5	35	27.67	6.52
Technology sourcing	83	11	52	28.39	11.32
Organization building	83	11	65	28.08	11.15
Legitimacy	83	11	59	31.33	11.23
Openness (composite indicator)	83	33	172	87.81	29.56
Consulting	83	1	7	2.80	2.18
Licensing	83	1	7	4.62	2.40
Product-based	83	1	7	4.78	2.35
Software	83	1	7	3.12	2.48
Age	83	2	10	5.96	1.94
Nanotechnology	83	0	1	0.10	0.31
Biotechnology	83	0	1	0.42	0.49
Energy	83	0	1	0.18	0.38
ICT technology	83	0	1	0.40	0.49
Offshore technology	83	0	1	0.14	0.35
Academic origin	83	2	14	8.13	2.73
Entrepreneurial experience	83	0	1	0.68	0.46
Valid N	82				

Source: Own study.

(TTO); the research department of origin (RES); other national research departments (RES-N); other international research departments (RES-I); seed and venture funds (SEED); customers (CUS); suppliers (SUP); the firm's board of directors (BOARD); students (STUD); and public support agencies (PUB). To explore each of the three hypothesis we listed the 11 actors and asked the respondent to indicate whether each actor had contributed to technology development (organization building/legitimacy) on a 7-point Likert scale (1 = no contribution, 7 = very large contribution). Our measures of openness are summary scales of the rated contribution from all 11 actors for each hypothesis and an overall sum score (see Table 8.1).

3.3.3 Control variables

We included a number of control variables to ensure that the effects of the dimensions of openness on the dependent variable are not due to omitted variable bias. An important control variable is the business model that the SBEFs pursue. Earlier studies have distinguished between four categories of business model (Druilhe and Garnsey 2004): consulting firms, technology development companies, product-based companies, and software companies. These four business models were measured by using four survey questions preceded by the following question stem: "Please indicate the extent to which your firm's business model builds on. . .: 'consultancy or research services', 'development of technology for sale or licensing', 'development and sale of product', and 'development and sale of software'. Respondents could tick from 1 (no extent) to 7 (to a high extent) for each of the four items.

Firm age is included as a control variable because it is related to the market value of new innovations. Firm age is measured as the number of years since the firm's registration in the Norwegian business register. Prior entrepreneurial experience is important for new start-up firms. The variable 'entrepreneurial experience' takes the value 1 if anyone in the management team has previously founded a firm, and 0 otherwise. We do not include other measures of the competence of the management team because the founders of SBEFs are all highly educated; most of them have a PhD degree and many years of research experience. Our sample is homogeneous in that respect.

We included a set of technological field dummy variables because the dynamics of technology development and innovation differ across technology fields (Malerba 2002). We distinguished between: nanotechnology (including material technology); biotechnology (including biomedicine); oil & offshore technology; ICT; and energy. We also measured whether the technology that the SBEFs are trying to commercialize has an academic origin. This summary scale called 'academic origin' consists of two questions about the extent to which the technology had its origin in the research group in which the SBEF had its origin and the extent to which the technology had its origin in another research group within another university or research institute. This control is added because it may be more challenging to commercialize technology with an academic origin compared to technology with an industrial origin (Zahra et al. 2007).

Lastly, we included a set of TTO dummy variables to control for the possibility that some TTOs may offer better services, funding possibilities, and access to networks than other TTOs, which may influence the SBEFs' technology transfer capability (Chapple et al. 2005). Because each TTO also serves specific universities and research institutes, the TTO dummy variables also control for the heterogeneity of the research environments in which the SBEFs have their origin. The university and research institution in which the SBEF has its origin can have a long-lasting influence on the firm's capabilities (Shane and Stuart 2002). A descriptive analysis of all the variables used in the OLS regression is provided in Table 8.1 (TTO dummy variable omitted due to space considerations).

4.   EMPIRICAL RESULTS

4.1   External Sourcing: A Correlation Analysis

A basic premise of this chapter is that openness can be conceptualized by three related dimensions of external sourcing: (1) technology; (2) resources needed to build the organization/firm around the technology; and (3) legitimacy. To explore the relationships between these dimensions, Tables 8.2 to 8.4 show whether and to what extent the same external actors add to the firm along all – or just some – of the openness dimensions.

Table 8.2 shows whether and to what extent the SBEFs in our sample source technology and legitimacy from the same external actors. The diagonal in Table 8.2 (in bold type) displays the Pearson's correlation coefficient between the questions 'to what extent have the following actors' contributed to the development of your firm's technology' and 'to what extent have the following actors' contributed to give your firm credibility and legitimacy'. We can observe a rather strong liner relationship between these two dimensions. An interpretation is that if firms for instance draw a lot from suppliers in their technology development they also get legitimacy and trust from suppliers (and vice versa). However, there are also rather high and positive correlations between these two dimensions across external actors. As an example, there is a 0.462 correlation between 'technology sourcing from industry partners' and 'external trust' from suppliers. Hence, technology sourcing and trust from external actors may be interrelated aspects of openness, especially for new technology based firms. Another example shows that there is a 0.395 correlation between 'external trust from public funding sources' and 'external technology sourcing from international research groups'.

Table 8.3 shows whether and to what extent the SBEFs in our sample source 'technology' and 'organization building' resources from the same external actors. Table 8.3 shows a rather strong linear relationship between these two dimensions, suggesting that when firms draw deeply on, for instance, customers in their technology development, they also get access to organization-building resources from customers to a rather high extent (and vice versa). As in Table 8.2, there are also rather high and positive correlations between these two dimensions across external actors. Hence, external technology sourcing and access to organization-building resources may be interrelated aspects of openness.

Table 8.4 shows whether and to what extent SBEFs in our sample gain 'legitimacy' and 'organization building' resources from the same

Table 8.2 Correlations between 'contributions to technology' (column) and 'contributions to legitimacy' (row) from external actors

	IND	TTO	RES	RES-N	RES-I	SEED	CUS	SUP	BOARD	STUD	PUB
IND	0.456**	0.167	-0.027	0.195	0.097	0.246*	0.400**	0.343**	0.160	0.005	0.286**
TTO	0.243*	0.422**	0.211	0.073	-0.061	0.089	0.108	0.211	0.032	0.145	0.167
RES	0.175	0.160	0.442**	0.161	0.032	0.153	0.204	0.167	0.163	0.258*	0.074
RES-N	0.073	0.177	-0.006	0.567**	0.292**	0.184	0.030	-0.067	0.372**	0.060	0.278*
RES-I	0.173	0.106	0.132	0.219*	0.525**	0.159	-0.058	0.081	0.336**	0.173	0.122
SEED	0.028	-0.006	-0.054	0.185	0.186	0.474**	0.030	-0.029	0.102	-0.130	0.134
CUS	0.159	0.108	-0.022	-0.127	-0.085	-0.074	0.475**	0.430**	-0.057	0.116	0.039
SUP	0.462**	0.046	0.046	-0.045	0.100	-0.095	0.403**	0.658**	0.131	0.152	0.153
BOARD	0.272*	0.019	0.171	0.230*	0.229*	0.117	0.059	0.128	0.571**	0.253*	0.299**
STUD	0.200	0.048	-0.011	-0.079	0.050	-0.102	0.145	0.160	0.067	0.626**	0.028
PUB	0.271*	0.072	0.001	0.245*	0.395**	0.103	0.186	0.272*	0.213	0.238*	0.465**

Notes:
* Correlation is significant at the 0.05 level.
** Correlation is significant at the 0.01 level.

Source: Own study.

Table 8.3   Correlations between 'contributions to technology' (column) and 'contributions to organization building' (row) from external actors

	IND	TTO	RES	RES-N	RES-I	SEED	CUS	SUP	BOARD	STUD	PUB
IND	**0.511****	0.322**	0.035	0.173	0.079	0.240*	0.500**	0.397**	0.134	0.000	0.264*
TTO	0.264*	**0.528****	0.243*	0.096	−0.106	0.152	0.121	0.143	0.115	0.172	0.142
RES	0.087	0.214	**0.471****	0.106	0.060	0.012	0.051	0.159	0.285**	0.219*	0.015
RES-N	0.105	0.087	−0.103	**0.471****	0.278*	0.176	0.030	0.018	0.318**	0.095	0.277*
RES-I	0.146	0.105	−0.068	0.109	**0.326****	0.073	0.041	0.046	0.168	0.128	0.190
SEED	0.042	−0.066	0.093	0.274*	0.103	**0.566****	0.132	−0.072	0.096	−0.106	0.123
CUS	0.298**	0.107	0.142	0.017	−0.048	0.183	**0.610****	0.274*	0.102	0.055	0.139
SUP	0.564**	0.214	−0.009	−0.044	0.018	0.057	**0.541****	**0.797****	0.086	0.078	0.153
BOARD	0.247*	−0.005	0.191	0.143	0.214	0.120	0.073	0.144	**0.519****	0.183	0.196
STUD	0.163	0.091	0.072	0.032	0.068	−0.023	0.159	0.181	0.097	**0.637****	0.144
PUB	0.151	0.118	0.062	0.260*	0.254*	0.164	0.292**	0.220*	0.216*	0.221*	**0.593****

Notes:
*   Correlation is significant at the 0.05 level.
** Correlation is significant at the 0.01 level.

Source: Own study.

Table 8.4 Correlations between 'contributions to legitimacy' (column) and 'contributions to organization building' (row) from external actors

	IND	TTO	RES	RES-N	RES-I	SEED	CUS	SUP	BOARD	STUD	PUB
IND	**0.603****	0.282**	0.053	0.263*	0.079	0.156	0.293**	0.231*	0.222*	0.083	0.219*
TTO	0.315***	**0.812****	0.321**	0.173	0.057	0.157	0.078	0.064	0.136	0.100	0.160
RES	0.039	0.123	**0.609****	0.106	0.153	-0.083	0.009	0.081	0.215	0.142	0.110
RES-N	0.271*	0.122	-0.003	**0.861****	0.261*	0.350**	0.014	-0.008	0.328**	0.173	0.380**
RES-I	0.244*	0.094	-0.034	0.591**	**0.390****	0.276*	0.062	0.018	0.242*	0.273*	0.289**
SEED	0.294**	0.092	0.088	0.223*	0.089	**0.750****	0.015	-0.126	0.215	-0.017	0.241*
CUS	0.507***	0.095	0.152	0.096	-0.008	0.118	**0.545****	0.294**	0.108	0.190	0.001
SUP	0.422**	0.267*	0.225*	0.059	0.013	0.078	0.364**	**0.573****	0.107	0.126	0.302**
BOARD	0.204	0.035	0.144	0.290**	0.219*	0.377**	0.047	0.154	**0.800****	0.210	0.334**
STUD	0.125	0.119	0.217*	0.197	0.084	0.008	0.185	0.171	0.308**	**0.608****	0.340**
PUB	0.366**	0.273*	0.211	0.262*	0.119	0.232*	0.246*	0.190	0.354**	0.141	**0.698****

Notes:
  * Correlation is significant at the 0.05 level.
  ** Correlation is significant at the 0.01 level.

Source: Own study.

external actors. Table 8.4 shows a rather strong linear relationship between these two dimensions, suggesting that when firms draw deeply on, for instance, the TTO for external trust and legitimacy they also acquire external resources that can be used to build the organization around the technology (and vice versa). However, there are also rather high and positive correlations between these two dimensions across external actors. Hence, sourcing external organization-building resources and access to external trust and legitimacy may be interrelated aspects of openness. Overall, the correlations displayed in the tables have shown that external sourcing of technology, organizational resources and legitimacy are highly correlated within the same actor – and even across types of actors. This may suggest that external sourcing of technology, organizational resources and legitimacy are interrelated aspects of OI, at least for SBEFs.

4.2   Econometric Analysis

This section reports the empirical results from four regression analyses. The three first regressions examine the external contributions to technology development (Cronbach's alpha = 0.76), organization building (Cronbach's alpha = 0.75) and legitimacy (Cronbach's alpha = 0.72) separately. The last regression analyses combine these three aspects of openness into a composite measure of openness which contains all three dimensions. This was done after a factor analysis which showed that all three dimensions were strongly correlated and loaded high on the same factor (Cronbach's alpha = 0.85).

Table 8.5 shows that the three dimensions of openness, when examined individually, have a positive and significant influence on the innovativeness of SBEFs. These findings offer empirical support for all hypotheses. The composite indicator of openness is also a positive and significant predictor of innovativeness. In addition, we find that older SBEFs are less innovative than younger SBEFs, that the degree to which basic science can be commercialized and introduced to industry by SBEFs seems to depend on technology fields, and that SBEFs commercializing basic science and technology with an academic origin are more innovative.

The four regression models explain from 48 per cent to 52 per cent of the variance in the dependent variable. Hence, the models have good explanatory power and can to a substantial extent account for why SBEFs have different technology transfer capabilities as reflected by differences in their innovativeness.

Table 8.5 *Regression analysis (standardized regression coefficients reported)*

Variables	Coef.	Coef.	Coef.	Coef.
Technology sourcing	0.326***	Not estimated	Not estimated	Not estimated
Organization building	Not estimated	0.331***	Not estimated	Not estimated
Legitimacy	Not estimated	Not estimated	0.220*	Not estimated
Openness (composite indicator)	Not estimated	Not estimated	Not estimated	0.360***
Consulting	0.020	−0.004	0.042	0.004
Licensing	0.305**	0.292**	0.326**	0.296**
Product-based	0.124	0.130	0.135	0.123
Software	0.351**	0.396**	0.391**	0.390**
Age	−0.256**	−0.195*	−0.213*	−0.209*
Nanotechnology	0.275**	0.242**	0.243**	0.268
Biotechnology	−0.211	−0.244	−0.192	−0.232
Energy	0.250**	0.235*	0.228	0.231*
ICT technology	−0.384**	−0.462***	−0.383***	−0.437***
Offshore technology	−0.090	−0.065	−0.076	−0.095
Academic origin	0.196**	0.254	0.262	0.223
Entrepreneurial experience	−0.040	−0.054	−0.033	−0.034
TTO dummies	Included	Included	Included	Included
R^2	50 %	51 %	48 %	52 %
N	82	82	82	82
Model	1	2	3	4

Note: * Significant at the 0.1 level; ** significant at the 0.05 level; *** significant at the 0.01 level.

Source: Own study.

5. CONCLUSIONS

The objective of this study was to examine the contributions from external actors to SBEFs that are converting scientific inventions into commercial applications. While science-based entrepreneurial firms (SBEFs) play a key role in converting scientific knowledge into new breakthrough products and services they must, like many other start-up firms, assemble resources and knowledge to survive and succeed. In this chapter we examined the role of openness for the ability of SBEFs to be innovative. We adopted an entrepreneurial perspective on the open innovation model that is particularly applicable to new firms. Openness was conceptualized as the external sourcing of (1) technology; (2) organization building; and

(3) legitimacy. Based on a sample of 84 SBEFs we found empirical support for our conceptualization of openness and that openness is a positive and significant predictor of the innovativeness of SBEFs.

The OI literature has traditionally focused on the role of technology sourcing from external actors. We offer a more comprehensive view on whether and how external actors contribute to the innovativeness of new ventures in general, and SBEFs in particular. This chapter has proposed three core dimensions related to external sourcing of (1) technology; (2) organizational resources; and (3) legitimacy from external actors as important dimensions of openness.

Our empirical analysis verifies that external sourcing of technology, organizational resources and legitimacy are interrelated aspects of openness, especially in the new venture context. First, it was shown that external sourcing of technology, organizational resources and legitimacy from the same external actor were highly correlated. Secondly, a principal components factor analysis verified that the three dimensions of external sourcing of resources identified one single factor with high factor loadings. Third, we found that the innovativeness of SBEFs is related to external sourcing of technology, organization building and legitimacy. When examined in isolation, as well as together in a composite measure of OI, these dimensions are positively and significantly related to innovativeness of SBEFs.

Overall, our results suggest that sourcing of resources for organization building and legitimacy are key aspects of open innovation together with external technology sourcing, at least in the new venture context. The results from this chapter suggest that openness in the innovation process is not restricted to external technology sourcing. A sole focus on external technology sourcing would in fact provide an incomplete assessment on the role of external actors in the technology commercialization process, at least from universities.

We further believe that our findings support the argument that to develop innovative technologies there is a need to conduct exploration that spans both technological and organizational boundaries (Rosenkopf and Nerkar 2001). In the case of SBEF this means that they have to search outside their own research institution and outside the specific industry context for developing innovative technologies. This underscores the crucial role for actors possessing knowledge and networks that can help refine the technology to bridge the gap between scientific inventions and commercial application.

Overall, our study contributes to the literature on innovation by looking at the contribution from external actors to resource acquisition in start-ups. Compared to large firms, start-ups have few resources, which may limit their ability to search for and integrate technological knowledge. It could therefore be questioned whether SBEFs that already possess advanced technologies would benefit from further technological exploration, or whether they should focus their limited time and resources on gaining market strength for their current innovation. Our findings suggest that further exploration is important for innovativeness. The importance of actors such as other national and international research institutions, investors, the board of directors, and public support for technology development indicates that a broad search path is preferable also in start-ups (Rosenkopf and Nerkar 2001). It might be that the identification of multiple market opportunities prior to entry would leave the nascent firm in a better position to select the most favourable alternative (Gruber et al. 2008).

The findings also have important implications for policy and entrepreneurs. Although most SBEFs in our sample are small, they are highly innovative and may have a potential for generating a larger impact in the future. To promote the innovativeness of SBEFs, policy makers should promote interaction with a broad set of external actors. Strategic network building should be a proactive task of new ventures (Lechner et al. 2006) and our findings have implications for what type of actors are most relevant for SBEFs. Prior studies have stressed the crucial role of industry contacts for SBEFs, such as customers and suppliers (de Jong and Marsili 2006), while our findings indicate that other sources play an even more important role. In particular, support schemes should promote contacts with intermediary actors that have not been connected to the research or to the industry, and therefore are able to provide alternative perspectives on technology development.

This study was exploratory and has several limitations but also implications for further research. Our results are based on responses from the CEOs of SBEFs, while a combination of data sources would be preferable to avoid common method biases and problems with relying on the subjective perceptions of the respondents. Moreover, our sample is small and consists of only Norwegian firms, while other contexts could reveal different findings.

The cross-sectional research design allows us to suggest a connection between openness and innovativeness, but the causality is unclear. Future longitudinal studies may test whether external sourcing of technology, organization building and legitimacy are related to higher innovativeness at a later point in time. This could preferably be done where both the innovativeness and openness of SBEFs has been measured over time, so that panel regressions techniques could be used to study this relationship. Another interesting avenue for future research would be to explore the dimensions used to measure openness proposed in this chapter. Although our research clearly suggests that openness includes three interrelated dimensions that positively influence innovativeness, it could be questioned whether our three dimensions are related to other dependent variables in the same way. In addition, future research could identify other important dimensions of openness that we have not considered in this chapter.

In this study we have argued for the positive implications of openness in the form of collaborating with many actors. In practice, however, openness may also have negative consequences related to the costs associated with maintaining many relationships and the risk of revealing technological secrets and strategies to competitors. Future research may therefore take a more nuanced view on openness by also including the negative effects.

REFERENCES

Aldrich, H. (1999), *Organizations Evolving*, Thousand Oaks, CA: Sage Publications.

Autio, E. and H. Yli-Renko (1998), 'New, technology-based firms as agents of technological rejuvenation', *Entrepreneurship and Regional Development*, **10** (1), 71–92.

Brush, C.G., P.G. Green and M.M. Hart (2001), 'From initial idea to unique advantage: the entrepreneurial challenge of constructing a resource base', *Academy of Management Executive*, **15** (1), 64–78.

Chapple, W., A. Lockett, D. Siegel and M. Wright (2005), 'Assessing the relative performance of UK university technology transfer offices: parametric and non-parametric evidence', *Research Policy*, **34** (3), 369–84.

Chesbrough, H. and R.S. Rosenbloom (2002), 'The role of the business model in capturing value from innovation: evidence from Xerox Corporation's technology spin-off companies', *Industrial and Corporate Change*, **11** (3), 529–55.

Chesbrough, H., W. Vanhaverbeke and J. West (2006), *Open Innovation: Researching a New Paradigm*, Oxford: Oxford University Press.

Cohen, W.M. and D.A. Levinthal (1990), 'Absorptive capacity: a new perspective on learning and innovation', *Administrative Science Quarterly*, **35** (1), 128–52.

Cohen, W.M., R.R. Nelson and J.P. Walsh (2002), 'Links and impacts: the influence of public research on industrial R&D', *Management Science*, **48** (1), 1–23.

Dahlander, L. and D.M. Gann (2010), 'How open is innovation?', *Research Policy*, **39** (6), 699–709.

de Jong, J.P.J. and O. Marsili (2006), 'The fruit flies of innovations: a taxonomy of innovative small firms', *Research Policy*, **35** (2), 213–29.

Delmar, F. and S. Shane (2004), 'Legitimating first: organizing activities and the survival of new ventures', *Journal of Business Venturing*, **19** (3), 385–410.

Druilhe, C. and E. Garnsey (2004), 'Do academic spin-outs differ and does it matter?', *The Journal of Technology Transfer*, **29** (3/4), 269–85.

Fang, E. (2008), 'Customer participation and the trade-off between new product innovativeness and speed to market', *Journal of Marketing*, **72** (4), 90–104.

Fleming, L. and O. Sorenson (2004), 'Science as a map in technological search', *Strategic Management Journal*, **25** (8–9), 909–28.

Freel, M.S. (2003), 'Sectoral patterns of small firm innovation, networking and proximity', *Research Policy*, **32** (5), 751–70.

Gruber, M., I.C. MacMillan and J.D. Thompson (2008), 'Look before you leap: market opportunity identification in emerging technology firms', *Management Science*, **54** (9), 1652–65.

Hanlon, D. and C. Saunders (2007), 'Marshaling resources to form small new ventures: toward a more holistic understanding of entrepreneurial support', *Entrepreneurship Theory and Practice*, **31** (4), 619–41.

Jensen, R. and M. Thursby (2001), 'Proofs and prototypes for sale: the licensing of university inventions', *American Economic Review*, **91** (1), 240–59.

Kotabe, M. and K.S. Swan (1995), 'The role of strategic alliances in high-technology new product development', *Strategic Management Journal*, **16** (8), 621–36.

Laursen, K. and A. Salter (2004), 'Searching high and low: what types of firms use universities as a source of innovation?', *Research Policy*, **33** (8), 1201–15.

Lechner, C., M. Dowling and I. Welpe (2006), 'Firm networks and firm development: the role of the relational mix', *Journal of Business Venturing*, **21** (4), 514–40.

Li, H. and K. Atuahene-Gima (2001), 'Product innovation strategy and the performance of new technology ventures in China', *The Academy of Management Journal*, **44** (6), 1123–34.

Malerba, F. (2002), 'Sectoral systems of innovation and production', *Research Policy*, **31** (2), 247–64.

Mosey, S. and M. Wright (2007), 'From human capital to social capital: a longitudinal study of technology-based academic entrepreneurs', *Entrepreneurship Theory and Practice*, **31**, 909–35.

Pittaway, L., M. Robertson, K. Munir, D. Denyer and A. Neely (2004), 'Networking and innovation: a systematic review of the evidence', *International Journal of Management Reviews*, **5–6** (3–4), 137–68.

Rasmussen, E. and O.J. Borch (2010), 'University capabilities in facilitating entrepreneurship: a longitudinal study of spin-off ventures at mid-range universities', *Research Policy*, **39** (5), 602–12.

Rasmussen, E., S. Mosey and M. Wright (2011), 'The evolution of entrepreneurial competencies: a longitudinal study of university spin-off venture emergence', *Journal of Management Studies*, **48** (6),1314–45.

Rickne, A. (2006), 'Connectivity and performance of science-based firms', *Small Business Economics*, **26** (4), 393–407.

Rosenkopf, L. and A. Nerkar (2001), 'Beyond local search: boundary-spanning, exploration, and impact in the optical disk industry', *Strategic Management Journal*, **22** (4), 287–306.

Shane, S. (2000), 'Prior knowledge and the discovery of entrepreneurial opportunities', *Organization Science*, **11** (4), 448–69.

Shane, S. and T. Stuart (2002), 'Organizational endowments and the performance of university start-ups', *Management Science*, **48** (1), 154–70.

Tether, B.S. (2002), 'Who co-operates for innovation, and why: an empirical analysis', *Research Policy*, **31** (6), 947–67.

Vohora, A., M. Wright and A. Lockett (2004), 'Critical junctures in the development of university high-tech spinout companies', *Research Policy*, **33** (1), 147–75.

Von Hippel, E. (1988), *The Sources of Innovation*, Oxford: Oxford University Press.

Wright, M., B. Clarysse, P. Mustar and A. Lockett (eds) (2007), *Academic Entrepreneurship in Europe*, Cheltenham, UK and Northampton, MA, USA: Edward Elgar Publishing.

Yli-Renko, H., E. Autio and H.J. Sapienza (2001), 'Social capital, knowledge acquisition and knowledge exploitation in young technology-based firms', *Strategic Management Journal*, **22** (6/7), 587–613.

Zahra, S.A. and A.P. Nielsen (2002), 'Sources of capabilities, integration and technology commercialization', *Strategic Management Journal*, **23** (5), 377–98.

Zahra, S.A., E. Van de Velde and B. Larraneta (2007), 'Knowledge conversion capability and the performance of corporate and university spin-offs', *Industrial and Corporate Change*, **16** (4), 569–608.

Zimmerman, M.A. and G.J. Zeitz (2002), 'Beyond survival: achieving new venture growth by building legitimacy', *Academy of Management Review*, **27** (3), 414–31.

9. Promoting corporate entrepreneurship within a large company: an in-depth case study

Olga Belousova and Benoit Gailly

1. INTRODUCTION

For modern companies it has become an imperative to innovate and to be different in order to outsmart one another (Johnston and Bate 2003). Thus, continuous innovation and organic growth appear on the agenda of many firms, and corporate entrepreneurship (CE) receives intense attention as an activity important for firms' vitality (Dess et al. 2003). A lot of research has focused on how being entrepreneurially oriented, that is being innovative, risk-taking and ready to pioneer, may contribute to firms' financial performance and strategic value (Covin and Slevin 1989; Dess et al. 1997; Lumpkin and Dess 2001; Wiklund and Shepherd 2005). Also, from the literature we have a good understanding regarding antecedents of CE (Birkinshaw 1999; Burgers et al. 2009; Heller 1999; Hornsby et al. 2002; Kuratko et al. 1990; Marvel et al. 2007; Zahra and Covin 1995). Nevertheless, continual appeals from scholars (Dess et al. 2003; Hornsby et al. 2002; Kuratko et al. 2005; Stopford and Baden-Fuller 1994) highlight a need for more in-depth understanding of the activities of individual corporate entrepreneurs. Why? Imagine a large industrial company with a traditional product and well defined procedures: at one point in time one of its business units (BU) comes up with an entrepreneurial initiative of introducing a new production process. Just two years later the team wins several innovation contests. Another two years and the BU's management makes entrepreneurship one of its strategic priorities. How can we explain this change in the BU's strategic objectives? Hornsby et al. (2002), Dess et al. (2003) and Kuratko et al. (2005) suggest that examining and documenting specific types of entrepreneurial activities in established corporations helps highlight their meaningful contribution to organizational success. Indeed, Stopford and Baden-Fuller (1994) argue that 'the attributes of behavior normally associated with individual entrepreneurs can infect the enterprise as a whole' (p. 521). More recent works emphasize the need to do this exercise for different levels of management (Hornsby et al. 2009; Kuratko 2007; Phan et al. 2009). They demonstrate that managers of different ranks may have different roles in the CE process and that they may perceive the stimuli for CE in different ways. Hence, understanding the behavioural aspect of CE is crucial for the companies that aim to stimulate innovation and put in place new management practices designed to encourage entrepreneurial behaviours of their people.

The current research aims to contribute to the discussion regarding activities and behaviours of employees that develop entrepreneurial initiatives within established organizations. In order to do so we analyse a case study that describes a sequence of CE undertakings within one BU of a European industrial company, starting out with a local initiative of a small team of managers, and resulting in a BU-wide entrepreneurship development programme (EDP). The primary questions that guide our analysis are: 'What activities were undertaken and how did managers of different ranks contribute to the process?' and 'What was the context and how was it leveraged by the entrepreneurs?' Indeed, 'entrepreneurial behaviour does not occur in a vacuum; rather, it takes place within the context of the organization's full array of actions' (Kuratko et al. 2005: 704). Our secondary objective is to analyse these initiatives as one single process of change leading to the decision of the management to introduce CE into the strategic values of the BU. The question that drives our thought here is 'How may some CE activities trigger change in an internal entrepreneurial environment?' Our understanding of the internal entrepreneurial environment is very close to what has been described previously as a corporate (Burgelman 1983a) or organizational (Birkinshaw 1999) context, or what has been discussed in the CE literature as an internal (also intrapreneurial or entrepreneurial) environment (Hornsby et al. 1999; Hornsby et al. 2002; Kuratko et al. 1990). Thus, we see it as a set of administrative and social mechanisms, such as management support, rewards, organizational boundaries, availability of resources and work discretion that shape the behaviours of actors in the organization, and over which management may have some control. We chose the 'internal entrepreneurial environment' in order to avoid confusion with the general notion of context which we use in our analysis, and also to highlight our focus on those variables within the organizational context that are relevant for CE. Ropo and Hunt (1995) and Shepherd et al. (2010) suggested that corporate entrepreneurs may influence their internal entrepreneurial environments by involving other organizational members, whose feedback may further stimulate or inhibit new CE initiatives. Shepherd et al.

(2010) modelled this action–feedback exchange as a spiral that represents co-evolution between CE initiatives and an organization's entrepreneurial culture. They define 'entrepreneurial culture' as a 'coalescence of . . . behavioral norms and cognitions shared by organizational members' (p. 62) and position it as a concept akin to the entrepreneurial environment (p. 60) by referring to the works of Hornsby et al. (1999) and Ireland et al. (2003). This allows us to apply their conceptualization in analysing our case. Hence, then we document and discuss activities of corporate entrepreneurs of different managerial ranks as they develop CE initiatives, and then proceed with the analysis of the whole case storyline in order to identify activities that led to the change in the internal entrepreneurial environment.

The rest of the chapter is structured as follows. We first develop a theoretical background of the study. We then outline our methodology and fieldwork and discuss the findings, contributions and limitations of the study in the final section.

2.   THEORETICAL DEVELOPMENT

CE is often recognized as beneficial for organizations and therefore it is important to understand how organizations may exploit it in a better way. The 'central and essential element in the entrepreneurial process' is behaviour (Covin and Slevin 1991: 8); however, different management ranks tend to play diverse roles in it (Hornsby et al. 2009; Kuratko 2007; Phan et al. 2009). They also have been demonstrated to react differently to the stimuli provided in the organizational environment (Hornsby et al. 2009). Therefore, the current study aims to address behaviours of corporate entrepreneurs from different managerial levels. We adopt a dispersed CE perspective (Birkinshaw 1997), assuming that an initiative and responsibility might come from anywhere within an organization. The primary manifestation of the dispersed CE is initiative. Birkinshaw (1997) defines 'initiative' as entrepreneurial challenge 'bounded by the identification of an opportunity at the front end and the commitment of resources to the undertaking at the back end' (p. 207). Thus, in the first part of our study we focus on a within-initiative time frame of analysis. In the second part of the chapter we look at the current case as a single process during a period of seven years, thus providing an opportunity to study the link between activities of corporate entrepreneurs and their internal entrepreneurial environment. The following two sections proceed accordingly.

2.1 Within-initiative Analysis

Aiming to answer the questions 'what activities are needed to develop an initiative' and 'how different management levels may contribute to this process' we reviewed the literature on these two dimensions: the process dimension and the hierarchical dimension. The process of developing entrepreneurial initiatives within established organizations has been a subject of considerable attention by scholars, and a variety of views on its stages have been introduced (Burgelman 1983b; Garud and Van de Ven 1992; Hornsby et al. 1993; Kanter 2004; Russell 1999; Zaltman et al. 1973). Diverse in the number of and labels for the stages picked out, these conceptualizations can be reduced to the one of Shane and Venkataraman (2000), who describe the generic entrepreneurial process as consisting of discovery, evaluation and exploitation of entrepreneurial opportunities with addition of another important category of CE action that is linked to promoting and legitimating initiatives (Kanter 1985; Prasad 1993; Russell 1999; Sarason et al. 2006; Van de Ven 1986). Thus, *discovery* involves seeing how entrepreneurial opportunities come into existence (Shane and Venkataraman 2000); *evaluation* is focused on normative assessment of an idea and its development into a valuable project (Shane and Venkataraman 2000; Mitchell et al. 2004); *legitimation* deals with getting attention, recognition and approval from the organization members and higher management in order to mobilize people and achieve their enrolment on the project (Kanter 2004; Prasad 1993; Van de Ven 1986); *exploitation* covers different action modes directed towards bringing the innovation to the market (Shane et al. 2003). These four categories of CE action comprise the process dimension of our analysis.

The second dimension reflects the contribution of different management ranks. The literature has traditionally highlighted the role of middle-level managers in developing CE initiatives because being the intermediates between strategic perspectives of the top level and implementation issues surfacing at lower levels allows them to keep their hands on the pulse of the organization (Dutton et al. 1997; Hornsby et al. 2002; Kuratko et al. 2005). However, a successful CE initiative involves a tuned collaboration of different management ranks (Floyd and Lane 2000; Kuratko et al. 2005; Kuratko 2007). Although different studies may focus on one or two levels, a three-level structure stands out from the literature: top, middle and operating level management (Hornsby et al. 2009; Kuratko 2007; Phan et al. 2009). Following these prominent authors, we employ the three-level approach.

Thus, the framework allows us to analyse the behavioural component of CE along two dimensions: the process dimension, which outlines key categories of CE action – discovery, evaluation, legitimation and exploitation; and a hierarchical dimension, which includes operating, middle and top levels of management. Thus we deepen our understanding of the very essence of the entrepreneurial process – the nature of entrepreneurial behaviour. The next section focuses on a larger picture by looking at the sequence of events during the whole timeline described in the case.

2.2 Across-initiatives Analysis

This lens of analysis allows the link between CE initiatives and their internal environment to be studied. Several authors have focused on this topic. For example, Crossan et al. (1999) and Mom et al. (2007) suggest that organizations can learn from individual entrepreneurial initiatives and that entrepreneurial cultures of both an individual and an organization co-evolve. Indeed, a large entrepreneurial development may involve a significant number of people across different departments of the company, thus introducing a significant change to the existing practices and perceptions of the business-as-usual. Ireland et al. (2009) suggest that if pro-entrepreneurship cognitions are broadly descriptive of organizational members, this influences the strength of cultural norms favouring entrepreneurial behaviour and is reflected in organizational culture. Ropo and Hunt (1995) first suggested applying the concept of spirals to study the individual–organization co-development linked to entrepreneurship. Shepherd et al. (2010) offered the idea of entrepreneurial spirals and defined them as an 'enduring, deviation amplifying relationship between the manager's attitude towards and ability for entrepreneurship and the organizational entrepreneurial culture' (p. 60).

According to Shepherd et al. (2010), a 'deviation-amplifying relationship between variables means that an increase in variable one causes an increase in variable two, which in turn causes an increase in variable one' (p. 60). A spiral can be considered enduring when there is a pattern of three or more consecutive feedback loops from the higher management to the organizational members and from the organizational members to the higher management. There are two mechanisms that can launch an entrepreneurial spiral. One is about a change in the perception of feasibility and desirability of CE by higher management (Shapero and Sokol 1982), who can give a signal to other organizational members that more initiative is feasible and desirable. In their turn organizational members may or may not support this call. The other mechanism implies that the spiral is started by middle or lower-level organizational members. Here, a change in the external or internal environment of the organization may drive more of their autonomous behaviours (Burgelman 1983b) and it is up to the higher management whether or not to support the initiative of the employees.

Thus, the idea of entrepreneurial spirals may help us analyse the three entrepreneurial initiatives described in the case as a development of a single entrepreneurial spiral and may provide deeper understanding of this evolution. The next section presents the methodology of the empirical study and describes the case in detail.

3.   METHODOLOGY

As this research aims to address activities and behaviours of corporate entrepreneurs in established organizations, an in-depth engaged investigation is an appropriate method. Yin (1994) suggests that case studies are useful in the situations where ongoing activities need to be studied within their context, are hardly separable from this context and the parameters of this context cannot be manipulated by the researcher. As 'entrepreneurial behaviour does not occur in a vacuum' (Kuratko et al. 2005: 704), we use a case study approach to trace the process of entrepreneurial development within a real-life context (Yin 1994).

We follow a theoretical case selection approach and present the case that, in our opinion, helps highlight behavioural aspects of CE. First, the initial environment can be characterized by weak norms and shared understandings for CE that had to be established through activities of corporate entrepreneurs. Second, the traditional nature of the business complicated the task of corporate entrepreneurs, thus making their activities more visible. Third, the sequence of initiatives reported in this case developed from a local small team scale, towards a BU-wide EDP. This makes the case particularly interesting in studying the potential link between CE and its internal entrepreneurial environment.

3.1   Research Setting

The research is conducted within a BU of a European based industrial company (ChemCo) operating in more than ten different areas concentrated in three business sectors. ChemCo employs more than 25 000 employees in about 50 countries worldwide. The BU in focus (UniChem) employs more than 1000 people and functions in ten countries. The case covers the development of a sequence of entrepreneurial initiatives: a cost-cutting initiative, GreenVenture initiative and EDP initiative, which took place both in and outside Europe during the period of 2003–2011. The data collection started in the beginning of 2009. Therefore some of the materials are retrospective, whereas the new developments are being observed in real time.

3.2   Data Collection

We collected data from several sources: (1) ten semi-structured interviews with the core GreenVenture team, business development and production managers of UniChem; (2) several observations and unstructured interviews during the EDP seminar; (3) multiple secondary sources such as press communications, internal presentations, personal observations and participation in meetings.

We recorded and fully transcribed all of the interviews, which each lasted between 90 minutes and two hours. We reviewed all of the interviews and created a common storyline to identify discrepancies between the reports of the interviewees. We then assembled a chronological list of events of the development, defining them as critical incidents in major functions related to the development (Garud and Rappa 1994), and verified it against the archival data evidence.

3.3   The Case

3.3.1   Initiative 1: Cost-cutting
The case's storyline starts in 2003, when a newly appointed UniChem Business Manager (BM) took over a business that was losing money. Aiming to understand more about the current situation, he engaged in studying different market reports and eventually came to an idea that the quality of their product portfolio appeared more than sufficient for the clients, and decreasing it to a sufficient level could help generate money. He explained the 'cost-cutting idea' to his colleagues and they set up a joint cross-country and cross-function team of managers to identify a future design for the initiative. Decreasing quality was not an idea that was welcome in the company known for its strategy of excellence in all spheres. Nevertheless, the initiative allowed a significant amount of money to be saved without losing customers (it has been replicated twice since then), and justified risk-taking for the potential gains of the business.

3.3.2   Initiative 2: GreenVenture
During the next months the BM had been further familiarizing himself with the nature of the business and the market situation for its products. Reports suggested that one of the product lines would no longer remain cost efficient and should soon be closed. However, under the new market

conditions another process became viable. It had been earlier described in the literature but its industrial development had never been made before. With this rough idea in mind the BM came to the R&D and production heads of UniChem, and although the discussion was absolutely informal, the R&D manager, together with a specialist from his lab, started reviewing the literature on the topic in order to design an economical and good quality solution.

Along with the first studies and experiments, the BM with the UniChem General Manager (GM1) began recruiting people for the future needs of the project: five more people joined the team (Team1) and started exploring their areas of responsibility, sharing findings and deciding on the next steps. Six months after the launch a set of successful tests and micro-pilots has proven that the first calculations were correct. Inspired by these results the BM started communicating the idea and the potential value of GreenVenture to the higher management in order to 'feel vibration'. Team1 meanwhile worked on testing the process on a larger scale with one of the existing production sites of ChemCo. They gathered preliminary information about the potential candidates, contacted them and invited them to participate in the contest for a cheaper and better solution. The proposal on the larger pilot with the contest winner was then submitted for management approval.

Sometime earlier, in 2005, during a business visit to the non-EU branch of ChemCo, the BM started discussing a potential development of GreenVenture in their area. At that time the idea did not go through; however in June 2006 together with the Business Development Manager of the non-EU area (TL2) they decided to build a small team and study the feasibility of this project. The non-EU team (Team2) started working on the future investment details; they employed a decentralized model which involved gathering information by creating a template and asking colleagues in other countries or departments to fill it in. When the information was collected, both teams together wrote another proposal asking for approval of the non-EU development. Before submitting it, though, they informally discussed this proposal with the Board members during one of their yearly non-EU visits: again, to 'feel vibration'. Meanwhile Team1 set out for the larger pilot. This involved establishing stronger links with specialized units (for example 'construction'), combining the project work with their everyday work, and making a lot of shortcuts in organizational procedures in order to keep pace with the development. Normally the communication with the specialized units would be delegated to the members of the team responsible for a corresponding part of the project. However, in order to speed up the development the BM and the GM1 jointly pushed managers of those units to give GreenVenture a priority status. This status meant that the best people would be devoted to the venture and that the resources would be available as fast as possible. With the Board's approval, recognition and prizes at several internal and external innovation contests, obtaining a priority status went more smoothly.

However, 2006 was not only the year of big starts, but also of big changes. In March, just a couple of months before submitting the formal request to the Board of ChemCo, a new General Manager (GM2) arrived to replace his retiring colleague. In order not to delay the development he allowed the BM to have direct contact with his boss, the Sector Manager. After several challenging discussions (including the one that dealt with a sudden doubling in the venture's investment costs) the latter presented the project proposal to the Board of ChemCo. The Board approved it. An interesting detail: as the GM2 arrived, the BM asked openly if he could keep the autonomy that the GM1 had granted him. The GM2 agreed and this conversation became one of the 'legends' of UniChem.

As 2007 went on, the market changed drastically and unpredictably. Funds were frozen until the team could come up with some explanations and an updated proposal. This market change negatively influenced the image of the venture; a lot of criticism and questioning followed. The team formed a special task force to re-prove the feasibility of the process and gathered extensive expertise in the market not only regarding their current approach, but also regarding other opportunities appearing on the market, pursued or abandoned by competitors. This first crisis also revealed the susceptibility of the venture: its dependency on the market price structure. One team member from a specialized unit started developing a new pricing policy for the raw material. First he initiated an intensive brainstorming session with his line manager, then he followed with an individual development with presentations to the team and the team's approval. However, it was not sufficient to only develop a new pricing policy. In order to regain the funding at least one potential partner needed to be convinced to work on the developed scheme. The team was able to regain the funding in April 2008. As they started signing factual contracts with partners, another crisis struck: 'September 2008 – what's happening? Crisis. Disaster' (TL2). Together with other new undertakings the venture was put on hold until its strategic role could be re-approved, and the team actively engaged in providing the necessary evidence. The funding was reinstated only in December 2009. Meanwhile the project underwent multiple structural changes (extending The Governing Board and transferring the project to another site). This delay allowed the teams to work on details of the implementation and potential future projects in other countries. Two of them were launched in 2010.

3.3.3   Initiative 3: Entrepreneurship Development Programme

Encouraged by the development of the GreenVenture in difficult times and urged by the global financial crisis, during one of the leadership team meetings in late November 2008 a notion of entrepreneurship came out. The old philosophy 'we are at home here' that had been in place for several previous years was to be changed: 'We needed a new philosophy that would unite the division' (GM1). Hence, the leadership team decided to develop this idea further. They also expected CE to be a tool for overcoming the gaps in performance that became more visible due to the financial crisis. One of the managers started gathering information about this concept by looking at available knowledge and collaborating with both internal and external experts. In September 2009 a special section on CE was included as a strategic objective of UniChem. Several smaller entrepreneurial projects that had been taking place in different sub-units of UniChem were revealed. The leadership team started 'putting some drops of oil' on the interfaces with other units to help these projects develop. In May 2010 the EDP gathered together second and third-tier managers of UniChem from all over the world for a three-day seminar. During the first two days the participants were asked to form groups and think about entrepreneurship, learn from the guest talks, develop their own understanding of CE and share feedback. The last day was reserved for developing new project ideas and a presentation of a future entrepreneurship support programme by the leadership team.

4.   FINDINGS

We organize the findings of the study in two temporal horizons: within and across initiatives.

4.1   Within Initiatives

In this category we classified our observations regarding CE activities in the course of developing each of the initiatives. We describe our findings using the analytical framework derived from the literature review in the first section. However, additional to the three-level, theoretically-driven model, the evidence from this case suggested that we differentiate between the top (Board) and the senior middle-management (GM1, GM2) activities. As we describe further, these two groups have demonstrated quite different patterns of behaviour.

4.1.1 Initiative 1: Cost-cutting

The cost-cutting initiative was an episodic local undertaking that took place within one of the businesses of UniChem and was developed without intervention of the top and senior management. The initiator and the key developer here was the middle level (the BM and peers). The key role of the GM1 was in providing autonomy. At this level of the development the GM1 performed the role traditionally assigned to the top management (Floyd and Lane 2000). The discovery was of a problem-solving nature. The methods of information gathering for the evaluation were formal and impersonal (studies); however, the proposal was made in the form of a discussion as the financial situation provided a natural legitimacy for trying to find a solution to the issue. The initiative was then transferred to operating managers for implementation.

4.1.2 Initiative 2: GreenVenture

This idea was both problem and opportunity oriented: the change in the market, on one hand, endangered the old process and stimulated a search for solutions; on the other, it provided an opportunity that was not viable before. Further, the idea was a co-product of the middle and operating level management: as a vision it was spotted by the BM, as an opportunity it was created and formulated by a mixed middle–operating-level team (the R&D manager and a specialist). It was evaluated in several steps: calculations on paper, lab tests, small pilots, larger pilots. Each of the steps was accompanied by a separate gathering of information involving different teams and methods of information search, including the 'vibration checks'. The dominant methods for gathering external information were formal impersonal searches for studies and market reports. However, both supply and marketing managers mentioned in their interviews that if they had to start the process again they would go and 'talk to people' earlier. Internally the team employed a decentralized approach and vigorously exchanged findings in the work-group meetings. Regarding legitimation, in order not to attract attention to the project, the team initially tried to respect the rules and assure non-collision of interests. They only started communicating the venture to the higher management levels when their resource requirements became high. At the later stages the communication was led by joint efforts of the senior–middle-level team.

Proposition 1a: In an organizational environment, not familiar with entrepreneurship, entrepreneurs will avoid extensive communication if the deviations from norms are not significant or funds can be obtained in informal ways.

Proposition 1b: If the initiative's resource requirements are significant, entrepreneurs will communicate and promote it extensively, thus potentially contributing to development of new values and norms favouring CE.

The methods used for the legitimation were largely informal (sounding out, 'feeling vibration', regular meetings of the core team and specialized units). The language used by both operating and middle managers was symbolic and was rich in metaphors. Still, during the periods of crisis (negative external context) the team had to come up with 'harder' proofs of GreenVenture's credibility and feasibility, namely additional studies, solid forecasts, signing up potential partners, and numerous formal approval processes.

Proposition 2a: Entrepreneurs who use informal methods of legitimation of an initiative and who let ideas percolate and transform the system of beliefs are more likely to contribute to development of new values and norms favouring CE.

Proposition 2b: Formal legitimating methods are more appropriate in hostile external environments and are aimed at protecting the initiative.

At this higher scale of development GM1 and GM2 helped to reinforce the position of the middle management, while the sponsoring, challenging and redefining roles were mostly performed at the top level.

4.1.3   Initiative 3: Entrepreneurship Development Programme

The discovery of the concept of CE by the management was a reaction to the 2008 global financial crisis and can be described as problem-solving oriented. The information gathering was primarily made by working with experts in CE and personnel development. As this idea was initiated by the senior–middle-level team, it has been extensively and openly communicated. Interestingly, the legitimizing was designed as co-creation of shared understanding of CE during the world-team seminar so that the concept would be anchored in managers' minds. To date, the team has not yet implemented the programme and therefore we cannot provide a discussion on the 'exploitation' stage.

The next section leads us to the across-the-case analysis.

4.2   Across Initiatives

This lens of analysis allows the whole time span of the UniChem case to be examined. The events described in it suggest that the first initiative

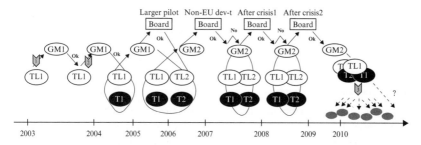

Notes: T1 – Team 1 (EU); T2 – Team 2 (non-EU); TL1 – Team Leader 1 (EU team); TL2 – Team Leader 2 (non-EU team); GM1 – General Manager 2003–2007; GM2 – General Manager 2007–2011.

Source: Adapted from Shepherd et al. (2010).

Figure 9.1   Enhancing spiral

provided legitimacy and resources for risk taking and experimentation, thus making possible the first steps of GreenVenture. Later, success, visibility and persistence of GreenVenture created expectations that CE might be an appropriate tool to bridge the performance gaps that UniChem faced. Eventually a mixed senior–middle management team designed, launched and sponsored the EDP. They explicitly communicated that more risk taking was expected from the employees, declared support and protection of higher management and devoted a certain envelope specifically for entrepreneurial developments. Thus, we can observe a certain shift in such elements of the entrepreneurial environment as managerial support, resource availability and organizational boundaries. What led to this shift? The propositions 1a, 1b, 2a and 2b have already highlighted the potential role of resource requirements, communication and the type of legitimation strategy employed by entrepreneurial teams. We now refer to the framework offered by Shepherd et al. (2010) as our key tool of analysis. Building on their approach, we schematically represent the spiral of the development in Figure 9.1.

The process presented in Figure 9.1 depicts the key participants and a schematic flow of feedback on CE initiatives between them. It has been in place for seven years and for the time being involves no less than one hundred people. The number of people involved in the project who accepted entrepreneurial values, is the proxy for the entrepreneurial culture (Ireland et al. 2009) we propose to use here. The spiral suggests that the number of people involved into CE increases non-linearly. Further, it suggests an additional detail to the spiral evolvement process: different levels of management may be involved gradually.

Proposition 3:   By attracting more entrepreneurial members, communicating entrepreneurship values and increasing desirability of being an entrepreneur, a CE initiative can contribute to development of new values and norms favouring CE.

Another aspect is the reaction of the team to some negative external events. The current case described two 'on hold' periods, each one lasting for more or less a year. These two periods we would characterize as negative feedback from the top management. Nevertheless, they were not able to stop the development: whenever the funds were frozen, the team continued to work on further details of the project. Eventually, seeing how entrepreneurial teams persisted in the face of difficult times, the GM2 has taken CE into the values and strategic objectives of UniChem.

Proposition 4:   Some negative external events may contribute to development of new values and norms favouring CE within organizations by forcing entrepreneurs to persist in order to keep the project alive.

According to Shepherd et al. (2010), negative feedback serves as a demotivator of entrepreneurial change and ultimately may cause diminishing and cancelling of an entrepreneurial spiral. However, Plowman et al. (2007) suggest that negative feedback serves a positive purpose of stabilizing the system, preventing it from entering vicious cycles generated by euphoria of initial successes. Thus it does not necessarily start a negative spiral and may serve as a signal for changing the course of action. Indeed, the case has demonstrated that, having received negative feedback, entrepreneurs resorted to more formal methods of legitimation. However, both of the 'on hold' periods occurred as reactions to the market fluctuations which, according to the BM, 'no one could foresee'. Thus, they reflect one type of potential negative feedback and lead us to our last (fourth) proposition.

5.   DISCUSSION AND CONCLUSION

Aiming to understand more about the behavioural aspect of CE, we analyse the activities and behaviours of different management levels involved in discovery, evaluation, legitimation and exploitation of entrepreneurial opportunities within a large company.

Interestingly, all three initiatives in this study came into existence as problem oriented although they were proposed by senior and middle-level managers. This suggests a departure from what the literature offers on this topic, highlighting the opportunities spotted by the middle and top-level management as rather visionary (Hornsby et al. 2009). Second, the case demonstrated a co-discovery or even co-creation of the opportunities by mixed-level teams (operating–middle in the case of GreenVenture and middle–senior in the case of the EDP). However, we are not aware of works studying in depth the process of opportunity co-discovery and co-creation within established organizations. We have further identified that the teams employed a variety of legitimating tactics. One of them was to achieve 'positive vibration' before entering into formal procedures. It was used primarily for getting the approval of the top management. In order to enrol peer and lower-level contributors in the project and to share entrepreneurial values with them another tactic was put in place. It could be characterized as co-creation and co-development through regular meetings or the EDP seminar. The last tactic – providing formal 'hard' proofs and using detailed predictions – was primarily used in negative market conditions in order to protect GreenVenture. These findings provide us with a deeper understanding regarding the diversity of potential strategies that corporate entrepreneurs may refer to. Interestingly, we observed that the senior management could perform both the role of the top management (in the first initiative) and the role of a 'reinforced' middle management (during the GreenVenture development). This suggests that it might not be sufficient simply to define managerial levels through their functions (Kuratko 2007), but that it may be necessary to investigate more thoroughly the contextual determination of the behavioural choices of employees from different hierarchical levels. Finally, we have explored the possibility to apply the entrepreneurial spiral approach to analysing entrepreneurial initiatives within UniChem.

Therefore this chapter makes a number of contributions to the existing research. First, by studying the behavioural aspect of CE, we are contributing to a better understanding of the nature of this process at different hierarchical levels of organization. Further, by studying a sequence of entrepreneurial initiatives of different scope and pace within one company, we aim to reveal a potential influence of CE activities on their internal environment. Indeed, a typical case of CE would end with the initiative and few studies look at preceding or subsequent developments within the same organization. The case discussed in this chapter shows a sequence of three initiatives where each previous one served to legitimate the next one, thus leading to an accumulated effect on its internal entrepreneurial environment by enrolling more people in developments, sharing and co-creating the projects with them. The chapter further made four propositions aimed at providing a more in-depth view on the influence that CE activities may have on the organizational environment.

Still, this study has a number of limitations. First, the case describes an entrepreneurial development within only one of the divisions of a large company. The BU has a specific profile of working with a very traditional product. Therefore, multiple case studies covering different contexts are desirable to increase the external validity of the study. A second limitation concerns the nature of the data collected. Although we tried to triangulate the information wherever possible, interpretation of the data depends heavily on the meaning assigned to it by the participants. Third, the data might suffer from the retrospectivity bias, when only successful interaction strategies are remembered and reported by the participants. However, accepting all the possible limitations of our approach, we still hope to obtain a useful insight into corporate entrepreneurial behaviours.

REFERENCES

Birkinshaw, J. (1997), 'Entrepreneurship in multinational corporations: the characteristics of subsidiary initiatives', *Strategic Management Journal*, **18** (3), 207–29.

Birkinshaw, J. (1999), 'The determinants and consequences of subsidiary initiative in multinational corporations', *Entrepreneurship Theory and Practice*, **24** (1), 9–36.

Burgelman, R.A. (1983a), 'A model of the interaction of strategic behavior, corporate context, and the concept of strategy', *Academy of Management Review*, **8** (1), 61–70.

Burgelman, R.A. (1983b), 'A process model of internal corporate venturing in the diversified major firm', *Administrative Science Quarterly*, **28** (2), 223–44.

Burgers, J.H., J.J.P. Jansen, F.A.J. Van den Bosch and H.W. Volberda (2009), 'Structural differentiation and corporate venturing: the moderating role of formal and informal integration mechanisms', *Journal of Business Venturing*, **24** (3), 206–20.

Covin, J.G. and D.P. Slevin (1989), 'Strategic management of small firms in hostile and benign environments', *Strategic Management Journal*, **10** (1), 75–87.

Covin, J.G. and D.P. Slevin (1991), 'A conceptual model of entrepreneurship as firm behavior', *Entrepreneurship Theory and Practice*, **16** (1), 7–25.

Crossan, M.M., H.W. Lane and R.E. White (1999), 'An organizational learning framework: from intuition to institution', *Academy of Management Review*, **24** (3), 522–37.

Dess, G.G., G.T. Lumpkin and J.G. Covin (1997), 'Entrepreneurial strategy making and firm performance: tests of contingency and configurational models', *Strategic Management Journal*, **18** (9), 677–95.

Dess, G.G., R.D. Ireland, S.A. Zahra, S.W. Floyd, J.J. Janney and P.J. Lane (2003), 'Emerging issues in corporate entrepreneurship', *Journal of Management*, **29** (3), 351–78.

Dutton, J.E., S.J. Ashford, R.M. O'Neill, E. Hayes and E.E. Wierba (1997), 'Reading the wind: how middle managers assess the context for selling issues to top managers', *Strategic Management Journal*, **18** (5), 407–23.

Floyd, St.W. and P.J. Lane (2000), 'Strategizing throughout the organization: managing role conflict in strategic renewal', *Academy of Management Review*, **25** (1), 154–77.

Garud, R. and M. Rappa (1994), 'A socio-cognitive model of technology evolution', *Organization Science*, **5** (3), 344–62.

Garud, R. and A. Van de Ven (1992), 'An empirical evaluation of the internal corporate venturing process', *Strategic Management Journal*, **13** (1), 93–109.

Heller, T. (1999), 'Loosely coupled systems for corporate entrepreneurship: imagining and managing the innovation project/host organization interface', *Entrepreneurship Theory and Practice*, **24** (2), 27–33.

Hornsby, J.S., D.F. Kuratko and R.V. Montagno (1999), 'Perception of internal factors for corporate entrepreneurship: a comparison of Canadian and US managers', *Entrepreneurship Theory and Practice*, **24** (2), 11–26.

Hornsby, J.S., D.F. Kuratko and S.A. Zahra (2002), 'Middle managers' perception of the internal environment for corporate entrepreneurship: assessing a measurement scale', *Journal of Business Venturing*, **17** (3), 253–73.

Hornsby, J.S., D.F. Kuratko, D.A. Shepherd and J.P. Bott (2009), 'Managers' corporate entrepreneurial actions: examining perception and position', *Journal of Business Venturing*, **24** (3), 236–47.

Hornsby, J.S., D.W. Naffziger, D.F. Kuratko and R.V. Montagno (1993), 'An interactive model of the corporate entrepreneurship process', *Entrepreneurship Theory and Practice*, **17** (2), 29–37.

Ireland, R.D., J.G. Covin and D.F. Kuratko (2009), 'Conceptualizing corporate entrepreneurship strategy', *Entrepreneurship Theory and Practice*, **33** (1), 19–46.

Ireland, R.D., M.A. Hitt and D.G. Sirmon (2003), 'A model of strategic entrepreneurship: the construct and its dimensions', *Journal of Management*, **29** (6), 963–89.

Johnston, R.E., Jr and J.D. Bate (2003), *The Power of Strategy Innovation: A New Way of Linking Creativity and Strategic Planning to Discover Great Business Opportunities*, New York: AMACOM.

Kanter, R.M. (1985), 'Supporting innovation and venture development in established companies', *Journal of Business Venturing*, **1** (1), 47–60.

Kanter, R.M. (2004), 'The middle manager as innovator', *Harvard Business Review*, **82** (7/8), 150–61.

Kuratko, D.F. (2007), 'Corporate entrepreneurship', *Foundations and Trends in Entrepreneurship*, **3** (2), 151–03.

Kuratko, D.F., R.V. Montagno and J.S. Hornsby (1990), 'Developing an intrapreneurial assessment instrument for an effective corporate entrepreneurial environment', *Strategic Management Journal*, **11** (Special Issue: Corporate Entrepreneurship), 49–58.

Kuratko, D.F., R.D. Ireland, J.G. Covin and J.S. Hornsby (2005), 'A model of middle-level managers' entrepreneurial behavior', *Entrepreneurship Theory and Practice*, **29** (6), 699–716.

Lumpkin, G.T. and G.G. Dess (2001), 'Linking two dimensions of entrepreneurial orientation to firm performance: the moderating role of environment and industry life cycle', *Journal of Business Venturing*, **16** (5), 429–51.

Marvel, M.R., A. Griffin, J. Hebda and B. Vojak (2007), 'Examining the technical corporate entrepreneurs' motivation: voices from the field', *Entrepreneurship Theory and Practice*, **31** (5), 753–68.

Mitchell, R.K., L. Busenitz, T. Lant, P.P. McDougall, E.A. Morse and J. Brock

Smith (2004), 'The distinctive and inclusive domain of entrepreneurial cognition research', *Entrepreneurship Theory and Practice*, **29** (2), 505–18.

Mom, T.J.M., F.A.J. van den Bosch and H.W. Volberda (2007), 'Investigating managers' exploration and exploitation activities: the influence of top-down, bottom-up, and horizontal knowledge inflows', *Journal of Management Studies*, **44** (6), 910–31.

Phan, P.H., M. Wright, D. Ucbasaran and W.-L. Tan (2009), 'Corporate entrepreneurship: current research and future directions', *Journal of Business Venturing*, **24** (3), 197–205.

Plowman, D.A., L.T. Baker, T.E. Beck, M. Kulkarni, S. Thomas Solansky and D. Villarreal Travis (2007), 'Radical change accidentally: the emergence and amplification of small change', *Academy of Management Journal*, **50** (3), 515–43.

Prasad, L. (1993), 'The etiology of organizational politics: implications for the intrapreneur', *SAM Advanced Management Journal*, **58** (3), 35–41.

Ropo, A. and J.G. Hunt (1995), 'Entrepreneurial processes as virtuous and vicious spirals in a changing opportunity structure: a paradoxical perspective', *Entrepreneurship Theory and Practice*, **19** (3), 91–111.

Russell, R.D. (1999), 'Developing a process model of intrapreneurial systems: a cognitive mapping approach', *Entrepreneurship Theory and Practice*, **23** (3), 65–84.

Sarason, Y., T. Dean and J.F. Dillard (2006), 'Entrepreneurship as the nexus of individual and opportunity: a structuration view', *Journal of Business Venturing*, **21** (3), 286–305.

Shane, S. and S. Venkataraman (2000), 'The promise of entrepreneurship as a field of research', *Academy of Management Review*, **25** (1), 217–28.

Shane, S., E.A. Locke and C.J. Collins (2003), 'Entrepreneurial motivation', *Human Resource Management Review*, **13** (2), 257–79.

Shapero, A. and L. Sokol (1982), 'The social dimensions of entrepreneurship', in C.A. Kent et al. (eds), *Encyclopedia of Entrepreneurship*, Englewood Cliffs, NJ: Prentice-Hall, pp. 72–90.

Shepherd, D.A., H. Patzelt and J.M. Haynie (2010), 'Entrepreneurial spirals: deviation-amplifying loops of an entrepreneurial mindset and organizational culture', *Entrepreneurship Theory and Practice*, **34** (1), 59–82.

Stopford, J.M. and C.W.F. Baden-Fuller (1994), 'Creating corporate entrepreneurship', *Strategic Management Journal*, **15** (1), 521–36.

Van de Ven, A.H. (1986), 'Central problems in the management of innovation', *Management Science*, **32** (5), 590–607.

Wiklund, J. and D. Shepherd (2005), 'Entrepreneurial orientation and small business performance: a configurational approach', *Journal of Business Venturing*, **20**, 71–91.

Yin, R.K. (1994), *Case Study Research: Design and Methods*, Beverly Hills, CA: Sage Publications.

Zahra, S.A. and J.G. Covin (1995), 'Contextual influences on the corporate entrepreneurship–performance relationship: a longitudinal analysis', *Journal of Business Venturing*, **10** (1), 43–58.

Zaltman, J., R. Duncan and J. Holbek (1973), *Innovations and Organizations*, New York: John Wiley and Sons.

10. The state of the art of knowledge research in entrepreneurship: a ten-year literature review

Alejandro Campos and Esther Hormiga

1. INTRODUCTION

This chapter presents an in-depth analysis of the different perspectives in which knowledge in the field of entrepreneurship has been studied and addressed during the last ten years – 2000 to 2010 – along with some conclusions and future research topics. Our aim is that this extensive literature review should serve as a reference point for researchers by establishing the state of the art of knowledge in the field of entrepreneurship.

Many researchers view companies as sets of resources systematically exploited and interrelated for producing and trading goods or services. For more than two decades now scholars have explored phenomena concerning companies and organizations, basing their research on an analysis of resources (Barney 2001; Conner and Prahalad 1996; Grant 1991; Wernerfelt 1984). After recognizing and categorizing company resources, researchers identified knowledge as one of the most important within a firm (Grant 1996; Wright et al. 2007). Its importance is so great that it has led to the development of new theories – derived from a resource-based viewpoint – specializing in studying knowledge management as a particular resource: knowledge-based theory (Grant 1996; Nickerson and Zenger 2004) and knowledge-management theory (Nonaka 1991; Nonaka and Takeuchi 1995; Thompson and Walsham 2004).

The case of entrepreneurship is no different. Entrepreneurship is a phenomenon that has received special attention from scholars worldwide over the last few decades. Of all the wide variety of resources and capabilities that give birth to a company, knowledge is undoubtedly one of the most explored assets in academic literature. In recent years knowledge has been closely related to the study of business creation in several ways and there are as many academic papers on this issue as topics relating to human beings and entrepreneurship.

Academic literature in the field of entrepreneurship presents different paths for analysing knowledge as an object of study or the knowledge management process. Some authors refer to a certain stock of knowledge, mostly represented by indicators such as education, experience, skills, training and a number of other terms that imply an accumulation of knowledge (Bosma et al. 2004; Dimov and Shepherd 2005; Kim et al. 2006; Rauch et al. 2005; Van Gelderen et al. 2005b; Williams 2004). Other authors refer to knowledge management in terms of the process whereby it is created or, to be more specific, in terms of the situations in which it is generated (Atherton and Price 2008; Cope 2005; Corbett 2007; Lee and Jones 2008; Minniti and Bygrave 2001; Schildt et al. 2005), while another group of researchers has analysed the dynamism of knowledge in the form of information-flows (Corbett 2007; George et al. 2002; Parker 2006; Totterman and Sten 2005; Westhead et al. 2005b; 2009).

Apart from the distinctions mentioned above, different forms or expressions of knowledge in entrepreneurship have been addressed by authors using several different theoretical perspectives. Theories naturally associated with different fields of study have been used to frame research about knowledge in entrepreneurship, specifically theories coming from neighbouring fields of study: psychology, sociology, economics, management and approaches to entrepreneurship.

Topics related to knowledge in entrepreneurship have been studied at different ontological levels too: entrepreneur knowledge at the individual level (Arthurs and Busenitz 2006; Dimov and Shepherd 2005; Parker 2006); entrepreneur knowledge at group level (Friar and Meyer 2003; Watson et al. 2003; West 2007); knowledge within the organization, i.e. organization level (Collinson 2000; Corbett et al. 2007; Deeds et al. 2000; Van Geenhuizen 2008); and the inter-organization level referring to knowledge flowing and being constructed among groups of organizations (Biggeiro 2006; O'Gorman and Kautonen 2004; Schildt et al. 2005).

As mentioned earlier, the great disparity among ways of addressing the topic of knowledge in the field of entrepreneurship is evident. For this reason a process needs to be started to standardize the definitions of certain concepts in order to thoroughly understand the important role of knowledge in entrepreneurship. To do this it is essential to have a clear idea of what has been done so far in terms of this subject. We have to know the state of the art of knowledge in entrepreneurship.

For the purposes of this chapter we propose a definition of entrepreneur knowledge as the set of understandings constructed by individuals – entrepreneurs – as a result of the combination of three main aspects. First, all the cognitive connections among the data obtained from educational activities that become a meaningful understanding stored by the subject. Second, the information gathered through different means and/or networks that become somehow useful and important to the individual, and third, all those meaningful experiences acquired through the performance of specific activities and shared amongst peers when interacting and evolving in a social context.

2. METHODOLOGY

The literature review carried out to produce this article covers the six major academic journals in the field of entrepreneurship in terms of impact. The journals analysed and their impact factors according to the Journal Citation Report (Thomson Reuters) (2010) are: *Journal of Business Venturing* (IF: 2.149), *Entrepreneurship Theory and Practice* (IF: 2.272), *International Small Business Journal* (IF: 0.927), *Small Business Economics* (IF: 1.555), *Journal of Small Business Management* (IF: 1.189) and *Entrepreneurship and Regional Development* (IF: 1.353). The articles included in this review were published in these academic journals between 2000 and 2010. Every academic paper or article explored in the review analyses the subject of knowledge in any form that may be described or addressed from any different theoretical framework, with any different purpose and at any different ontological level. A total of 143 academic articles have been retrieved from these journals. Each article was reviewed according to the parameters included in a self-developed database, searching for specific characteristics: author, year of publication, title, journal, main subject, methodology, type of work, academic theories used to support the study, indicators, sample used for analysis, size of company, ontological level of learning and main conclusions as a dependent or independent variable.

The data collected are organized and filtered in order to recognize first the role knowledge plays as an object of study (stock of knowledge, knowledge acquisition through learning, knowledge transference, and so on), then those articles that address knowledge at each of the four ontological levels (individual, group, organization and inter-organization), and then each group of articles is analysed in terms of the academic theory on which the article is based. Conclusions, limitations and future research topics are presented in the final section.

3. KNOWLEDGE IN ENTREPRENEURSHIP AS AN OBJECT OF STUDY

In this section we perform an epistemological analysis of knowledge to review the way in which researchers address it to explore either its construction process or its impact on other variables. Epistemology offers a philosophical orientation to explain the way knowledge is defined, constructed, owned, shared, disseminated and recognized. We find through our analysis that knowledge has been studied in several different ways and the thoroughness of the analysis depends on the indicators used by researchers to measure it or its effect on some other variable.

In the following sections we will look at the most common ways in which knowledge has been addressed as well as the indicators used in the entrepreneurship literature over the last decade. Most of the articles do not refer to knowledge as such; instead they just use certain indicators to make analyses. In order to have a clearer perspective on the epistemology of knowledge, we will classify the articles according to the knowledge indicator categories proposed by Smith et al. (2009): stock of knowledge, knowledge creation and knowledge transfer.

3.1   Stock of Knowledge

The stock of knowledge is defined by Grossman and Helpman (1990) as the general state of scientific, engineering and industrial know-how of the employees in a company. Stocks of knowledge are the accumulated knowledge assets which are internal to the firm and are enriched with the acquisition and assimilation of more knowledge (De Carolis and Deeds 1999). For the purposes of this chapter, the stock of knowledge refers to the amount of experience, education, skills and previous knowledge that an entrepreneur possesses. It is the accumulated knowledge gained over the years that is available in the entrepreneur's memory (Smith et al. 2009).

3.1.1   Education and experience

One of the most common ways in which knowledge has been measured or represented is in terms of the number of years a person has been educated, their maximum level of education and/or the number of years they have spent performing a particular activity. Indeed, the word 'knowledge' has often been substituted by education and/or experience when researchers have examined it as a demographic variable (Ferrante 2005; Hindle and Cutting 2002; Johnson 2000; Mueller 2006; Nziramasanga and Lee 2001; Peña 2004; Seawright et al. 2008; Thomas 2009; Thompson et al. 2010; Van Praag 2003; Vinogradov and Kolvereid 2007). In all these and a number of other studies, education and experience were addressed as independent variables.

Education and experience are the most common indicators linked to knowledge in terms of human capital in the entrepreneurship literature during the last decade. These indicators have been used to measure the impact of human capital on variables such as performance (Bosma et al. 2004; Williams 2004); economic growth (Peña 2004); employment growth (Rauch et al. 2005); and the success of firms either in terms of survival (Dimov and Shepherd 2005; Van Gelderen et al. 2005a); patenting (Allen et al. 2007); funding (Zarutskie 2010); or profitability (Honig 2001a; Watson et al. 2003). Since both education and experience are indicators regularly considered to be personal characteristics, it is not uncommon to find that the inclusion of these components in the measurement of any dependent variable in all cases involves studies of the impact of knowledge at the individual level. Findings in most of the articles show that the formula *Education+Experience* has proved to have a positive impact on performance and stability variables in new ventures (Astebro and Bernhardt 2005; Peña 2004;Watson et al. 2003). However, one of the most revealing and consistent findings in the literature is that on some occasions education and experience were measured separately as demographic variables, and education showed contradictory results, with poor or null significant impact levels for dependent variables such as self-employment, entrepreneurship activity, performance and survival (De Clerq and Arenius 2006; Kim et al. 2006; Mueller 2006; Nziramasanga and Lee 2001).

Researchers have also used experience by itself, not as a demographic variable addressing the expertise acquired by entrepreneurs or firms, but as regards a specific subject, market, strategy or situation. Like studies using experience as a demographic variable, these studies tend to use it as an independent variable when measuring the variables mentioned above. Bosma et al. (2004) conclude that not all types of experience and education have the same influence on the performance of new ventures. In this respect they studied experience at different levels of business ownership, experience in the industry, experience as an employee and level of education.

Apart from the formula *education+experience*, when researchers have referred to experience as the only component of knowledge and measured its impact on different variables, they have done it mostly at the individual level. According to the results of most of the papers analysed in this review, we find that experience seems to have a greater impact than education on the firm's performance.

3.1.2   Skills or abilities as knowledge indicators

Another way in which researchers have addressed knowledge is by including indicators that refer to the possession or acquisition of specialized knowledge in their studies. Among these indicators we find all kinds of skills, abilities, training, and so on with the common characteristic that they are provided or acquired for a specific purpose, depending on the sector or need that the entrepreneur faces at a particular moment. The mix of indicators results in knowledge and specific competences generated through the implementation of effective knowledge management practices in new ventures. According to Palacios et al. (2009), introducing a knowledge management programme into the organization has an effect on the generation of innovation distinctive competences. The abilities that knowledge management helps to develop are skills in investment and knowledge flow management, the acquisition of internal knowledge, the transfer, dissemination and internal application of accumulated knowledge, and an increase in the variety of organizational memory.

Based on a longitudinal study conducted in Germany by Rauch et al. (2005), we can state that the human capital of business owners has effects on employment growth and that developing human resources has a positive impact on success; developing and exploiting human resources includes training/development of employees, decision-making involvement, goal communication and support for personal initiative. As mentioned by Rauch et al. (2005), the fact that many business start-ups have only a few employees does not mean that personnel practices can be ignored. Human resources are essentially important and an optimal utilization of skills and knowledge increases small business growth. The probability of success in business can be improved by increasing human capital in a firm and by developing and utilizing human resources.

In this respect we have come across knowledge indicators such as skills (Almor and Lerner 2002; Beerepoot 2008; Koellinger 2008; Koellinger and Minniti 2006; Ladzani and Van Vuuren 2002; Williams and Chaston 2004) and specific knowledge (Acs et al. 2009; Gilbert et al. 2008; Gorman et al. 2005; Kelley and Rice 2002; Junkunc 2007; Mosey and Wright 2007; Politis 2005; Ravasi and Turati 2005; Sapienza et al. 2004; Shepherd and Zacharakis 2003; Sternberg 2004). These kinds of knowledge indicators present a constant positive effect on any measured dependent variable. We can assume, then, that knowledge specifically oriented toward the proper subject or activity will help to improve a firm's performance (Henry et al. 2004; Gilbert et al. 2008; Ladzani and Van Vuuren 2002).

3.2   Knowledge Creation: Learning as a Knowledge Acquisition Process

As stated in the previous sections, knowledge in the field of entrepreneurship is a phenomenon that has been explored in a number of different ways. Researchers over the last decade have used different terms and words referring to the intangible asset of knowledge. Knowledge has been also referred to as the result of a learning process, for individuals, (Cope 2005; Minniti and Bygrave 2001), and as the creation stage of a knowledge management process, for organizations, (Nonaka and Takeuchi 1995). Many authors have explored the way it was acquired (Atherton and Price 2008; Corbett et al. 2007; Cope 2005; Lee and Jones 2008; Minniti and Bygrave 2001; Schildt et al. 2005) or have referred to learning activities as an independent variable affecting others.

When knowledge has been considered the result of a number of learning processes and the analysis includes a review of the factors involved in these processes, different approaches to how knowledge is constructed are raised. There are differences in the way researchers conceive or explain knowledge in terms of the elements it comprises, and the lack of a standardized theory for entrepreneurial learning is evident (Cope 2005; Minniti and Bygrave 2001).

As mentioned before, the learning process has also been taken into account when explaining some of the other variables in entrepreneurial firms. Learning is conceived by Chandler and Lyon (2009) as a process involving education, experience and search-and-notice activities. In this sense, the correlation between education and the two separate variables is significant. However, when the three are included in the model measuring a firm's performance, education becomes insignificant (Chandler and Lyon 2009). This supports the statements in the previous section about experience having a higher impact than education on different aspects of entrepreneurship phenomena.

Knowledge acquired through learning refers not only to individuals but to groups, organizations or even groups of organizations. Organizational learning refers to the practices implemented by organizations to create new knowledge by conducting a proper management of the knowledge possessed by the individuals within the organization and making this knowledge available to others (Nonaka 1991). Learning may apply and affect the same variables of entrepreneurs or companies. A study conducted by Lumpkin and Lichtenstein (2005) reveals that the more organizational learning practices enacted by entrepreneurs, the higher the likelihood that new opportunities will be recognized, and the more organizational learning practices enacted by entrepreneurial firms, the higher the likelihood that new opportunities will be recognized.

The types of learning activities developed by entrepreneurs or organizations and the impacts these styles may have on ventures have also been analysed. In 2008 Dutta and Thornhill described how the cognitive style of a member of the managerial team may affect other members' ways of learning and have certain effects on how firms develop or implement growth intentions. Style of learning was examined by Pittaway and Cope (2007) searching for policy implications. Acceptance and perception from managers of e-learning practices in the firm is explained in the work carried out by Admiraal and Lockhorst in 2009. When authors address learning as a process of knowledge acquisition, studies have been performed at different ontological levels and not only at the individual level.

3.3   Knowledge Transfer: Information Flows and Agglomeration

Knowledge transfer is an aspect of the knowledge management process that has been gaining in importance as the knowledge economy makes organizations search for knowledge as an intangible asset and a source of competitive advantage. At any ontological level, knowledge management, and particularly knowledge transfer, is one of the easiest and possibly richest methods of new knowledge acquisition. Knowledge – in the form of information – permanently flows within certain spaces, and many articles in this review address the topic by analysing different situations related to the knowledge management process and specifically to the transference of knowledge and information.

Information available to entrepreneurs or companies is another knowledge indicator used to study the impact of knowledge on various entrepreneurial phenomena. This information is acquired by entrepreneurs or companies from different sources and is used to seek higher levels of performance or even to recognize and exploit business opportunities. In this respect knowledge was also measured during the last decade as both an independent and a dependent variable. Researchers highlight the importance of information as a crucial component of a firm's success or survival. Biggeiro (2006) states that the geographical location of a firm is a fundamental factor for its development. When a firm is well located it is possible to acquire knowledge from analysing the goods and services surrounding it, and the more intensive the information exchange that occurs in a specific location, the more knowledge the new firm will be able to generate. Information, according to Parker (2006), is a kind of knowledge that allows entrepreneurs to make decisions and create certain expectations. Even when this study shows that entrepreneurs consider previous experience more important, information is also exploited by them to form expectations and scenarios for a business. New information is also a kind of knowledge that is more important for young entrepreneurs than for older ones (Parker 2006).

In the literature there are well-identified environments where information flow represents an accumulation of knowledge that is completely exploitable and truly useful for new ventures. Among these environments, higher education institutions figure as the most popular, along with information access providers generating spaces like research centres, technology transfer offices, business incubators or small business development centres. A study by George et al. (2002) reported that companies with university links had significantly more technology alliances than companies with no links. Firms with university links will have significantly more new products under development, significantly more patents, and spend less (per employee) on R&D than firms without these links.

Some business owners are confident that belonging to the incubator network has enabled them to receive critical information much earlier than external individuals would be able to receive it. They recognize the benefits of participating in the incubator community because they are able to share information, experiences and knowledge concerning specific problems and interests. The main reason for being a part of an incubator is to build successful enterprises and information relationships with other business owners in the community. These in turn are needed in order to access a wider network of information (Totterman and Sten 2005). The information flow in incubators tends to be dynamic simply because of the nature of the incubating environment. However, when incubator managers are able to involve business owners in specific information-sharing practices, it makes the knowledge flow continuously and permanently available (Fang et al. 2010). Other recognized environments where information can flow dynamically are clusters. Here information is constantly transferred from one firm to another, giving the members the chance to connect with new trends, technology, processes and experiences that represent a set of exploitable knowledge (Hervas-Oliver and Albors-Garrigos 2007; 2008).

One of the most traditional theories on entrepreneurship states that information is an important component of knowledge and the natural way of obtaining it is through the networks the entrepreneur joins, forms or participates in (Collinson 2000; Kristiansen et al. 2005; Lorentzen 2008; Waxell and Malmberg 2007). Other approaches consider that knowledge is embedded in a region's economic activity and just needs to be spread in the form of information and adjusted to the needs of new ventures (Braunerhjelm et al. 2010; O'Gorman and Kautonen 2004; Van Geenhuizen 2008).

Within companies, the way information is stored and kept has a direct effect on the level of knowledge diffusion and the amount of knowledge shared among company members (Tsang 2002). At the individual level, information is a factor that affects the identification of opportunities, and the exploitation of available information drives the intensity of business creation among different types of entrepreneur: novice, serial and portfolio entrepreneurs (Westhead et al. 2005b; 2009).

4.   ONTOLOGICAL LEVELS OF KNOWLEDGE ANALYSIS IN ENTREPRENEURSHIP

In order to know what has been covered on the subject of knowledge in the field of entrepreneurship, it is important to recognize the ontological dimension of the work carried out. Ontology refers to the philosophical study of beings, the basic categories of beings and the existence of specific entities within a phenomenon. In this sense, ontological levels of knowledge in entrepreneurship will state the categorization of the entities that create or exploit knowledge during entrepreneurship phenomena. Ontology offers a philosophical orientation to clarify who is/ are generating, sharing or exploiting knowledge in the entrepreneurial process. In this sense we will focus on the four main ontological levels recognized during this literature review: individual, group, organization and inter-organization.

4.1   Individual Level

Most researchers over the last decade focused their studies of knowledge on entrepreneurship at the individual level. A total of 79 articles out of the 143 covered by this chapter – 55 per cent – were identified as analysing knowledge as a result of an entrepreneur's individual process or as an individual intangible asset affecting other variables. We highlight the importance of the individual level in particular because at this level the analysis focuses on the processes whereby the entrepreneur constructs, exploits or applies knowledge in new business.

In entrepreneurship, unlike in other fields of study, individual knowledge plays a fundamental role due to the extremely close relationship between the company and the individual founder during the first years of business. The importance of knowledge in the field of entrepreneurship is also higher because in most cases entrepreneurial activity is conducted by individuals. Access to financing and certain other benefits is very closely related to the reputation and prestige of the business founder, often measured in terms of the knowledge they possess (Arthurs and Busenitz 2006; Dimov and Shepherd 2005; Parker 2006).

The other knowledge levels – group, organization and inter-organization – are very closely related to the individual level. Big firms and consolidated organizations support creative individuals, providing them with the proper conditions to stimulate the creation of new knowledge (Nonaka 1991).

4.2 Group Level

We understand the group ontological level of knowledge in entrepreneurship as the knowledge created, possessed or exploited by a number of individuals that collectively perform a given action. Group-level learning, according to Moreno-Luzón and Lloria (2008), comes from a phenomenon whereby information received from outside the group and information shared within the group is passed through a learning process resulting in new group understandings.

At this level, knowledge has not been explored thoroughly enough. Few articles were identified by this review using knowledge or knowledge indicators to measure different dependent variables and basing their studies on different theoretical perspectives. Friar and Meyer (2003) used knowledge indicators such as the experience and education of all the group members to measure expected company growth, and highlighted the importance of the variety of team member skills. Their findings showed that if there were few differences in skills, the result would be slower business growth.

In 2006, Lester et al. measured the valuation by investors of a business opportunity in terms of the capabilities of the entrepreneur group. The work is based on organizational theory and its findings show that the prestige of the team in terms of educational background, experience and specialized knowledge provides investors with a certain amount of trust for investment decision-making.

West (2007) defined entrepreneurial team collective cognition as a critical but poorly understood link between individual cognition and team decisions leading to new venture survival and growth. The researcher concludes that new venture strategy can be viewed as a function of the composition of the top management team, and that changes in new venture strategy may also result from changes in the team composition.

4.3 Organization Level

A considerable number of researchers have examined either the way in which learning takes place in organizations or the role that an organization's knowledge plays in performance, growth, survival and other variables (Table 10.1). As for the individual level, many theories coming from different fields of study have served as a framework for analysing learning or knowledge at organization level. However, it is usual to find that theories from the field of management are clearly dominant at this level.

There are differences in the way organizational knowledge has been conceived over the last decade. Organizational learning has been addressed by a number of authors and some of them have explained the way in which knowledge is constructed. Harrison and Leitch (2005) state that an organization's learning is experiential and that this process has a permanent effect on the way the organization behaves. According to these authors, an organization's learning is basically individual learning taking place in a social context, and this learning is organized by existing standard operating procedures, practices and other organizational rules and routines.

Lorentzen (2008) measures organizational learning as a function of regional innovation. In this article, innovative regions are spatial sources of knowledge and this knowledge must be accessed by the organization through its networks. Tolstoy (2009) explains the construction of organizational knowledge as a process of combination of diverse knowledge accessed from its different networks and prior business relationships.

4.4   Inter-organization Level

The inter-organization level of analysis of knowledge is a relatively new topic in the field of entrepreneurship. The first article in our sample to address the existence of collective learning within a group of organizations producing a knowledge agglomeration appeared in 2004.

O'Gorman and Kautonen (2004) explain that for a knowledge-intensive agglomeration to occur in a locality there must be the necessary knowledge base, local market opportunities and access to the resources necessary for using new knowledge to exploit local market opportunities. Additionally, there must be both a continuous flow of knowledge and entrepreneurial activity. Schildt et al. (2005) state that factors such as collaboration activities with companies that operate in industries that are customers of the focal company, the similarity of the partner's technological base, the similarity of the companies' technological competences, and the relatedness of the type of learning outcomes are fundamental to the process of inter-organization learning.

From 2006 the topic of inter-organizational learning started to become more popular among researchers, and factors such as the importance of strategies such as company relocation were analysed (Biggeiro 2006). The study of knowledge creation and flow within clusters became a major topic in the entrepreneurship field. Many different studies addressed these phenomena and interesting findings were presented during the second half of the decade (Hervas-Oliver and Albors-Garrigos 2008; Parrilli and Sachetti 2008; Waxell and Malmberg 2007).

Other authors have also explored inter-organization learning within clusters (Beerepoot 2008; Gilbert et al. 2008), but inter-organization learning is not a phenomenon exclusive to clusters: it can also come about naturally in certain other environments.

Some authors have recently explored inter-organization learning in spaces such as university incubators (Fang et al. 2010) and geographical regions and counties (Atherton and Price 2008; Audretsch et al. 2008). At this level of knowledge analysis, most of the articles measure inter-organization knowledge as a dependent variable.

Most of the articles have referred to knowledge or indicators related to knowledge as independent variables to explain other factors of entrepreneurial phenomena. In this sense, and responding to the great variety of perspectives and ways of addressing knowledge identified during this review, we consider it important to analyse in greater depth all those academic theories that have framed the studies referring to knowledge in entrepreneurship in the last decade.

5. ANALYSIS OF THEORIES DURING THE LAST DECADE

Knowledge in entrepreneurship has been addressed by authors from different theoretical perspectives. This diversity includes theories and approaches originating in different fields of study and involves the depth of the study of knowledge, the objectives they pursue or the intensity of its relatedness to entrepreneurship. In order to have a clear idea of what theories have been used to frame recent studies of knowledge in entrepreneurship, we classified the theoretical framework found during the literature review according to the field of study the theories came from or that they naturally belong to: psychology, sociology, economics, management or entrepreneurship.

5.1 Psychological Theories

In order to contextualize the analysis of psychological theories we have to understand that the learning and construction of knowledge are considered natural areas of study belonging to the field of psychology. It is therefore logical that we find many articles studying knowledge in entrepreneurship at the individual level using psychological theories or approaches adapted from the field of psychology.

During the 1970s and 1980s psychological approaches to entrepreneurship were some of the most commonly used theoretical frameworks in the field of entrepreneurship (Hormiga et al. 2006: 44). Psychological approaches have been used to analyse both the personal characteristics and the cognitive processes of entrepreneurs. The human capacity to process new information, the tendency to minimize cognitive efforts and mental efforts and various other human cognitive behaviours are closely related to entrepreneurial activity (Baron 1998). In this respect the cognitive approach has been used by researchers over the last ten years to support theoretical and empirical analyses of knowledge or, at least, to introduce an indicator of knowledge into the field of new business creation.

Several studies have aimed to measure the influence of knowledge on other variables in the new venture under the umbrella of cognitive theories (De Carolis and Saparito 2006; Foo 2010; Simon et al. 2000; Shepherd and Zacharakis 2003; Van Gelderen et al. 2005a; Westhead et al. 2009; Zacharakis and Shepherd 2001, amongst others).

Knowledge theory is explored by some authors in order to explain the importance and effects of specific knowledge on company performance, internal decision-making or even on the pure decision to start up (De Clercq and Arenius 2006; Williams and Chaston 2004). Learning theories were also addressed to explaining the effects of individual knowledge on entrepreneurial phenomena (Admiraal and Lockhorst 2009; Corbett 2005; 2007; Dutta and Crossan 2005). Knowledge and learning-based theories are the most common ones supporting the analysis of knowledge at organization level.

Education theory served as a theoretical framework for articles measuring the impact of education as a demographic indicator on dependent variables related to the entrepreneurial phenomenon (Hindle and Cutting 2002; Pittaway and Cope 2007; Thompson et al. 2010).

Souitaris et al. (2007) and De Tienne and Cardon (2010) presented innovative theoretical approaches to explain the entrepreneur's decision-making process based on psychological theories. The theory of planned behaviour and threshold theory presented respectively by the above authors explore dependent variables such as the intention to start up a business and strategies to exit the market, taking into account traditional knowledge indicators like education and experience.

Finally, the theory of constructivism was the framework used by Krueger (2007) to explain the process of the entrepreneur's knowledge construction based on indicators like information, prior knowledge and experience.

5.2 Sociological Theories

We found few studies based on theories from the field of sociology. However, these theories help researchers explain important phenomena in entrepreneurship. Middleman minority theory, for example, was used by Chaganti and Greene (2002) to analyse the social context of the entrepreneurial phenomenon.

Empirical studies based on theories from the field of sociology have been carried out by Bhagavatula et al. (2010) to measure the mobilization of resources and recognition of opportunities through networks; by Westhead et al. (2005a), who developed a study based on network theory to analyse the number of sources and amounts of information shared and gathered by novice, serial and portfolio entrepreneurs; and by Lee and Jones (2008), who used social communication theory and included education and experience indicators to explain that continuous online interaction promotes a reflective learning style – shared experiences – and helps transform negative communication into tangible outcomes for bridging into diverse resources. Information and support are mobilized through heterogeneous vertical actors (industry contacts/venture capitalists), which can be achieved by a more instrumental form of networking.

5.3 Economic Theories

Economic theories are not used as extensively in the knowledge area by researchers in entrepreneurship. Since economic theories are more related to the development of a specific environment, it is understandable that of the six articles based on these theories, four are concerned with organization level and two with inter-organization level.

The evolutionary approach to organizational change drives changes in the organizations and organizational routines that characterize a given organizational population. In evolutionary models of entrepreneurship, entrepreneurs generate variation by founding new firms, pursuing different strategies and attempting to combine different bundles of assets to do so (Baum and Silverman 2004). Baum and Silverman (2004) used this approach to analyse the impact of organizational knowledge on access to financing from venture capitalists. The evolutionary approach was also used to study certain factors regarding organizations in their environment. Shepherd et al. (2000) explain how the environmental pressures of market and economy may affect the development of organizations and how the knowledge possessed by members plays a fundamental role in these situations.

The theory of knowledge in regional development addressed by Huggins (2008) serves as a framework for studying the relationships between higher education institutions and organizations. This study analyses the development of organizations receiving funding or collaboration from universities and explores the relation between funding and knowledge transfer.

Audretsch et al. (2008) framed a paper around the theory of endogenous growth. In it the authors measured how regional economic development is affected by knowledge-based entrepreneurial activity, knowledge spill-overs and regional innovation. The same theory and some of the same indicators were analysed by Acs et al. (2009) in order to measure the entrepreneurial activity in a region as a catalyst for economic development. This approach was also used by Braunerhjelm et al. (2010) to measure regional endogenous growth in itself.

5.4   Management Theories

Management theories predominate among academic studies of knowledge in entrepreneurship. At the individual level different theories traditionally used in management research have been adapted to the entrepreneurial phenomenon.

As stated in the introduction, the resource-based view of the company is considered one of the most influential theoretical frameworks for strategic management in firms (Barney et al. 2001). The idea that competitive advantage derives from the resources and capabilities a firm controls that are valuable, rare, imperfectly imitable and not substitutable, has been set up as one of the most common perspectives for analysing knowledge in entrepreneurship. Some researchers in the field have supported their work on resource-based theory (Arthurs et al. 2009; West and Noel 2009).

Resource-based theory is the basis for articles that consider knowledge, learning practices, the education of organization members, knowledge management practices, knowledge acquisition activities and so on as dependent variables for measuring dependent variables such as financial reward (Shepherd and De Tienne 2005); organization performance (Arthurs and Busenitz 2006; Thornhill 2006), training activities needed (Newbert 2005) and product development and innovation (Deeds et al. 2000; Palacios et al. 2009).

Human capital theory is the dominant approach among theories originating in management studies. Two out of three articles present analyses supported by human capital theory. The concept of human capital pertains to individuals' knowledge and abilities that allow for changes in action and economic growth. Human capital may be developed through formal training and education aimed at updating and renewing one's capabilities in order to do well in society. In this sense it is natural that we find several academic articles addressing knowledge in entrepreneurship where researchers support their studies on human capital theory (Åstebro and Bernhardt 2005; Corbett et al. 2007; Sharder and Siegel 2007; Stanworth et al. 2004).

5.5   Approaches to Entrepreneurship

To a lesser extent but showing a constant trend in the course of the last decade we find approaches from various theories specially oriented and applied to the field of entrepreneurship. The 'theory of entrepreneurship' has been used mainly to analyse the personal characteristics and needs entrepreneurs have in order to start up a business (Arenius and Minniti 2005; Johnson 2000; Jones and Tullous 2002; Smith et al. 2009; Mueller 2006; Van Praag 2003). This same theory of entrepreneurship is used to analyse the phenomenon at organizational level (Dew et al. 2004; Lee and Osteryoung 2004; Shane 2002; Tolstoy 2009). Other approaches to entrepreneurship have been used as a framework for different studies over the last decade: the theory of self-employment (Koellinger and Minniti 2006; Nziramasanga and Lee 2001); entrepreneur environment theory (Kozan et al. 2006); the theory of on-the-job search (Hyytinen and Ilmakunnas 2007); and the theory of immigrant entrepreneurship (Vinogradov and Kolvereid 2007). We should highlight the fact that all the studies using theories adapted to the field of entrepreneurship as a framework have considered more or less the same knowledge indicators – education, experience and prior knowledge – to measure different dependent variables.

6.   CONCLUSIONS AND IMPLICATIONS

6.1   Conclusions

Over the last decade researchers have used different definitions, theories and ontological levels to address all kinds of issues related to knowledge in entrepreneurship. During this review we have identified the tendency of scholars to explore knowledge in the field of entrepreneurship as an asset possessed by and sometimes transferred among entrepreneurs or organizations. We should highlight the fact that 59 per cent of the articles included in this review explore the stock of knowledge in terms of the experience, skills or level of education held by entrepreneurs individually or collectively. In this sense we recognize that the most popular way of conceiving knowledge in entrepreneurship is by taking into account indicators like experience, education and skills as an intangible asset. Other authors have decided to refer to knowledge by taking into account the knowledge transfer processes possessed by an entrepreneur or organization. These articles – 25 per cent of the sample – do not concern themselves much with the amount or type of knowledge possessed by an individual or group but do refer to the transfer processes of this asset.

The last group of articles comprises those papers that refer to knowledge in terms of the ways in which an entrepreneur or organization acquires new knowledge or learning. This classification is aimed at bringing together all the articles in the sample that explores learning processes or strategies for knowledge construction. Despite the recognized importance of knowledge as a key intangible asset for new business, it is surprising that only 16 per cent of the articles in the sample have addressed knowledge from the perspective of its creation during the last decade.

Entrepreneurship is a field of study clearly dominated by articles analysing knowledge at the individual level: 58 per cent of academic work in the field has aimed to explore individual attainment of knowledge, 29 per cent has been done at organization level, and only a few papers have looked at group (4 per cent) and inter-organization (9 per cent) levels. It is worth mentioning that work at inter-organization level has been gaining in popularity during the second half of the decade.

Regarding the theories that have framed the studies about knowledge in entrepreneurship during the last decade, we observe that most of the articles include theories that come from the fields of psychology and management. We also found theories belonging to other fields of study such as economics and sociology, but to a lesser degree.

In Table 10.1 we present the taxonomy of the articles in the sample. This allows us to observe and recognize clear tendencies of researchers working on the subject of knowledge in entrepreneurship.

First of all we conclude that when authors refer to knowledge in entrepreneurship, they tend to be referring to the stock of knowledge possessed by the entrepreneur as an individual and commonly employ theories related to the field of management or approaches to entrepreneurship to address this phenomenon.

Secondly, when researchers talk about the way in which entrepreneurs and organizations create knowledge, the theories are more oriented toward the field of psychology. This may be due to the relatedness between learning processes and psychology.

When articles have referred to the transfer of knowledge, there is a clear increase in the number of papers analysing the phenomenon at inter-organization level. Mostly during the second half of the decade, papers referring to knowledge transfer have become more popular and there have been more papers about clusters, industrial districts, university transfer offices and incubators.

This review has led us to extract two main conclusions related to the academic research on entrepreneur knowledge in the last decade. First we find that research papers that use the concept of knowledge display a clear disparity in the indicators that form the construct. There is no generally

Table 10.1 Taxonomy of articles referring to knowledge in entrepreneurship, 2000–2010

		Psychology	Management	Sociology	Economy	Approaches to entrepreneurship
Stock of knowledge	Individual	3, 17, 26, 31, 37, 44, 45, 47, 50, 69, 88, 127, 132, 141, 142, 143	16, 20, 21, 32, 38, 61, 62, 63, 70, 76, 77, 79, 92, 103, 105, 116, 119, 120, 121, 123, 124, 125, 129, 130, 140	33, 78, 139	–	6, 12, 27, 34, 41, 86, 90, 91, 96, 111, 113, 131, 134, 135
	Group		24, 39, 40			25
	Organization	15, 23, 35, 101, 108	22, 42, 52, 55, 57, 64, 65, 68, 81, 84, 97, 136	–	48, 74	10, 28, 115
	Inter-organization	–	–	–	138	–
Knowledge creation	Individual	13, 29, 46, 56, 58, 66, 75, 94, 98, 104, 106, 114, 126, 133	59, 60, 95	118	–	71, 112
	Group	83	–			
	Organization	30, 36, 43, 53, 73, 128	2, 7, 100	1	–	107
	Inter-organization	5, 51	11	–	–	–
Knowledge transfer	Individual	87	–	–	–	–
	Group	–	–	–	–	–
	Organization	14, 122	19, 67, 72, 85, 110	4, 8	99, 137	54, 80
	Inter-organization	9, 89, 109, 117	18, 49, 82, 93	–	102	–

Table 10.1 (continued)

Key:
1. Anderson and Jack (2002)
2. Collinson (2000)
3. Simon et al. (2000)
4. George et al. (2002)
5. O'Gorman and Kautonen (2004)
6. Johnson (2000)
7. Kristiansen et al. (2005)
8. Totterman and Sten (2005)
9. Biggeiro (2006)
10. Kuemmerle (2000)
11. Parrilli and Sacchetti (2008)
12. Lin et al. (2000)
13. Minniti and Bygrave (2001)
14. Lockett et al. (2009)
15. Kelley and Rice (2002)
16. Kundu and Katz (2003)
17. Parker (2006)
18. Waxell and Malmberg (2007)
19. Noronha Vaz and Nijkamp (2009)
20. Honig (2001a)
21. Honig (2001b)
22. Cowling and Taylor (2001)
23. Bierly and Daly (2007)
24. Friar and Meyer (2003)
25. West (2007)

49. Hervás-Oliver and
    Albors-Garrigós (2007)
50. Mitchell et al. (2004)
51. Schildt et al. (2005)
52. Shepherd and DeTienne (2005)
53. Sternberg (2004)
54. Markman et al. (2005)
55. Arthurs and Busenitz (2006)
56. Williams and Chaston (2004)
57. Gorman et al. (2005)
58. Dutta and Thornhill (2008)
59. Henry et al. (2004)
60. Dakhli and De Clercq (2004)
61. Williams (2004)
62. Chrisman and McMullan (2004)
63. Peña (2004)
64. Newbert (2005)
65. Thornhill (2006)
66. Politis (2005)
67. Bosma et al. (2004)
68. Deeds et al. (2000)
69. Corbett (2005)
70. Rauch et al. (2005)
71. Cope (2005)
72. Lorentzen (2008)

95. Kim et al. (2006)
96. Mueller (2006)
97. Sharder and Siegel (2007)
98. Souitaris et al. (2007)
99. Huggins (2008)
100. Corbett et al. (2007)
101. Wang (2008)
102. Audretsch et al. (2008)
103. Mosey and Wright (2007)
104. Corbett (2007)
105. Allen et al. (2007)
106. Pittaway and Cope (2007)
107. Tolstoy (2009)
108. Krueger (2007)
109. Gilbert et al. (2008)
110. Audretsch and Lehmann (2006)
111. Hyytinen and Ilmakunnas (2007)
112. Katz (2008)
113. Vinogradov and Kolvereid (2007)
114. MacDonald et al. (2007)
115. Lee and Osteryoung (2004)
116. Marvel and Lumpkin (2007)
117. Beerepoot (2008)
118. Lee and Jones (2008)
119. Koellinger (2008)

26. Zacharakis and Shepherd (2001)
27. Nziramasanga and Lee (2001)
28. Dew et al. (2004)
29. Ladzani and Van Vuuren (2002)
30. Harrison and Leitch (2005)
31. Hindle and Cutting (2002)
32. Lerner and Almor (2002)
33. Chaganti and Greene (2002)
34. Jones and Tullous (2002)
35. Sapienza et al. (2004)
36. Sapienza et al. (2005)
37. Shepherd and Zacharakis (2003)
38. Davidsson and Honig (2003)
39. Lester et al. (2006)
40. Watson et al. (2003)
41. Van Praag (2003)
42. Stanworth et al. (2004)
43. Lumpkin and Lichtenstein (2005)
44. Dutta and Crossan (2005)
45. Baron and Ward, (2004)
46. Hindle (2004)
47. Ward (2004)
48. Baum and Silverman (2004)

73. Tsang (2002)
74. Shepherd et al. (2000)
75. Ravasi and Turati (2005)
76. Dimov and Shepherd (2005)
77. Westhead et al. (2005a)
78. Westhead et al. (2005b)
79. Ferrante (2005)
80. Shane (2002)
81. Junkunc (2007)
82. Hervás-Oliver and Albors-Garrigós (2008)
83. Van Gelderen et al. (2005a)
84. Åstebro and Bernhardt (2005)
85. Van Geenhuizen (2008)
86. Arenius and Minniti (2005)
87. Van Gelderen et al. (2005b)
88. De Carolis and Saparito (2006)
89. Fang et al. (2010)
90. Kozan et al. (2006)
91. Koellinger and Minniti (2006)
92. Poon et al. (2006)
93. Atherton and Price (2008)
94. De Clercq and Arenius (2006)

120. Backes-Gellner and Werner (2007)
121. Ucbasaran et al. (2008)
122. Cegarra-Navarro and Wensley (2009)
123. Seawright et al. (2008)
124. Moen et al. (2008)
125. Arthurs et al. (2009)
126. Kickul et al. (2009)
127. Westhead et al. (2009)
128. Chandler and Lyon (2009)
129. Fernández and Fuentes (2009)
130. West and Noel (2009)
131. Smith et al. (2009)
132. Haynie and Shepherd (2009)
133. Admiraal and Lockhorst (2009)
134. Gatewood et al. (2009)
135. Thomas (2009)
136. Palacios et al. (2009)
137. Acs et al. (2009)
138. Braunerhjelm et al. (2010)
139. Bhagavatula et al. (2010)
140. Zarutskie (2010)
141. Foo (2010)
142. De Tienne and Cardon (2010)
143. Thompson et al. (2010)

Source: Authors.

accepted theory for addressing the role of knowledge in entrepreneurship and there is no agreement as to the way knowledge is conceived. Secondly, there are many different theories addressing the subject of knowledge in entrepreneurship, and in our opinion there should be a specialized theory to at least explain the entrepreneur knowledge construction process, that is a theory to help us answer the question 'how do entrepreneurs construct new knowledge?'

Despite agreement among the academic community as to the importance of knowledge for companies, the papers that analyse this phenomenon in new ventures and specifically the entrepreneur's knowledge do not converge at a common point when trying to define it. This leads the authors to measure the same constructs using different indicators, resulting in significant differences in the way the entrepreneur's knowledge is conceived.

These differences lead to a wide range of problems, such as the use of the same concepts in different ways, varying traditions of theory building, data collection and data analysis, different theoretical languages, or widely varying basic epistemological positions. Due to this disparity of concepts we find that the entrepreneur's experience for some authors is not the same as it is for others and vice versa. The same happens with concepts like the entrepreneur's education, information, and thus with the whole conception of the entrepreneur's knowledge.

In this respect, based on our analysis of the 143 articles included in this review and following the basics of the theory of constructivism, we support the definition of knowledge stated at the beginning of this article.

6.2 Implications for Theory and Practice

This chapter has worked through and structured the research carried out over the last ten years on a fundamental topic in the field of entrepreneurship: knowledge. This review provides researchers addressing this topic with a clear map of the academic tendencies in the field of entrepreneurship during the last decade.

This study identifies the areas currently being explored as regards knowledge in the field of entrepreneurship and enables researchers to recognize the gaps and the needs related to the phenomenon. Here we are able to recognize the theories that have served as a theoretical foundation for papers on knowledge in the field of entrepreneurship. Theorists may recognize first the lack of depth in the study of the knowledge construction process in entrepreneurship, and secondly, the lack of a standard definition of knowledge in the field.

For practitioners, the chapter offers the opportunity to review the results of various pieces of research in terms of the effect of knowledge-related practices in companies, and subsequently to evaluate the need to apply these practices in their own businesses.

6.3   Limitations and Future Research Topics

Based on all the needs detected in this review, the limitations found represent future research topics. The number and diversity of the theories that have been used to frame academic work about knowledge in the field of entrepreneurship represent a limitation to this study, which has had to group them according to the field of study in which they originated. However, it also represents a future research topic in so far as a more in-depth analysis of these theories is needed and may use different categorization criteria. This article includes a literature review of the most important journals in the field of entrepreneurship and gives us a view of the state of the art of knowledge in the field. However, a review of the subject of knowledge in top management journals could bring a broader perspective.

Future research areas must also cover the evolution of subjects and theories over the last ten years. An efficient theory able to clearly identify the process of knowledge construction in the field of entrepreneurship needs to be found, along with a proposal for a model of the knowledge construction process to help researchers to be certain about the components of knowledge and to what extent these components play a fundamental role in the process. The importance, nature and effects of knowledge transfer could be a relevant research topic for the future. The factors that externally affect the process of knowledge construction in terms of its orientation and application and its impact on company development and also the role of external factors such as personal, cultural and sector values also need to be analysed in future research work.

REFERENCES

Acs, Z., P. Braunerhjelm, D. Audretsch and B. Carlsson (2009), 'The knowledge spillover theory of entrepreneurship', *Small Business Economics*, **32** (1), 15–30.
Admiraal, W. and D. Lockhorst (2009), 'E-learning in small and medium-sized enterprises across Europe: attitudes towards technology, learning and training', *International Small Business Journal*, **27** (6), 743–67.
Allen, S., A. Link and D. Rosenbaum (2007), 'Entrepreneurship and human capital: evidence of patenting activity from the academic sector', *Entrepreneurship Theory and Practice*, **31** (6), 937–53.
Almor, T. and M. Lerner (2002), 'Relationships among strategic capabilities and

the performance of women-owned small ventures', *Journal of Small Business Management*, **40** (2), 109–25.

Anderson, A. and S. Jack (2002), 'The articulation of social capital in entrepreneurial networks: a glue or a lubricant?', *Entrepreneurship and Regional Development*, **14** (1), 193–210.

Arenius, P. and M. Minniti (2005), 'Perceptual variables and nascent entrepreneurship', *Small Business Economics*, **24** (1), 233–47.

Arthurs, J. and L. Busenitz (2006), 'Dynamic capabilities and venture performance: the effects of venture capitalists', *Journal of Business Venturing*, **21** (2), 195–215.

Arthurs, J., L. Busenitz, R. Hoskisson and R. Johnson (2009), 'Firm-specific human capital and governance in IPO firms: addressing agency and resource dependence concerns', *Entrepreneurship Theory and Practice*, **33** (4), 845–67.

Åstebro, T. and I. Bernhardt (2005), 'The winner's curse of human capital', *Small Business Economics*, **24** (1), 63–78.

Atherton, A. and L. Price (2008), 'Can experiential knowledge and localised learning in start-up policy and practice be transferred between regions? The case of the START network', *Entrepreneurship and Regional Development*, **20** (1), 367–85.

Audretsch, D.B. and E. Lehmann (2006), 'Entrepreneurial access and absorption of knowledge spillovers: strategic board and managerial composition for competitive advantage', *Journal of Small Business Management*, **44** (2), 155–66.

Audretsch, D., W. Bönte and M. Keilbach (2008), 'Entrepreneurship capital and its impact on knowledge diffusion and economic performance', *Journal of Business Venturing*, **23** (6), 687–98.

Backes-Gelner, U. and A. Werner (2007), 'Entrepreneurial signaling via education: a success factor in innovative start-ups', *Small Business Economics*, **29** (2), 173–90.

Barney, J. (2001), 'Resource-based theories of competitive advantage: a ten year retrospective on the resource-based view', *Journal of Management*, **27** (4), 643–50.

Barney, J., M. Wright and D. Ketchen (2001), 'A resource-based view of the firm: ten years after 1991', *Journal of Management*, **27** (4), 625–41.

Baron, R. (1998), 'Cognitive mechanisms in entrepreneurship: why and when entrepreneurs think differently than other people', *Journal of Business Venturing*, **13** (2), 275–94.

Baron, R. and T.B. Ward (2004), 'Expanding entrepreneurial cognition's toolbox: potential contributions from the field of cognitive science', *Entrepreneurship Theory and Practice*, **28** (6), 553–73.

Baum, J. and B. Silverman (2004), 'Picking winners or building them? Alliance, intellectual, and human capital as selection criteria in venture financing and performance of biotechnology startups', *Journal of Business Venturing*, **19** (3), 411–36.

Beerepoot, N. (2008), 'Diffusion of knowledge and skills through labour markets: evidence from the furniture cluster in metro cebu (the Philippines)', *Entrepreneurship and Regional Development*, **20**, 67–88.

Bhagavatula, S., T. Elfring, A. Van Tilburg and G. Van de Bunt (2010), 'How social and human capital influence opportunity recognition and resource mobilization in India's handloom industry', *Journal of Business Venturing*, **25** (3), 245–60.

Bierly, P. and P. Daly (2007), 'Alternative knowledge strategies, competitive environment, and organizational performance in small manufacturing firms', *Entrepreneurship Theory and Practice*, **31** (4), 493–518.

Biggeiro, L. (2006), 'Industrial and knowledge relocation strategies under the challenges of globalization and digitalization: the move of small and medium enterprises among territorial systems', *Entrepreneurship and Regional Development*, **18**, 443–71.

Bosma, N., M. van Praag, R. Thurik and G. de Wit (2004), 'The value of human and social capital investments for the business performance of startups', *Small Business Economics*, **23** (2), 227–36.

Braunerhjelm, P., Z. Acs, D. Audretsch and B. Carlsson (2010), 'The missing link: knowledge diffusion and entrepreneurship in endogenous growth', *Small Business Economics*, **34** (1), 105–25.

Cegarra-Navarro, J. and A. Wensley (2009), 'Congenital learning in the Spanish telecommunication industry', *Journal of Business Venturing*, **24** (6), 533–43.

Chaganti, R. and P.G. Greene (2002), 'Who are ethnic entrepreneurs? A study of entrepreneurs' ethnic involvement and business characteristics', *Journal of Small Business Management*, **40** (2), 126–43.

Chandler, A. and D. Lyon (2009), 'Involvement in knowledge-acquisition activities by venture team members and venture performance', *Entrepreneurship Theory and Practice*, **33** (3), 571–94.

Chrisman, J.J. and W.E. McMullan (2004), 'Outsider assistance as a knowledge resource for new venture survival', *Journal of Small Business Management*, **42** (3), 229–44.

Collinson, S. (2000), 'Knowledge networks for innovation in small Scottish software firms', *Entrepreneurship and Regional Development*, **12**, 217–44.

Conner, K. and C. Prahalad (1996), 'A resource-based theory of the firm: knowledge versus opportunism', *Organization Science*, **7** (5), 477–501.

Cope, J. (2005), 'Toward a dynamic learning perspective of entrepreneurship', *Entrepreneurship Theory and Practice*, **29** (4), 373–97.

Corbett, A. (2005), 'Experiential learning within the process of opportunity identification and exploitation', *Entrepreneurship Theory and Practice*, **29** (4), 473–91.

Corbett, A. (2007), 'Learning asymmetries and the discovery of entrepreneurial opportunities', *Journal of Business Venturing*, **22**, 97–118.

Corbett, A., H. Neck and D. De Tienne (2007), 'How corporate entrepreneurs learn from fledgling innovation initiatives: cognition and the development of a termination script', *Entrepreneurship Theory and Practice*, **31** (6), 829–56.

Cowling, M. and M. Taylor (2001), 'Entrepreneurial women and men: two different species?', *Small Business Economics*, **16** (2), 167–75.

Dakhli, M. and D. De Clercq (2004), 'Human capital, social capital, and innovation: a multicountry study', *Entrepreneurship and Regional Development*, **16**, 107–28.

Davidsson, P. and B. Honig (2003), 'The role of social and human capital among nascent entrepreneurs', *Journal of Business Venturing*, **18** (2), 301–31.

De Carolis, D. and D. Deeds (1999), 'The impact of stocks and flows of organizational knowledge on firm performance: an empirical evaluation of the biotechnology industry', *Strategic Management Journal*, **20** (10), 953–68.

De Carolis, D. and P. Saparito (2006), 'Social capital, cognition, and entrepreneurial opportunities: a theoretical framework', *Entrepreneurship Theory and Practice*, **30** (1), 41–58.

De Clercq, D. and P. Arenius (2006), 'The role of knowledge in business start-up activity', *International Small Business Journal*, **24** (4), 339–58.

De Tienne, D. and M. Cardon (2010), 'Impact of founder experience on exit intentions', *Small Business Economics*, forthcoming, accepted 19 March 2010.

Deeds, D., D. De Carolis and J. Coombs (2000), 'Dynamic capabilities and new product development in high technology ventures: an empirical analysis of new biotechnology firms', *Journal of Business Venturing*, **15** (3), 211–29.

Dew, N., S. Velamuri and S. Venkataraman (2004), 'Dispersed knowledge and an entrepreneurial theory of the firm', *Journal of Business Venturing*, **19** (5), 659–79.

Dimov, D. (2007), 'Beyond the single-person, single-insight attribution in understanding entrepreneurial opportunities', *Entrepreneurship Theory and Practice*, **31** (5), 713–31.

Dimov, D. and D. Shepherd (2005), 'Human capital theory and venture capital firms: exploring "home runs" and "strike outs"', *Journal of Business Venturing*, **20** (1), 1–21.

Dutta, D. and M. Crossan (2005), 'The nature of entrepreneurial opportunities: understanding the process using the 4I organizational learning framework', *Entrepreneurship Theory and Practice*, **29** (4), 425–52.

Dutta, D. and S. Thornhill (2008), 'The evolution of growth intentions: toward a cognition-based model', *Journal of Business Venturing*, **23** (2), 307–32.

Fang, S., F. Tsai and J. Lin (2010), 'Leveraging tenant-incubator social capital for organizational learning and performance in incubation programme', *International Small Business Journal*, **28** (1), 90–115.

Fernández, R. and G. Fuentes (2009), 'Influence of the capacities of top management on the internationalization of SMEs', *Entrepreneurship and Regional Development*, **21** (2), 131–54.

Ferrante, F. (2005), 'Revealing entrepreneurial talent', *Small Business Economics*, **25** (2), 159–74.

Foo, M. (2010), 'Member experience, use of external assistance and evaluation of business ideas', *Journal of Small Business Management*, **48** (1), 32–43.

Friar, J. and M. Meyer (2003), 'Entrepreneurship and start-ups in the Boston region: factors differentiating high-growth ventures from micro-ventures', *Small Business Economics*, **21** (2), 145–52.

Gatewood, E., C. Brush, N. Carter, P.G. Greene and M. Hart (2009), 'Diana: a symbol of women entrepreneurs' hunt for knowledge, money, and the rewards of entrepreneurship', *Small Business Economics*, **32** (2), 129–44.

George, G., S. Zahra and D. Wood (2002), 'The effects of business–university alliances on innovative output and financial performance: a study of publicly traded biotechnology companies', *Journal of Business Venturing*, **17** (4), 577–609.

Gilbert, B., P. McDougall and D. Audretsch (2008), 'Clusters, knowledge spillovers and new venture performance: an empirical examination', *Journal of Business Venturing*, **23** (3), 405–22.

Gorman, G., P. Rosa and A. Faseruk (2005), 'Institutional lending to knowledge-based businesses', *Journal of Business Venturing*, **20** (6), 793–819.

Grant, R. (1991), 'The resource-based theory of competitive advantage: implications for strategy formulation', *California Management Review*, **33** (3), 114–36.

Grant, R. (1996), 'Toward a knowledge-based theory of the firm', *Strategic Management Journal*, **17**, 109–22.

Grossman, G. and E. Helpman (1990), 'Trade, knowledge spillovers and growth', *National Bureau of Economic Research*, **3485** (October), 1–17.

Harrison, R. and C. Leitch (2005), 'Entrepreneurial learning: researching the interface between learning and the entrepreneurial context', *Entrepreneurship Theory and Practice*, **29** (4), 351–74.

Haynie, M. and D. Shepherd (2009), 'A measure of adaptive cognition for entrepreneurship research', *Entrepreneurship Theory and Practice*, **33** (3), 695–716.

Henry, C., F. Hill and C. Leitch (2004), 'The effectiveness of training for new business creation', *International Small Business Journal*, **22** (3), 249–71.

Hervas-Oliver, J. and J. Albors-Garrigos (2007), 'Do clusters capabilities matter? An empirical application of the resource-based view in clusters', *Entrepreneurship and Regional Development*, **19** (1), 113–36.

Hervas-Oliver, J. and J. Albors-Garrigos (2008), 'Local knowledge domains and the role of MNE affiliates in bridging and complementing a cluster's knowledge', *Entrepreneurship and Regional Development*, **20**, 581–98.

Hindle, K. (2004), 'Choosing qualitative methods for entrepreneurial cognition research: a canonical development approach', *Entrepreneurship Theory and Practice*, **28** (6), 575–609.

Hindle, K. and N. Cutting (2002), 'Can applied entrepreneurship education enhance job satisfaction and financial performance? An empirical investigation in the Australian pharmacy profession', *Journal of Small Business Management*, **40** (2), 162–7.

Honig, B. (2001a), 'Human capital and structural upheaval: a study of manufacturing firms in the West Bank', *Journal of Business Venturing*, **16** (5), 575–94.

Honig, B. (2001b), 'Learning strategies and resources for entrepreneurs and intrapreneurs', *Entrepreneurship Theory and Practice*, **26** (1), 21–37.

Hormiga, E., R.M. Batista and A. Sánchez (2006), *El Capital Intelectual en las Empresas de Nueva Creación: Influencias de los Activos Intangibles en el Éxito Empresarial*, Gran Canarias: Fundación Formación y Desarrollo Profesional.

Huggins, R. (2008), 'Universities and knowledge-based venturing: finance, management and networks in London', *Entrepreneurship and Regional Development*, **20** (1), 185–206.

Hyytinen, A. and P. Ilmakunnas (2007), 'Entrepreneurial aspirations: another form of job search?', *Small Business Economics*, **29** (1), 63–80.

Johnson, P. (2000), 'Ethnic differences in self-employment among Southeast Asian refugees in Canada', *Journal of Small Business Management*, **38** (4), 78–86.

Jones, K. and R. Tullous (2002), 'Behaviors of pre-venture entrepreneurs and perceptions of their financial needs', *Journal of Small Business Management*, **40** (3), 233–49.

Junkunc, M. (2007), 'Managing radical innovation: the importance of specialized knowledge in the biotech revolution', *Journal of Business Venturing*, **22** (3), 388–411.

Katz, J.A. (2008), 'Fully mature but not fully legitimate: a different perspective on the state of entrepreneurship education', *Journal of Small Business Management*, **46** (4), 550–66.

Kelley, J.D. and M.P. Rice (2002), 'Leveraging the value of proprietary technologies', *Journal of Small Business Management*, **40** (1), 1–16.

Kickul, J., L. Gundry, S. Barbosa and L. Whitcanack (2009), 'Intuition versus analysis? Testing differential models of cognitive style on entrepreneurial self-efficacy and the new venture creation process', *Entrepreneurship Theory and Practice*, **33** (2), 439–67.

Kim, P., H. Aldrich and L. Keister (2006), 'Access (not) denied: the impact of financial, human, and cultural capital on entrepreneurial entry in the United States', *Small Business Economics*, **27** (1), 5–22.

Koellinger, P. (2008), 'Why are some entrepreneurs more innovative than others?', *Small Business Economics*, **31** (1), 21–37.

Koellinger, P. and M. Minniti (2006), 'Not for lack of trying: American entrepreneurship in black and white', *Small Business Economics*, **27** (1), 59–79.

Kozan, K., D. Öksoy, and O. Özsoy (2006), 'Growth plans of small businesses in Turkey: individual and environmental influences', *Journal of Small Business Management*, **44** (1), 114–29.

Kristiansen, S., J. Kimeme, A. Mbwambo and F. Wahid (2005), 'Information flows and adaptation in Tanzanian cottage industries', *Entrepreneurship and Regional Development*, **17** (5), 365–88.

Krueger, N. (2007), 'What lies beneath? The experiential essence of entrepreneurial thinking', *Entrepreneurship Theory and Practice*, **31** (1), 123–38.

Kuemmerle, W. (2002), 'Home base and knowledge management in international ventures', *Journal of Business Venturing*, **17** (2), 99–122.

Kundu, S. and J. Katz (2003), 'Born-international SMEs: BI-level impacts of resources and intentions', *Small Business Economics*, **20** (1), 25–47.

Ladzani, W.M. and J.J. Van Vuuren (2002), 'Entrepreneurship training for entering SMEs in South Africa', *Journal of Small Business Management*, **40** (2), 154–61.

Lee, R. and O. Jones (2008), 'Networks, communication and learning during business start-up: the creation of cognitive social capital', *International Small Business Journal*, **26** (5), 559–94.

Lee, S.S. and J.S. Osteryoung (2004), 'A comparison of critical success factors for effective operations of university business incubators in the United States and Korea', *Journal of Small Business Management*, **42** (4), 418–26.

Lerner, M. and T. Almor (2002), 'Relationships among strategic capabilities and the performance of women-owned small ventures', *Journal of Small Business Management*, **40** (2), 109–25.

Lester, R.S., S.T. Certo, C.M. Dalton, D.R. Dalton and A.A. Cannella Jr (2006), 'Initial public offering investor valuations: an examination of top management team prestige and environmental uncertainty', *Journal of Small Business Management*, **44** (1), 1–26.

Lin, Z., G. Picot and J. Compton (2000), 'The entry and exit dynamics of self-employment in Canada', *Small Business Economics*, **15** (1), 105–25.

Lockett, N., F. Cave, R. Kerr and S. Robinson (2009), 'The influence of co-location in higher education institutions on small firms' perspectives of knowledge transfer', *Entrepreneurship and Regional Development*, **21** (3), 265–83.

Lorentzen, A. (2008), 'Knowledge networks in local and global space', *Entrepreneurship and Regional Development*, **20** (6), 533–45.

Lumpkin, G.T. and B. Lichtenstein (2005), 'The role of organizational learning in the opportunity-recognition process', *Entrepreneurship Theory and Practice*, **29** (4), 451–75.

Macdonald, S., D. Assimakopoulos and P. Anderson (2007), 'Education and training for innovation in SMEs: a tale of exploitation', *International Small Business Journal*, **25** (1), 77–97.

Markman, G., P.H. Phan, D. Balkin and P. Gianiodis (2005), 'Entrepreneurship and university-based technology transfer', *Journal of Business Venturing*, **20** (2), 241–63.

Marvel, M. and G.T. Lumpkin (2007), 'Technology entrepreneurs' human capital and its effects on innovation radicalness', *Entrepreneurship Theory and Practice*, **31** (6), 807.

Minniti, M. and W. Bygrave (2001), 'A dynamic model of entrepreneurial learning', *Entrepreneurship Theory and Practice*, **5** (3), 5–18.

Mitchell, R., L. Busenitz, T. Lant, P. McDougall, E. Morse and J. Smith (2004), 'The distinctive and inclusive domain of entrepreneurial cognition research', *Entrepreneurship Theory and Practice*, **58** (6), 505–18.

Moen, O., R. Sørheim and T. Erikson (2008), 'Born global firms and informal investors: examining investor characteristics', *Journal of Small Business Management*, **46** (4), 536–49.

Moreno Luzón, M. and M. Lloria (2008), 'The role of non-structural and informal mechanisms of integration and coordination as forces in knowledge creation', *British Journal of Management*, **19** (3), 250–76.

Mosey, S. and M. Wright (2007), 'From human capital to social capital: a longitudinal study of technology-based academic entrepreneurs', *Entrepreneurship Theory and Practice*, **29** (6), 909–37.

Mueller, P. (2006), 'Entrepreneurship in the region: breeding ground for nascent entrepreneurs?', *Small Business Economics*, **27** (1), 41–58.

Newbert, S.L. (2005), 'New firm formation: a dynamic capability perspective', *Journal of Small Business Management*, **55** (1), 55–77.

Nickerson, J. and T. Zenger (2004), 'A knowledge-based theory of the firm: the problem-solving perspective', *Organization Science*, **15** (6), 617–32.

Nonaka, I. (1991), 'The knowledge-creating company', *Harvard Business Review*, **69** (6), 96–104.

Nonaka, I. and H. Takeuchi (1995), *The Knowledge Creating Company: How Japanese Companies Create the Dynamics of Innovation*, New York: Oxford University Press.

Noronha, T. and P. Nijkamp (2009), 'Knowledge and innovation: the strings between global and local dimensions of sustainable growth', *Entrepreneurship and Regional Development*, **21** (4), 441–55.

Nziramasanga, M. and M. Lee (2001), 'Duration of self-employment in developing countries: evidence from small enterprises in Zimbabwe', *Small Business Economics*, **17** (2), 239–53.

O'Gorman, C. and M. Kautonen (2004), 'Policies to promote new knowledge-intensive industrial agglomerations', *Entrepreneurship and Regional Development*, **16** (6), 459–79.

Palacios, D., I. Gil and F. Garrigos (2009), 'The impact of knowledge management on innovation and entrepreneurship in the biotechnology and telecommunications industries', *Small Business Economics*, **32** (3), 291–301.

Parker, S. (2006), 'Learning about the unknown: how fast do entrepreneurs adjust their beliefs?', *Journal of Business Venturing*, **21** (1), 1–26.

Parrilli, M. and S. Sacchetti (2008), 'Linking learning with governance in networks and clusters: key issues for analysis and policy', *Entrepreneurship and Regional Development*, **20** (4), 387–408.

Peña, I. (2004), 'Business incubation centers and new firm growth in the Basque country', *Small Business Economics*, **22** (2), 223–36.

Pittaway, L. and J. Cope (2007), 'Entrepreneurship education: a systematic review of the evidence', *International Small Business Journal*, **25** (4), 479–512.

Politis, D. (2005), 'The process of entrepreneurial learning: a conceptual framework', *Entrepreneurship Theory and Practice*, **29** (4), 399–420.

Poon, J., A. Ainuddin and S. Junit (2006), 'Effects of self-concept traits and entrepreneurial orientation on firm performance', *International Small Business Journal*, **24** (1), 61–84.

Rauch, A., M. Frese and A. Utsch (2005), 'Effects of human capital and long-term human resources development and utilization on employment growth of small-scale businesses: a causal analysis', *Entrepreneurship Theory and Practice*, **29** (6), 681–700.

Ravasi, D. and C. Turati (2005), 'Exploring entrepreneurial learning: a comparative study of technology development projects', *Journal of Business Venturing*, **20** (2), 137–64.

Rubenstein-Montano, B., J. Liebowitz, J. Buchwalter, D.N. McCaw and K. Rebeck (2001), 'A systems thinking framework for knowledge management', *Decision Support Systems*, **31** (1), 5–16.

Sapienza, H., D. De Clercq and W. Sandberg (2005), 'Antecedents of international and domestic learning effort', *Journal of Business Venturing*, **20** (4), 437–57.

Sapienza, H., A. Parhankangas and E. Autio (2004), 'Knowledge relatedness and post-spin-off growth', *Journal of Business Venturing*, **19** (6), 809–29.

Schildt, H., M. Maula and T. Keil (2005), 'Explorative and exploitative learning from external corporate ventures', *Entrepreneurship Theory and Practice*, **29** (4), 493–515.

Seawright, K., R. Mitchell and J. Brock Smith (2008), 'Comparative entrepreneurial cognitions and lagging Russian new venture formation: a tale of two countries', *Journal of Small Business Management*, **46** (4), 512–35.

Shane, S. (2002), 'Executive forum: university technology transfer to entrepreneurial companies', *Journal of Business Venturing*, **17** (4), 537–52.

Sharder, R. and D. Siegel (2007), 'Assessing the relationship between human capital and firm performance: evidence from technology-based new ventures', *Entrepreneurship Theory and Practice*, **31** (6), 893–910.

Shepherd, D.A. and A. Zacharakis (2003), 'A new venture's cognitive legitimacy: an assessment by customers', *Journal of Small Business Management*, **41** (2), 148–67.

Shepherd, D. and D. De Tienne (2005), 'Prior knowledge, potential financial reward, and opportunity identification', *Entrepreneurship Theory and Practice*, **29** (1), 1–24.

Shepherd, D., E. Douglas and M. Shanley (2000), 'New venture survival: ignorance, external shocks and risk reduction strategies', *Journal of Business Venturing*, **15** (3), 393–410.

Simon, M., S. Houghton and K. Aquino (2000), 'Cognitive biases, risk perception, and venture formation: how individuals decide to start a company', *Journal of Business Venturing*, **15** (1), 113–34.

Smith, B.R., C.H. Matthews and M.T. Schenkel (2009), 'Differences in entrepreneurial opportunities: the role of tacitness and codification in opportunity identification', *Journal of Small Business Management*, **47** (1), 38–57.

Souitaris, V., S. Zerbinati and A. Al-Laham (2007), 'Do entrepreneurship programmes raise entrepreneurial intention of science and engineering students? The effect of learning, inspiration and resources', *Journal of Business Venturing*, **22** (5), 566–91.

Stanworth, J., C. Stanworth, A. Watson, D. Purdy and S. Healeas (2004), 'Franchising as a small business growth strategy', *International Small Business Journal*, **22** (6), 539–59.

Sternberg, R. (2004), 'Successful intelligence as a basis for entrepreneurship', *Journal of Business Venturing*, **19** (2), 189–201.

Thomas, M. (2009), 'The impact of education histories on the decision to become self-employed: a study of young, aspiring, minority business owners', *Small Business Economics*, **33** (4), 455–66.

Thompson, M. and G. Walsham (2004), 'Placing knowledge management in context', *Journal of Management Studies*, **41** (5), 725–48.

Thompson, P., D. Jones-Evans and C. Kwong (2010), 'Education and entrepreneurial activity: a comparison of white and South Asian men', *International Small Business Journal*, **28** (2), 147–64.

Thornhill, S. (2006), 'Knowledge, innovation and firm performance in high- and low-technology regimes', *Journal of Business Venturing*, **21** (6), 687–703.

Tolstoy, D. (2009), 'Knowledge combination and knowledge creation in a foreign-market network', *Journal of Small Business Management*, **47** (2), 202–20.

Totterman, H. and J. Sten (2005), 'Start-ups: business incubation and social capital', *International Small Business Journal*, **23** (5), 487–511.

Tsang, E. (2002), 'Learning from overseas venturing experience the case of Chinese family businesses', *Journal of Business Venturing*, **17** (1), 21–40.

Ucbasaran, D., P. Westhead and M. Wright (2008), 'Opportunity identification and pursuit: does an entrepreneur's human capital matter?', *Small Business Economics*, **30** (2), 153–73.

Van Geenhuizen, M. (2008), 'Knowledge networks of young innovators in the urban economy: biotechnology as a case study', *Entrepreneurship and Regional Development*, **20** (2), 161–83.

Van Gelderen, M., R. Thurik and N. Bosma (2005a), 'Success and risk factors in the pre-startup phase', *Small Business Economics*, **24** (3), 365–80.

Van Gelderen, M., L. Van der Sluis and P. Jansen (2005b), 'Learning opportunities and learning behaviours of small business starters: relations with goal achievement, skill development and satisfaction', *Small Business Economics*, **25** (1), 97–108.

Van Praag, M. (2003), 'Business survival and success of young small business owners', *Small Business Economics*, **21** (1), 1–17.

Vinogradov, E. and L. Kolvereid (2007), 'Cultural background, human capital and self-employment rates among immigrants in Norway', *Entrepreneurship and Regional Development*, **19** (4), 359–76.

Wang, C. (2008), 'Entrepreneurial orientation, learning orientation, and firm performance', *Entrepreneurship Theory and Practice*, **32** (4), 635–59.

Ward, T. (2004), 'Cognition, creativity and entrepreneurship', *Journal of Business Venturing*, **19** (1), 173–88.

Watson, W., W. Stewart and A. BarNir (2003), 'The effects of human capital, organizational demography, and interpersonal processes on venture partner perceptions of firm profit and growth', *Journal of Business Venturing*, **18** (2), 145–64.

Waxell, A. and A. Malmberg (2007), 'What is global and what is local in knowledge-generating interaction? The case of the biotech cluster in Uppsala, Sweden', *Entrepreneurship and Regional Development*, **19** (2), 137–59.

Wernerfelt, B. (1984), 'A resource-based view of the firm', *Strategic Management Journal*, **5** (2), 171–80.

West, G.P. (2007), 'Collective cognition: when entrepreneurial teams, not individuals, make decisions', *Entrepreneurship Theory and Practice*, **31** (1), 77–104.

West, G.P. and T.W. Noel (2009), 'The impact of knowledge resources on new venture performance', *Journal of Small Business Management*, **47** (1), 1–22.

Westhead, P., D. Ucbasaran and M. Wright (2005a), 'Experience and cognition: do novice, serial and portfolio entrepreneurs differ?', *International Small Business Journal*, **23** (1), 72–98.

Westhead, P., D. Ucbasaran and M. Wright (2005b), 'Decisions, actions, and performance: do novice, serial, and portfolio entrepreneurs differ?', *Journal of Small Business Management*, **43** (4), 393–417.

Westhead, P., D. Ucbasaran and M. Wright (2009), 'Information search and opportunity identification', *International Small Business Journal*, **27** (6), 659–80.

Williams, D. (2004), 'Youth self-employment: its nature and consequences', *Small Business Economics*, **23** (3), 323–36.

Williams, J. and I. Chaston (2004), 'Links between the linguistic ability and international experience of export managers and their export marketing intelligence behaviour', *International Small Business Journal*, **22** (5), 463–86.

Wright, M., K. Hmieleski, D. Siegel and M. Ensley (2007), 'The role of human capital in technological entrepreneurship', *Entrepreneurship Theory and Practice*, **31** (6), 791–808.

Zacharakis, A. and D. Shepherd (2001), 'The nature of information and overconfidence on venture capitalists' decision making', *Journal of Business Venturing*, **16** (2), 311–32.

Zarutskie, R. (2010), 'The role of top management team human capital in venture capital markets: evidence from first-time funds', *Journal of Business Venturing*, **25** (2), 155–72.

Index

Titles of publications are in *italics*.
Abbreviations used: MBOs (management buyouts)
                      SBEFs (science-based entrepreneurial firms)